LITERARY/CULTURAL THEORY

JACQUES LACAN

Literary/Cultural Theory provides concise and lucid introductions to a range of key concepts and theorists in contemporary literary and cultural theory. Original and contemporary in presentation, and eschewing jargon, each book in the series presents students of humanities and social sciences exhaustive overviews of theories and theorists, while also introducing them to the mechanics of reading literary/cultural texts using critical tools. Each book also carries glossaries of key terms and ideas, and pointers for further reading and research. Written by scholar-teachers who have taught critical theory for years, and vetted by some of the foremost experts in the field, the series Literary/Cultural Theory is indispensable to students and teachers.

Also in the series

Psychoanalytic Theory and Criticism
Feminisms
Ecocriticism
Queer Studies
Dalit Literature and Criticism
New Historicism
Masculinities
Marxist Literary and Cultural Theory
Modernisms
Postmodernisms
Mikhail Bakhtin
Popular Culture
Diaspora Studies
Postcolonialisms

LITERARY/CULTURAL THEORY

JACQUES LACAN

FROM CLINIC TO CULTURE

MAHITOSH MANDAL
Presidency University, Kolkata

Edited by
SUMIT CHAKRABARTI
Presidency University, Kolkata

Orient BlackSwan

Publisher's Acknowledgements

"'Eyes a man could drown in': Phallic Myth and Femininity in John Fowles's *The French Lieutenant's Woman*," by Mahitosh Mandal. First published in *Interdisciplinary Literary Studies*, Vol. 19, No. 3, 2017. Copyright © 2017 The Pennsylvania State University, University Park, PA. This article is used by permission of The Pennsylvania State University Press.

Every effort has been made to trace copyright holders and to obtain their permission for the use of copyright material. The publisher apologises for any errors or omissions made, and would be grateful if notified of any corrections that should be incorporated in future reprints or editions of this book.

JACQUES LACAN: FROM CLINIC TO CULTURE

ORIENT BLACKSWAN PRIVATE LIMITED

Registered Office
3-6-752 Himayatnagar, Hyderabad 500 029, Telangana, India
Email: centraloffice@orientblackswan.com

Other Offices
Bengaluru, Bhopal, Chennai, Guwahati, Hyderabad, Jaipur, Kolkata, Lucknow, Mumbai, New Delhi, Noida, Patna, Vijayawada

First published 2018

026639

ISBN 978 93 5287 190 2

Typeset in Aldine 401 BT 10.5/13 *by*
Akhil Offset Printers
Hyderabad 500 020

Printed at
Graphica Printers & Binders,
Hyderabad 500 013

Published by
Orient Blackswan Private Limited
3-6-752, Himayatnagar, Hyderabad 500 029, Telangana, India
Email: info@orientblackswan.com

Dedicated to my parents, who let me pursue my dreams

Contents

Acknowledgements *ix*
Editor's Preface *xi*
List of Figures *xiv*

Introduction 1

1. An Outline of Lacan's Teachings 6

2. The Subject in Lacan 53

3. The Clinical Structures: Psychosis, Neurosis, Perversion 93

4. Literature with Lacan 131

5. Lacan in the Field of Culture 166

Conclusion 202

Glossary 204
Texts for Further Reading 214
Index 218

Acknowledgements

Three of my teachers from the Department of English, Jadavpur University, have played an instrumental role in the writing of this book: Dr Santanu Biswas, Dr Nandini Saha and Dr Chandreyee Niyogi. Dr Biswas, a Lacanian scholar and a practicing Lacanian analyst, sparked my interest in Lacan through a number of undergraduate and postgraduate courses (which I attended between 2006 and 2010) on the interface between literature and Lacanian psychoanalysis. Dr Saha, who worked on the English novelist John Fowles, supervised my MPhil dissertation on a Lacanian study of Fowles. Dr Niyogi, who is currently supervising my PhD thesis on Swami Vivekananda, encouraged me to write this book even though doing so meant I had to take some time off from writing my thesis.

Dr Sumit Chakrabarti, my senior colleague at the Department of English, Presidency University, and the series editor, gave me the opportunity to write this book and offered invaluable advice while putting up with my deferrals.

I am also indebted to the following colleagues of mine from the Department of English, Presidency University, for their constant support and encouragement: Dr Shanta Dutta, Dr Purna Banerjee, Dr Souvik Mukherjee, Dr Amrita Sen, Dr Anupama Mohan, Dr Suddhasheel Sen, Dr Shuhita Bhattacharjee, Kalyan Das and Anirban Ray.

Swami Suparnananda, secretary of Ramakrishna Mission Institute of Culture, Golpark, and Dr Angshuman Bhattacharjee, Professor of Philosophy at Ramakrishna Mission Residential College, Narendrapur, have shaped my life in more ways than one.

Teaching Lacan to my students at Presidency University has been a rewarding experience. Their questions and the clarifications they sought led me to delve deep into the subject.

For some time I was associated with and benefitted from two study groups: (1) The Lacan Study Group, run under my supervision at Presidency University, which comprised the following Lacan enthusiasts – Sayantika Chakraborty, Prabaha Tarafder, Sanjay Dey, Subham Chowdhury, Samudranil Gupta, Swayamdipta Das, Sauryendu Dasgupta, Subhayu Bhattacharjee, Souvik Mukherjee and Soumili Mandal. Sayantika, in particular, made important contributions to the LSG and ensured it ran smoothly for two long years. And (2) The Lacan Study Circle, Kolkata, which was run under the supervision of Dr Biswas and included the following colleagues and friends – Anindya Sengupta, Samya Seth, Dipanjan Maitra, Arka Chattopadhyay, Anik Samanta, Sukhaloka Mukherjee and Arijit Mitra.

Anushree Das, studying Mathematics at Presidency University, helped me by clarifying some of the mathematical concepts used by Lacan.

My experience of working with the team at Orient BlackSwan, in particular with Sreenath Sreedharan and Bikram Sharma, has been enriching.

I express my heartfelt gratitude to each of them.

The section on *The French Lieutenant's Woman* in Chapter Four is a reprint of my article published in *Interdisciplinary Literary Studies: A Journal of Criticism and Theory*, Vol. 19, No. 3 (2017). I am grateful to The Pennsylvania State University Press for granting me permission to use the article in this book.

Editor's Preface

This book on Jacques Lacan emerges directly, yet reflexively, out of literary practice. Both the author and the editor are students (and also teachers) of literature. There is a complex interconnectedness between many modernities discussed and/or practised in the humanities classroom, and in spite of shifts within narratives of engagement with the political nature of the study of the humanities, subjecthood has remained a central problem. The prevarications of postmodernity (and this is not a pejorative overture), with their emphases on contingency and parody, have rarely been able to occlude certain generic disclaimers on the question of the subject. Psychoanalysis, to use the term loosely, has therefore remained, in spite of shifting epistemes, as a modernist marker of our engagement with the question of the 'human'. A considerable part of psychoanalytic practice is irreducibly assigned, in Derridean interpretations, to the prioritisation of logocentrism within clinical praxes, a symptomatic positivism founded, if not on faith, on practical compulsion. This book is a grounded critique of such a reductive reading of the psychoanalytic. The world of language, characterised by logocentrism and phallogocentrism, predominantly constitutes only one of the three Lacanian registers – that of the symbolic. There are two more psychical registers – the imaginary and the real – which are by no means 'logocentric'. These three registers variously contribute to the formation of human subjectivity, according to Lacan, but one must note their differences. For instance, while the symbolic structures sexual desire, the real registers the traumatic and the imaginary is what determines how human fantasy works. The traumatic is neither experienced nor fully articulated through the *logos*, rather it ruptures and exposes the limitations of the same. Mahitosh Mandal has argued that if logocentrism is used to explain away the Lacanian, one will be unable to explain his emphasis on the nothingness of our being or the void that constitutes our subjectivity. 'How then would one explain affect, *jouissance*, *lalangue*, and *lituraterre*?' Mandal asks me in private correspondence during the making of this volume.

The old-school technique of the clinic – the analyst and the patient in proximate contact – has been under much scrutiny and critique in recent times. Particularly so because of radical developments in brain-science research, the growing popularity of the cognitivist-neurological-biological model of mapping the impulses of the human brain and revolutionary revisionism in the way one comprehends sexual ethics in the twenty-first century. However, while the post-theoretical subject has almost decidedly shifted towards the pill for happiness, the clinic has remained as a sensitive (even though tentative) marker of the humanness of our existence. Methodological implications aside, one may not easily dismiss the possibility of a counter-intuitive and ever-increasing return to the clinic in the near future. The immediate socio-psychological connect between the analyst and the analysand, I daresay, shall have its own proliferating use in a post-truth world. Also, in order to trace the genealogy of the study of the human mind, principally within (and outside of) the framework of modernity, one has to inevitably go back to a close reading of the works of Sigmund Freud and Jacques Lacan.

Predictably, the reader begins with Freud. Apart from Freud's own oeuvre, there is a whole body of criticism and literature that discusses Freud in great detail. In comparison, it is sometimes not easy for the scholar of the humanities and the social sciences to lay their hands on a volume that discusses Lacan's works. Neither his *écrits* nor the seminars are available as a comprehensive body of work. Much of his work is also only available in French, and there are differences within the academy about the authenticity of such translations. Additionally, the sometimes deliberate 'unreadability' of Lacan's *écrits* – which are only available, as Jean-Claude Milner has pointed out, to an elite inner circle – has often made his work inaccessible to many readers. In short, there are major difficulties in attempting to write a critical volume on the work of Jacques Lacan.

Mandal has planned the volume keeping in mind not only those already introduced to the work of Lacan, but also the scholar, the teacher or the student who uses Lacan in the classroom. The first three chapters attempt a categorical understanding of Lacan's oeuvre, while the two concluding chapters engage with the inter-disciplinary possibilities of using Lacan's seminars and *écrits* as a tool in the classroom. However, Mandal also adds a retrospective caveat in his introduction to the volume: 'While exploring the significance of Lacan in the clinical and cultural fields, the book reminds the reader of the gap between academic pedagogy and clinical practice.' This will remain an important reminder about the implications of a serious engagement for the reader/user of Lacan's works.

Mandal's volume is perhaps the first comprehensive attempt to make the work of Lacan accessible to a wide readership within the subcontinent. In fact, this was the principal reason why we chose to bring out a volume on Lacan within this series. While Lacan is read and discussed in the humanities and social sciences, engagement with his work is, more often than not, sketchy and tentative. We hope that this volume will help offer a fuller understanding of the feel and texture of Lacanian psychoanalysis, and incite enough interest in the reader to engage more comprehensively with the entire available body of Lacan's works.

Sumit Chakrabarti

List of Figures

Figure 1	Moebius strip (Image by courtesy of Wikimedia Commons)	page no. 30
Figure 2	Borromean knot (Image by courtesy of Wikimedia Commons)	page no. 37
Figure 3	Escort card (Image by courtesy of Wikimedia Commons)	page no. 44
Figure 4	Paternal metaphor	page no. 64
Figure 5	Saussurean algorithm	page no. 75
Figure 6	Saussure's linguistic sign	page no. 75
Figure 7	Formula of metaphor	page no. 77
Figure 8	Formula of metonymy	page no. 77
Figure 9	Saussure's linguistic sign (another version)	page no. 150

Introduction

> The end of my teaching is, well, to train psychoanalysts who are capable of fulfilling the function known as the subject, because it so happens that it is only from this point of view that we can really see what is at stake in psychoanalysis.
>
> Jacques Lacan, *My Teaching*

Psychoanalysis, in the precise Lacanian sense, is a clinical practice. Jacques Lacan's approach to this practice was, to say the least, a highly critical one. On the one hand, in his lectures (seminars) and writings (*écrits*) he engaged in an exhaustive and innovative critique of Sigmund Freud, to whom, unlike then-contemporary psychoanalysts, he had famously 'returned'. On the other hand, in the clinical field he introduced the controversial 'variable-length session', which deviated from the standard forty-five-minute analytic session as fixed by the International Psychoanalytic Association (IPA). Since he did not conform to the IPA's rules, Lacan's name was struck from the list of 'training analysts'. However, Lacan founded his own school of psychoanalysis, was joined by hundreds of analysts and trainee analysts and continued his psychoanalytic teaching and clinical practice. In time, his ideas exerted a powerful impact on both clinical and cultural fields. Although in his final public address at Caracas he continued to call himself a Freudian, Lacan's teachings gave birth to an entirely new terrain – the Lacanian orientation of clinical psychoanalysis.

The birth of Lacan's ideas took place at two sites – the couch and the seminar hall. Lacan treated and trained many analysands and delivered a substantial number of 'seminars' (collected into twenty-seven books) on the subject of psychoanalysis. These seminars were part of the curricula of the psychoanalytic societies and schools that Lacan was a member of or headed. A significant part of the audience for these seminars were analysts-in-training and, in many cases, the same analysands being analysed by Lacan in his clinic. There thus took place, both for the audience and the speaker, an emotive and cognitive exchange between the couch and the seminar hall. The mechanisms of the unconscious, the function of the analyst and the technique and goal of psychoanalysis were all themes which were discussed against the backdrop of a clinical experience shared by the speaker and the audience. When readers from non-clinical backgrounds engage with the texts of Lacan's seminars, they tend to miss this specific context in which these lectures were delivered.

In addition to the seminars, Lacan also wrote on psychoanalytic themes. However, these writings were largely derived from his seminars as most of them were written *for* the seminars, or were elaborate rewritings of issues discussed *in* the seminars. To differentiate his writings from his seminars and to highlight their specific nature (clinical context, writing as different from speech and so on), Lacan called them *écrits*. '*Écrits*' translates into 'writings', but the word is kept untranslated in English for its unique connotations. Lacan's *écrits* are as difficult to read as his seminars (if not more so). It may be argued, modifying John P. Muller and William J. Richardson's ideas, that both his *écrits* and his seminars are marked by a unique style; they not only theorise the unconscious – the central psychoanalytic concept – but also mimic the technique of 'free association', which is fundamental to psychoanalysis (Gallop 37; Muller 3). Difficulties also derive from the fact that, be it his seminars or his *écrits*, Lacan's implied addressees were analysts and analysands. This is something that Lacan insisted upon even when his audience dramatically increased in later years and large numbers of the Parisian intellectual community gathered to listen to him. Reading Lacan, without being aware of the clinical context, can therefore be very challenging.

It is the clinical orientation of Lacan's ideas which makes his teaching (*enseignement*) different from the conventional notion of teaching as understood within university discourse. Even though Lacan had become the 'master' for the majority of his followers, his constant focus was on the difficulty in 'mastering' the unconscious. This is why Lacan hesitated to use the word 'theory' in 'psychoanalytic theory', as theory implies a closed framework of thinking (Miller).

The key to the analytic experience, according to Freud and Lacan, is repeated encounters with the limits of the theoretical framework. This is indicated by Freud himself, who constantly revised his earlier theories and concepts. One obvious example would be Freud's replacement of his topographical model of the human mind (defined in terms of the unconscious, the preconscious, and the perception-consciousness systems constituting 'psychical localities') with the structural model (defined in terms of the id, the ego and the super-ego constituting 'psychical agencies'). In his strategic 'return to Freud' – which he emphasised right from the beginning of his teachings and which was strategic because the psychoanalysts of the 1940s and 1950s were moving away from Freud's texts – Lacan's emphasis was on bringing to the fore the implications of Freud's discoveries, which Freud himself was unaware of, or the impasses that Freud had encountered as a clinician. Throughout his career, Lacan too engaged in reformulating his earlier concepts and making accentual shifts. It is their clinical orientation that marks Lacan's texts as significantly different from those of other structuralist and poststructuralist theorists.

The present book is addressed to students, teachers and scholars of the humanities and social sciences. Presumably, the addressees of this book are largely, if not wholly, without any clinical orientation. Undergoing analysis under the supervision of a senior analyst, recognising one's symptoms and how they relate to the subject of the unconscious, witnessing the diagnosis of clinical structures, becoming a psychoanalyst and engaging in the discussion and study of case reports and theoretical works in groups are some of the essentials for a nuanced understanding of Lacan's teaching. While exploring the significance of Lacan in the clinical and cultural fields, this book aims to remind the reader of the gap which exists between academic pedagogy and clinical practice.

The book is divided into five chapters. Chapter One offers a survey of Lacan's teachings, especially focusing on his twenty-seven books which serve as a collection of his seminars. In view of the fact that Lacan's texts are largely unavailable in print (many of these have not yet been officially published or translated), the first chapter attempts to outline the scope of Lacan's teachings.

Chapter Two explains the various ways in which Lacan makes sense of the human subject. The discussion develops around the imaginary, symbolic and real (RSI) dimensions of subjectivity. It highlights the concept of the subject of the unconscious and ends with a description of the status of the subject at the end of a successful psychoanalysis.

Chapter Three is devoted to a discussion of the clinical structures of psychosis, neurosis and perversion. The clinical cases of Aimée, Wolf Man, Schreber, Dora and Little Hans, and the case of James Joyce, and Lacan's readings of them, are presented in detail. The three structures are also explained in terms of their mutual differences.

To say that the 'clinical' is all that is in Lacan's teachings would be misleading. Even though almost everything in Lacan is clinically oriented, he did not confine himself to clinical cases. A major part of Lacan's teachings is a commentary on philosophy, linguistics, arts, politics, literature, history, religion, mathematics and so on. In fact, Lacan modifies his psychoanalytic vocabulary in relation to these disciplines while, at the same time, thought-provokingly critiquing and exposing their limits. Lacan's teachings in this regard are very much informed by what can be called the 'cultural' (as different from the 'clinical'). Lacan's thoughts on cultural texts and concerns need to be engaged with as they are extremely valuable. Lacan's ideas have quite justifiably not remained confined to the clinical field. Even during his lifetime, he tremendously influenced academicians, intellectuals and theoreticians from various fields. Over time, such influence has visibly increased. The fourth and fifth chapters of the book attempt to demonstrate Lacan's relation to the field of culture.

Chapter Four is specifically devoted to explicating Lacan's understanding of literature and his formulation of psychoanalytic literary criticism. The basic coordinates of Lacanian criticism are outlined in terms of explaining how literary narratives can be, and have been, read in relation to the three Lacanian registers, three clinical structures, and 'sexuation'. An analysis of Lacan's seminal text 'Lituraterre' (1971) has been attempted in order to explain Lacan's term *lituraterre* and how the literature of Edgar Allan Poe, James Joyce, avant-garde writers and Samuel Beckett tend towards *lituraterre*. Thereafter, to demonstrate how Lacanian criticism works, a detailed analysis of John Fowles's *The French Lieutenant's Woman* (1969) has been done with close reference to the concepts of 'phallic myth', 'femininity' and 'sexual non-rapport'.

Chapter Five extends the question of engaging with Lacan beyond the clinical context by examining how Lacan has been read in the domains of film studies, gender studies, postcolonial studies and deconstruction. The section on film studies explicates Žižek's reading of Hitchcock, particularly the film *Psycho* (1960), to give an idea of Lacanian film criticism. The section on gender studies explains how Lacan has been criticised by feminists but how, nevertheless, his insights have been considered useful for feminism. The section on postcolonial studies focuses on how Lacan has particularly been used in the conceptualisation of the postcolonial o/Other, Manichaeism and in the reading of colonial narratives (especially by Abdul R. JanMohamed). The final section on Lacan and deconstruction traces the debate over the reading of Poe's 'The Purloined Letter' (1844) by Lacan, Jacques Derrida, Barbara Johnson and Slavoj Žižek.

In general, the book aims at a close reading of selected texts by Lacan and Lacanian theorists.

REFERENCES

Gallop, Jane. *Reading Lacan*. Ithaca: Cornell UP, 1985. Print.

Lacan, Jacques. *My Teaching*. Trans. David Macey. London: Verso, 2008. Print.

Miller, Jacques-Alain. 'Lacan's Later Teaching.' *Lacan Dot Com*. Trans. Barbara P. Fulks. Web. 5 September 2017. <http://www.lacan.com/frameXXI2.htm>

Muller, John P. and William J. Richardson. *Lacan and Language: A Reader's Guide to Écrits*. New York: International UP, 1982. Print.

Chapter One

An Outline of Lacan's Teachings

> The first thing to note, then, is that there is no James Strachey, no 'Standard Edition', for Lacan in English. Moreover, there have been few efforts to coordinate the translations, with as a result a fair degree of variation between them, both in terms of the way certain words are translated and in the style and 'feel' of the translations themselves. However, these variations are not, in themselves, serious deficiencies. The real problem is that some are not very reliable.
>
> Russell Grigg, 'Lacan in Translation'

Jacques Marie Émile Lacan was born to a Parisian-Catholic family on 13 April 1901. He completed his primary and secondary education at the prestigious Collège Stanislas de Paris (1907–19). In 1919, he started studying medicine at the Paris Medical Faculty. After completing his study, he engaged in clinical training in psychiatry at several places: in 1927, at the Sainte-Anne Hospital, Paris, under the supervision of Henri Claude; in 1928, at the Paris Police Special Infirmary for the Insane, under the direction of the famous psychiatrist Gaëtan Gatian de Clérambault; and from 1929 to 1931, at Hôpital Henri Rousselle. Additionally, in 1930, he took a two-month training course at the Burghölzli Psychiatric Clinic in Zürich. He became a licensed forensic psychiatrist in 1931 and received his doctorate in psychiatry in 1932, which was the same year when his growing interest in psychoanalysis, evident in his doctoral thesis, came to fruition as he started his 'training analysis' – the training one needs to undergo to become a psychoanalyst – with the psychoanalyst Rudolph Loewenstein. In 1934, he became a 'candidate member' of the Psychoanalytic Society of Paris (*Société psychanalytique de Paris*, SPP), which was founded in 1926, and when his analysis with Loewenstein ended in 1938, Lacan was made a 'full member' of the SPP. The SPP was temporarily disbanded during the Second World War and in 1945, for a period of five weeks, Lacan visited England to study British psychiatry and how it was put into practice during the war. The SPP resumed its activities in 1946, and in 1948, Lacan became a member of its teaching committee. However, in 1953, when Lacan had come to be known as the most formidable psychoanalyst of the SPP and elected its president, he resigned. Lacan's resignation was triggered by disagreements with some of the SPP members due to various reasons including Lacan opposing 'medicalis(ing) psychoanalytic training as a sub-discipline of neurobiology', promoting the rights of non-medical students to train and practice psychoanalysis and his practice of the 'short session' (Clark 'Biography'). Following his resignation, he immediately joined a new group called the French Society of Psychoanalysis (*Société française de psychanalyse*, SFP). But in 1963, less than a decade later, he would resign from the SFP following the IPA's demand that for the SFP to get official accreditation, Lacan, the practitioner of 'variable-length sessions', had to be deprived of the right to train new analysts. In 1964, Lacan founded his own school called the Freudian School of Paris (*École freudienne de Paris*, EFP), and remained its president till 1980, when it was dissolved by Lacan himself. In October 1980, shortly before his death in 1981, Lacan founded a new school called the School of Freudian Cause (*École de la cause freudienne*, ECF). It may be mentioned that during his various resignations Lacan was supported by many of his followers. Solidly trained as a psychiatrist and psychoanalyst, with the most enviable command over psychoanalytic theory and practice, Lacan attracted hundreds of Parisians and was a central figure in intellectual circles. However, the offshoot of his often controversial and uncompromising decisions was that he created a number of enemies and divided his followers.

Even before he started his public seminars in 1953, Lacan had already produced a substantial amount of psychoanalytic work. For instance, in 1931, he translated into French Freud's 'Some Neurotic Mechanisms in Jealousy, Paranoia and Homosexuality' (1922). This is a key Freudian text which Lacan engages with in his doctoral thesis, *Paranoiac Psychosis in its Relation to Personality* (*De la psychose paranoïaque dans ses rapports avec la personnalité*, 1932). In his thesis, Lacan writes about a psychotic woman whom he names Aimée and diagnoses as suffering from 'self-punishment paranoia', a new clinical category that Lacan proposed (Evans 137). The real name of the patient was Marguerite Anzieu and she had, in 1931, attempted to stab the famous actress Huguette Duflos at the stage door of a theatre. This incident became front-page news in Paris. It may be mentioned in passing that the bibliography of Lacan's doctoral thesis was so huge that Professor Heuyer wrote to Lacan saying, 'If you've read all that, I pity you'. Lacan's response was to say, 'In fact, I had read it all' (*Écrits* 486). In 1933, his article 'Motives of Paranoiac Crime: The Crime of the Papin Sisters' (*Motifs du crime paranoïaque: le crime des soeurs Papin*) was published in the surrealist journal *Minotaure*, which also published another article by Lacan. In this text, Lacan discusses the mysterious 1933 case of the Papin sisters who, while working as maids in the town of Le Mans, murdered the daughter and wife of their employer. The cases of Aimée and the Papin sisters contain instances of delusions and hallucinations and showcase Lacan's innovative critique. They also attest to the impact surrealism had on Lacan, and his bond with surrealists like Salvador Dalí who, for instance, developed and used the famous paranoiac-critical method in his paintings. In 1936, Lacan's 'Beyond the "Reality Principle"' (*Au-delà du 'principe de réalité'*) was published. This text alludes to Freud's *Beyond the Pleasure Principle* (1920). In the same year, Lacan presented his first analytic report at the fourteenth IPA Congress, which took place in Marienbad, on the theme of the mirror stage. Midway through his presentation, the IPA President Ernest Jones had to stop him since he had crossed his time-limit. Lacanians' only significant memory associated with this presentation is that Lacan, thus prevented from completing his presentation, left the conference and went to see the

Berlin Olympic Games. This was perhaps the beginning of Lacan's state of disagreement with the IPA. In 1938, Lacan's article on 'The Family Complex' (*Les complexes familiaux*, inappropriately translated as *La famille*) was published in the eighth volume of the *Encyclopédie Française*. In this text, Lacan develops, among other things, his ideas on the weaning complex, intrusion complex, Oedipus complex and castration complex – the four determining stages in the life of a child (discussed in Chapter Two). In 1945, Lacan published 'British Psychiatry and the War' (*La Psychiatrique anglaise et la guerre*), in the journal *Evolution Psychiatrique*. This article was based on his visit to England immediately after the Second World War. In 1949, he presented, at the sixteenth IPA Congress in Zurich, a new paper on the mirror stage. In this text, Lacan develops the notion of the imaginary. Finally, in 1952, Lacan delivered a lecture on psychoanalysis and dialectic ('La psychanalyse, dialectique?') wherein he defended the use of variable-length sessions – that which had raised a lot of objections from SPP members. In 1953, as a member of the newly founded SFP, Lacan delivered the famous 'Rome Discourse', in which, in terms of developing his theory on the function and field of speech and language in psychoanalysis, he challenged the prevalent politics of medicalising psychoanalysis by linking it to neurobiology.

Four common threads stand out in these otherwise diverse 'pre-seminar texts'. First, Lacan engages with and is influenced by the surrealist movement – which was derived from Freud's discovery of the unconscious and its various 'formations' including dreams (discussed in Chapter Two). Second, having rigorously engaged with clinical psychiatry over the years, Lacan starts to take issue with certain psychiatric theories and techniques and explores the possibilities of synthesising clinical psychiatry with Freudian teachings (Roudinesco 32). Third, Lacan, frequently in dialogue with Freud, is found to have problems with existing theories and techniques of psychoanalysis. Fourth, Lacan's major psychoanalytic contributions in these years include the conception of the mirror stage (*Le stade du miroir*) and paranoia, which would predominantly figure in the early stages of his oral teachings.

A BRIEF SURVEY OF LACAN'S SEMINARS

The very concept of the 'psychoanalytic seminars' was formulated by Lacan quite clearly on two occasions. In the 1949 statutes of the SPP which he had written, he divided the curriculum of the Society into four categories – '*commentaries* of the official texts (particularly Freud's), courses on controlled technique, clinical and phenomenological critique, and child analysis' ('Chronology'; italics mine). In the foundational act of the EFP, Lacan divided the School into three sections – 'a section of "pure psychoanalysis", which would be responsible for the training of new analysts; a clinical section; and . . . a section to . . . *an homage to the Freudian field*, which would *explore connections* between psychoanalysis and other disciplines' (Clark 'Biography'; italics mine). What is evident from these formulations is that the seminars and the analytic praxis were supposed to intimately inform each other.

In 1951, at his apartment in Paris, Lacan started organising weekly private seminars with small groups of analysts. Between 1951 and 1952, he discussed Freud's case history of 'Wolf Man' and between 1952 and 1953, he spoke on 'Rat Man'. No shorthand versions of these seminars exist. In 1953, Lacan shifted his seminars to the medical-school clinic of Sainte-Anne Hospital, where he worked and where his first ten Seminars were delivered. In 1963, Lacan resigned from the SFP, with the consequence that the Seminar of that year, which was on the theme of the Name-of-the-Father, ended after only one session. This incomplete Seminar is called *The Non-existent Seminar* (*Le séminaire inexistant*). Immediately after his resignation, École Pratique des Hautes Études (EPHE) institutionally sponsored Lacan's seminars, which he delivered at the Dusanne lecture theatre of the École Normale Supérieure (ENS). At the ENS, six Seminars (from *Seminar Book XI* to *Seminar Book XVI*) were delivered. In 1969, after a disagreement with the director of the ENS, who accused Lacan of instigating student riots, Lacan changed the venue, this time to the Faculté de Droit at the Pantheon, where the rest of his Seminars (from *Seminar Book XVII* to *Seminar Book XXVII*) were delivered.

Lacan's weekly deliberations were called seminars (or sometimes 'lessons' or 'sessions' due to their analytic significance). Seminars based on an annual theme constituted the book of seminars for that particular year. The seminars were delivered over twenty-seven years and there are thus twenty-seven books of seminars. In this book, 'Seminar' with an uppercase 'S' refers to a particular book of seminars, and 'seminar' with a lowercase 's' refers to a specific lecture delivered by Lacan. Even though Lacan took up a different theme each year, the Seminars are, in one way or the other, interconnected. Véronique Voruz and Bogdan Woolf, in *The Later Lacan: An Introduction* (2007), observe that these Seminars can be chronologically divided into three phases – the imaginary phase, the symbolic phase, and the real phase, where these three terms, abbreviated as RSI, constitute the 'three registers of analytic experience' (viii). The two editors have suggested that even though Lacan simultaneously referred to all three terms in the beginning of his career, he made accentual shifts over time. From *Seminar Book I* to *Seminar Book X*, the accent is on the notion of the imaginary. Some of the key concerns of this phase include 'mirror stage, narcissism, identification – and so the formation of the ego' (viii). It should be noted, however, that Lacan's interest in the mirror stage can be traced back to his 1936 IPA presentation which was interrupted by the IPA President. From *Seminar Book XI* to *Seminar Book XIX* – where the accent is on the symbolic – Lacan continues, in various ways, to 'formalise the object of anxiety as object *a*' and as far as the object *a* is the 'residual real caught in the symbolic', his attempt in these Seminars is to 'absorb, treat, or at least account for' the real vis-à-vis the symbolic (ix). Once again, Lacan's interest in the symbolic can be traced back to his 1953 lecture, the 'Rome Discourse'. From *Seminar Book XX* to *Seminar Book XXVII* – where the accent is explicitly on the real qua real – Lacan is no longer concerned with the 'residual real caught in the symbolic' but instead recognises the real as irreducible to the symbolic (ix). The key concerns of this phase include *jouissance*, *sinthome* and sexual non-rapport.

The Real, the Symbolic and the Imaginary

In Lacan, the real, the symbolic and the imaginary constitute the three registers of psychical life. Simply put, the imaginary order is the world of images and visuals (mirror image of oneself, semblable images of siblings, 'imago' of the mother's breast and so on) which the child identifies with to develop his sense of selfhood. This imaginary identification leads to the formation of the ego. The symbolic order is the world of law, norms and prohibition (the 'no' and 'names' of the father) that the child has to identify with due to his entry into the network of language. This symbolic identification is opposed to the imaginary identification and involves the substitution of the 'desire of the mother' (the desire to be the imaginary object of the mother's desire and thereby preserve the original oneness with the mother) with the 'Name-of-the-Father'. The real order is both pre-symbolic and extra-symbolic and, as Slavoj Žižek explains in *Enjoy Your Symptom!* (2012), is linked to both life and death which are, in a sense, alien to the symbolic world. The core of human life is enjoyment, but civilisation (the symbolic order) puts a limit to it – unlimited enjoyment is forbidden. Lacan uses the term *jouissance* to designate the notion of pleasure that is considered transgressive, that is, pleasure which transcends the idea of 'pure pleasure' and transgresses into the realms of pain. *Jouissance* is pre-symbolic in the sense that it is related to the body and is there even before symbolic identification takes place. Lacan talks about two kinds of *jouissance* – phallic *jouissance* and feminine *jouissance*. Phallic *jouissance* is what can be articulated through language, but feminine *jouissance* is an experience which exceeds the symbolic order and thus 'ek-sists' it (exists outside but insists on the symbolic order). The real order is also linked to death in the sense that it relates to void, nothingness and trauma. At the end of a successful psychoanalysis, for instance, the analysand has an encounter with the real as he realises that behind all his imaginary and symbolic identifications he is ultimately defined by nothingness. In a sense, the imaginary and symbolic function as veils that save the subject from encountering the real, whereas it is the creation of *sinthome* at the end of analysis that helps the subject to both realise and be equipped to come to terms with his experience of nothingness.

Although *Seminar Book XXII* is on the RSI, it should be noted that in July 1953, Lacan had delivered a lecture on the 'symbolic, the imaginary and the real' at the SFP's inaugural meeting (Evans xxi). In other words, this was not the first time Lacan talked about the interrelation between these registers. This third phase of Lacan's teachings, which is clearly different from the first two phases, has been designated as 'later teaching'. However, for Jacques-Alain Miller, who coined the expression 'later teaching of Lacan' (*Le dernier enseignement de Lacan*) and divided Lacan's career into four stages, the third stage of Lacan's teachings begins with *Seminar Book XXI* – not *Seminar Book XX* – and ends with *Seminar Book XXIII* (Biswas). The fourth or final stage of Lacan's teachings, which Miller called the 'latest Lacan' (*Le tout dernier Lacan*), would correspond to *Seminar Books XXIV–XXVII*. In this stage, Lacan is emphatically concerned with the topological conception of psychoanalysis, especially with the topology of knots. However, as is obvious, any such classification of Lacan's teachings or his psychoanalytic output across his career is just for preliminary guidance. Lacan returned to his earlier concepts in his later days, developed the same over the course of his teachings and, overall, reformulated ideas without ever rejecting any of them. His teachings, in general, resist classification.

Structurally speaking, a survey of Lacan's Seminars – each collection delivered approximately between November and June of every academic year – reveals a recurrent underlying pattern. For every annual Seminar, Lacan isolated a major theme pertaining to his conception of psychoanalysis which he developed in relation to (a) philosophy, literature, arts and other disciplines, (b) Freud's texts, (c) his own analytic experience and his take on clinical psychoanalysis and (d) structural linguistics, 'mathemes' (algebraic symbols) and topology frequently used to formulate psychoanalytic discoveries. Another noticeable pattern is that a concept is never static in Lacan's works – it is endowed with new implications over the course of his Seminars. For instance, the Cartesian *cogito ergo sum* (I think therefore I am), critiqued from the beginning of Lacan's teachings in relation to the Freudian 'barred subject', is reformulated over the years into *cogito ergo es* (I think therefore you are, or I think therefore Id is, where *es* is Latin for 'you are' and German for 'Id') (discussed in *Seminar Book XIV*). Lacan's critique of Descartes derives, as elaborated on in Chapter Two, from the Freudian idea that the subject is not a unified something but an entity split between thinking and being, between something and nothing or between the symbolic/imaginary identifications and experiences of the real. Another example of concepts imbued with new implications is when Lacan discussed the notion of anxiety in various Seminars before devoting an entire Seminar, namely *Seminar Book X*, to this theme. A reading of any given concept in Lacan must take into consideration all its implications as developed over the years. Dylan Evans, naturally, had to adopt such an approach in his invaluable *A Dictionary of Lacanian Psychoanalysis* (1996). But the unavailability of some of Lacan's Seminars has occasionally prevented scholars, including Evans, from perfecting such an approach. Such is the case with Michael Clark's *Jacques Lacan: An Annotated Bibliography in Two Volumes* (1988). Due to their unavailability, Clark could not annotate six of Lacan's Seminars in his well-researched book.

Lacan spoke and wrote in French. Although his last seminar was delivered in 1980, some of the transcripts of his Seminars are still to be translated or published. For instance, *Seminar Book*s *IX, XII, XIII, XIV, XV, XXI, XXV* and *XXVI* are yet to be published in French. While excerpts have been published in the French-language Lacanian journal *Ornicar?*, *Seminar Book*s *XXII*, *XXIV* and *XXVII* are yet to be published in French as independent volumes. Furthermore, *Seminar Book*s *IV*, *VI*, *XVI*, *XVIII* and *XIX*, though published in French, have not been officially translated into English apart from a few excerpts. So, virtually sixteen of Lacan's twenty-seven books of seminars remain officially unavailable to the English-speaking world. Cormac Gallagher, an Irish Lacanian who attended Lacan's seminars in person, has produced unofficial translations of many of the Seminars, and these translations are widely used, but Gallagher's translations are based on unedited French transcripts. As challenged as an English-speaking reader is in this instance, an attempt is made here to offer a thematic survey of the twenty-seven Seminars which constitute the bedrock of Lacan's teachings. The survey is based on a reading of the available official and unofficial versions of Lacan's Seminars, as well as the relevant critical approaches to the same.

Seminar Book I

Seminar Book I, titled *Freud's Papers on Technique (Les écrits techniques de Freud)*, is a collection of seminars delivered during 1953–54 and critiques the psychoanalytic method as discussed by Freud, particularly his writings from 1904 to 1919 which were published in a single German volume called *Zur technik der psychoanalyse und zur metapsychologie* (1924). Even though Lacan refers to these specific texts by Freud, which include five of Freud's case histories (Dora, Little Hans, Rat Man, the Schreber case and Wolf Man), he reminds his audience that Freud, at every turn, talked about the psychoanalytic technique (*Book I* 13). According to Lacan, Freud's papers on technique engage with the 'notions fundamental to the mode of operation of the analytic therapy, the notion of resistance and the function of transference' (8). Lacan returns to Freud's texts with an apparently simple question – 'what do we do when we do psychoanalysis?' (10). As such, the larger objective of this Seminar is to mutually inform or critique Freudian ideas on the psychoanalytic method and Lacan's and his analyst-audience's immediate clinical experiences. Some related issues addressed by Lacan in this context include the idea of the 'reconstruction of the subject's history' (13), the three formations of the ego (super-ego, ego-ideal and ideal-ego), the concepts of narcissism, the imaginary, *méconnaissance*, the idea of ego analysis and its relation to discourse analysis, the significance of the symbolic order, and the function of speech in psychoanalysis. Some of these concepts are discussed in Chapter Two.

Seminar Book II

Seminar Book II, titled *The Ego in Freud's Theory and the Technique of Psychoanalysis* (*Le moi dans la théorie de Freud et dans la technique de la psychanalyse*), collects seminars delivered between 1954 and 1955. Lacan announces the broader aim of the Seminar in the following words:

> So this year we will pursue the examination and criticism of the notion of the ego in Freud's theory, we will clarify its meaning in relation to Freud's discovery and to the technique of psychoanalysis, all through studying side by side some of its current uses, which are tied to a certain manner of conceiving

> the relation of one individual to another in analysis. (*Book II* 12)

The Seminar begins by placing Freud's take on the ego in opposition to pre-analytical notions of the ego as found in the philosophies of Socrates, René Descartes, John Locke, G. W. F. Hegel, Immanuel Kant and Friedrich Nietzsche. Among these, Lacan would time and again return to and criticise the Cartesian notion of the *cogito*. One of Lacan's primary reasons for criticising Descartes was that he believed the 'I' in Descartes's 'I think' was not the same as the 'I' in 'I am', since there is an unrecognised split on a number of levels – between thinking and being, between the unconscious and consciousness, between subject as something and subject as nothing (this issue is discussed in detail in Chapter Two). It is this division which turns the individual into a 'barred subject' – barred from knowing his unconscious thoughts or from realising his being as nothing (Evans 16, 198). The domains of consciousness and ego, as conceived of in philosophy, are deeply problematic from the point of view of psychoanalysis since, among other things, these domains constitute a 'circle of certainties'. Lacan hence states in this Seminar:

> The unconscious completely eludes that circle of certainties by which man recognises himself as ego. There is something outside this field which has every right to speak as *I*, and which makes this right manifest by coming into the world speaking as an *I*. It is precisely what is most misconstrued by the domain of the ego which, in analysis, comes to be formulated as properly speaking being the *I*. (*Book II* 8)

The ego is but the 'being I' and there is an 'I' outside the field of the ego which is thus different from the ego. Lacan hence makes statements like – '*I* is an other . . . the real *I* is not the ego' (*Book II* 7), the subject is excentric vis-à-vis the ego, and the 'I' is an other to the 'being I' (44). Although, the 'I' that speaks and thinks – this 'I' that is distinct from the 'being I' – is the domain of the unconscious, this does not mean that the ego or the 'being I' is identical to the domain of consciousness. The 'more Freud's works progress', states Lacan, 'the less easy he finds it to locate consciousness, and he has to admit that it is in the end unlocalisable' (8). According to Lacan, the psychoanalytic critique of the ego and consciousness, as proposed by Freud, not only replaces a psychical universe dominated by the ego with one dominated by the unconscious, but also interrogates the very notion of consciousness. It is a situation analogous to the replacement of the theory of a geocentric/Ptolemaic universe with the theory of a heliocentric/Copernican universe. Lacan concludes: 'In relation to this conception, the Freudian discovery has exactly the same implication of decentring as that brought about by the Copernican discovery' (7).

In this context, Lacan strongly criticises the theories of the school of ego psychology which avoid what he believed to be the most crucial questions related to the theory of the ego and the technique of psychoanalysis. As opposed to the ego psychologists, who place a misguided emphasis on the notion of the ego, Lacan questions why Freud had to introduce the structural notion of the human mind (comprising the psychical 'agencies' – the id, the ego and the super-ego) in the place of his earlier topographical model of the human mind (comprising psychical 'localities' – the systems of the unconscious, the pre-conscious and the perceptual-conscious), and relates the formulation of these new notions to the 'crisis in technique which had to be overcome' by Freud (*Book II* 11). To make sense of this clinical crisis, as well as the newly discovered notions, Lacan suggests an attentive reading of Freud's works from 1920 onwards – his 'last metapsychological period' of which *Beyond the Pleasure Principle* is the 'primary text, pivotal work' and the 'most difficult' to fathom (12). By asking why this text was written before other texts of this period which theorised the ego, Lacan engages in an analysis of the clinical impasse that Freud himself had encountered. Such an analysis does not, however, remain confined to this one text; Lacan, for instance, goes on to offer some invaluable insight into Freud's presentation of the 'Dream of Irma's Injection' from *The Interpretation of Dreams* (1899). Other issues addressed in *Seminar Book II* include: a reading of Edgar Allan Poe's short story 'The Purloined Letter' in conjunction with *Beyond the Pleasure Principle*, and Lacan's glorification of Poe's story as 'an absolutely sensational short story, which could even be considered as essential for a psychoanalyst' (179); the introduction of the big Other and Schema L ('Schema L' takes its name from the upper case Greek *lambda* and represents how the symbolic relation between the subject and Other is blocked by the imaginary relation between the ego and the specular image) (172); a discussion of the RSI; and the relation between psychoanalysis and cybernetics.

Seminar Book III

Seminar Book III, titled *The Psychoses* (*Les Psychoses*), collects seminars delivered from 1955 to 1956. This is a major treatise on 'madness', as Lacan himself states at the outset: 'The psychoses . . . correspond to what has always been called and legitimately continues to be called *madness*' (4). Psychosis has also been an old interest of Lacan's and here he refers to his doctoral thesis on paranoiac psychosis which he wrote as a young psychiatrist. While engaging in a thorough investigation of psychosis in this Seminar, Lacan explores the differences between neurosis and psychosis (which, along with perversion, constitute the 'three clinical structures' in Lacanian nosography). In one sense, these clinical structures are mutually different in terms of their fundamental operations; neurosis is defined by repression (*Verdrängung*), perversion is defined by disavowal (*Verleugnung*) and psychosis is defined by foreclosure (*Verwerfung*). What is foreclosed in psychosis, says Lacan, is the 'Name-of-the-Father'. The 'Name-of-the-Father' is understood primarily as the first signifier that the child has access to (the 'no' and the 'name' of the father), as the primary signifier which names and positions the subject in the symbolic order and as the signifier of law, logic and language that constitute social reality. The absence of the Name-of-the-Father, derived from the malfunctioning of the Oedipus complex (discussed in Chapters Two and Three), is what leaves a hole in the symbolic order and a prevalence of the imaginary (image of the father as opposed to the 'Name-of-the-Father') occurs. Hallucinations and delusions, symptoms of psychosis, are said to be triggered by the reappearance in the real of what is repudiated in the symbolic. Obviously, Lacan's analysis of psychosis is directly related to his conception of the three psychical registers – the real, the symbolic and the imaginary. But, at this stage, his thrust remains on the 'absolute necessity of isolating that essential articulation of symbolism which is called the signifier, in order to understand anything at all, analytically speaking, of the strictly paranoiac field of the psychoses' ('Book IV' 21 November 1956). Over the course of the Seminar, Lacan engages in a detailed critique of Freud's 1911 study of the Schreber case based on Daniel Paul Schreber's autobiographical account of his paranoid delusions. Some of the related issues addressed in this Seminar include the significance of Freud's 'The Loss of Reality in Neurosis and Psychosis' (1924) and 'Neurosis and Psychosis' (1924), the differences between masculine and feminine hysteria vis-à-vis the Dora case, and the notion of *points de capiton* or the quilting/anchoring point which knots or ties together the signifier and the signified for the subject. *Seminar Book III* is discussed in detail in Chapter Three of this book.

Seminar Book IV

Seminar Book IV, titled *The Object Relation and the Freudian Structures* (*La relation d'objet et les structures freudiennes*), collects the lectures of 1956–57. The title alludes to the theories of the object relations school of psychoanalysis. In this Seminar, Lacan engages in a rigorous criticism of the flawed theories of this school, as propounded by D. W. Winnicott and other members of the Middle Group of British Psychoanalytic Society and as defended by the members of the SPP, including Maurice Bouvet (Evans 128). The thrust of the Seminar, Lacan tells us, is the following:

> I tried to show that there is no object that is not metonymical, the object of desire being the object of the desire of the other, and desire always being desire of something else, precisely of what is lacking in the object that has been primordially lost, in so far as Freud shows it as something that has always to be rediscovered. ('Book V' 6 November 1957)

This would have the following implications. First, Lacan does not talk about the object – he talks about the lost object – and he also reminds us that Freud's concern is not the object but the lack of the object. Here, the object is understood both as the mother (the object of the child's desire) and the object of the mother's desire (which the child considers to be the 'phallus' and which he wants to embody to maintain his oneness with her). For Lacan, the object, in both these senses, has to be sacrificed by the child in order to be socialised, and the stage of castration is what helps the child sacrifice the object in relation to the 'desire for/of the mother' and accept the 'name/law of the father' (this is examined in further detail in Chapter Two). During the course of his discussion, Lacan talks about the subjective manifestations of the lost object in three forms, namely, castration, frustration and privation. According to Evans's interpretation of this issue, frustration may be defined as an 'imaginary lack of a real object' involving the child's experience of a lack or refusal of the mother's love (symbolised by a breast, for instance). Privation may be defined as a 'real lack of a symbolic object', involving the child thinking that the mother suffers a deprivation of the phallus due to incest taboos. Castration may be defined as a 'symbolic lack of an imaginary object' involving the repression of the child's desire to embody the imaginary phallus, which is posited as an answer to 'what does the mother lack?' Obviously, all three events are related to different kinds of 'lack of the object' (Evans 22–23).

Second, as opposed to the notion of the object as something that satisfies a biological need, Lacan defines the object on the level of desire, which is fundamentally linked to the order of language. The object of desire is 'metonymical' (a term which can be traced back to Roman Jakobson's formalist ideas of language, which Lacan makes ample use of) because it is always 'part object' or substitute object, since the original object is primordially lost. This metonymical object does not fulfil desire but causes it – in fact, it is the *source* of desire. Lacan hence talks about 'object cause' (*objet petit a*) instead of the object per se. Indeed, over time Lacan articulates more explicitly the notion of desire as something that seeks recognition, not fulfilment, and therefore depends on the 'object cause'. Other related issues explored in this Seminar include the function of the object in relation to phobia and fetishism, the notions of motherhood, love, and feminine homosexuality, a fresh approach to the Dora case and the Little Hans case, the differences between the real phallus, the symbolic phallus and the imaginary phallus, and the paradox of *jouissance*. Some of these concepts are discussed in Chapter Two.

Seminar Book V

Seminar Book V, titled *The Formations of the Unconscious* (*Les formations de l'inconscient*), collects seminars delivered during 1957–58. According to Freud, formations of the unconscious – which manifest the unconscious as well as its logic – are four in number: dream, wit, parapraxes and symptom. The formations obey the rules of condensation and displacement. In this Seminar, Lacan shows how each of these formations is structured by language and how the mechanisms of condensation and displacement are similar to the linguistic mechanisms of metaphor and metonymy (this is further elaborated on in Chapter Two). To emphasise the centrality of language in the formation(s) of the unconscious, Lacan asks his audience to read his 1957 text 'The Instance of the Letter in the Unconscious', which he continually refers to during the course of the Seminar. He emphasises that witticism (according to Freud, *witz*) is the best way of getting into the subject matter of the formations of the unconscious – it is the 'most brilliant form in which Freud himself shows the relationship of the unconscious to the signifier and to its techniques' ('Book V' 6 November 1957). Jokes reveal signifying techniques and unconscious mechanisms by facilitating particular kinds of articulation and enjoyment which are otherwise not socially permissible. In this context, Lacan closely reads Freud's text *Wit and its Relation to the Unconscious* (1905). In terms of elaborating the ideas of Czech formalists and literary theory, Lacan explains how, from the beginning, Freud situated himself at the level of the structural theory of the signifier. Among other things, in this Seminar, Lacan engages in a reappraisal of the Oedipus complex and an exposition on the formation of the subject.

Seminar Book VI

Seminar Book VI, titled *Desire and its Interpretation* (*Le désir et son interprétation*), collects seminars delivered from 1958 to 1959. In this Seminar, Lacan highlights the essentially linguistic dimension of desire and its centrality in clinical praxis, while also exploring the notion of desire in philosophy and in poetry. Perhaps one of the more significant contributions made by Lacan in this Seminar is his detailed psychoanalytic critique of William Shakespeare's play, *Hamlet* (1609), in conjunction with the notion of the 'graph of desire'. Lacan considers *Hamlet* not as a revenge tragedy but as a 'tragedy of desire', since Hamlet's suffering begins with the discovery of his mother's hasty remarriage and not with the discovery of his father's murder. For Lacan, Hamlet is suspended in the desire of the mother, a desire which puts Hamlet's time 'out of joint', compelling him to vacillate between hesitation and haste.[1] Lacan dismisses the theory that Hamlet procrastinates and highlights the fact that while there are some moments in the play when Hamlet hesitates, there are other moments when he hastens. Based on a close reading of the play, Lacan defines Hamlet's behaviour as derived from his being suspended in the time of the Other, which can be formulated as: Hamlet hastens when the Other (mother/Claudius) hesitates, and Hamlet hesitates when the Other hastens. The attempt to rescue his time and desire from the grasps of the Other inevitably ends in the subject/Hamlet receiving a mortal wound. In a way, to get rid of the symbolic and imaginary identifications which constitute subjectivity is to suffer wounds, experience death/nothingness or encounter the real. During the course of this immensely insightful and provocative analysis of *Hamlet*, Lacan goes on to explicate the stages in Hamlet and Ophelia's relationship, Ophelia's madness, Laertes as Hamlet's ideal ego, the relation of the dead king to the notion of the phallus, the desire of Gertrude and the larger clinical implications of the play. Related issues addressed in this Seminar include Lacan's precise formulation of psychoanalysis as a technique which 'essentially shows us what we will call man's capture in the components of the signifying chain', his distinction between desire and the phallus – 'desire is the metonymy of being in the subject; the phallus is the metonymy of the subject in being' ('Book VI' 12 November 1958) – an exploration of the relation between subject and the Other vis-à-vis desire and language, and the reformulation of Saussurean linguistics.

SHORT TAKES

The Phallus

The notion of the phallus (which has caused controversy, as discussed in Chapter Five) is formulated by Lacan on three levels: the real phallus, the symbolic phallus and the imaginary phallus. The imaginary phallus is something that the child, at the pre-Oedipal stage, imagines the mother to be lacking and that he wants to embody or identify with so as to become the object of the mother's desire. The symbolic phallus is the signifier – in fact, the first signifier the child encounters (the 'no'/'name' of the father) – that anchors his entire symbolic universe. The symbolic dimension of the phallus also comprises discourse or myths of male supremacy. The real phallus is described as being linked to the 'real father'. Due to the anxiety-provoking presence of the 'real father', the child has to sacrifice his fantasy of oneness with the mother during the moment of castration. The 'real father' is the 'potent father' or the bearer of the organ. However, Lacan suggests that ultimately the biological organ has a symbolic value – the 'real father' is discovered as the bearer of the organ and is thereby seen as the bearer of the law. Lacan is not promoting the real father or the real phallus here, he is simply articulating a clinical finding which reveals the different ways the formation of the (feminine/masculine) subject is affected by the imaginary, symbolic and real dimensions of the phallus. Such a finding can, in fact, be used to critique patriarchy.

SHORT TAKES

Other/other

The concept of the Other/other (*Autre/autre*) is to be understood on the level of the three registers. The 'other' with a lowercase 'o' (the 'little other') is the imaginary other. The subject's earliest encounter with the imaginary other takes place at the mirror stage. The mirror stage is described as occurring between six and eighteen months when the child is yet to develop proper motor coordination. At this stage, the child derives pleasure from looking at his image in the mirror. He considers the image to be himself; he identifies with it by thinking 'I am that'. According to Lacan, this is the moment of construction of the 'I' or the ego (or the imaginary order of subjectivity). Such a construction of selfhood is both paradoxical and misleading – paradoxical because there is a difference between the subject and the image of the subject, and misleading because it is with reference to something that is external to the child that his selfhood is constituted. It is the imaginary other that constructs the self. Such an idea of selfhood is described by Lacan as illusory. The 'Other' with an uppercase 'O' (the 'big Other') is the symbolic Other. The symbolic Other is the locus of speech and language. The otherness of the Other cannot be reduced into the subject's own terms – the subject is always under the Other's sway. The symbolic order of subjectivity (the formation of the subject of the unconscious) is created in terms of the subject's relation to the Other. The 'Other', with a capital 'O', also designates the real order as it stands for the 'Other sex' and 'Other *jouissance*' – that is, femininity and feminine *jouissance*. In his later teachings, Lacan highlights that 'The woman does not exist' and that feminine *jouissance* is 'beyond the phallus' (*Seminar Book XX* 7, 74). In both these contexts, Lacan's emphasis is on the distinction between the symbolic and the real. The symbolic is the phallic domain and the woman does not exist in this domain; she ek-sists the symbolic (or verges on the real). In the same sense, the Other *jouissance* is in the real since it ek-sists in the symbolic qua the phallic.

Seminar Book VII

Seminar Book VII, titled *The Ethics of Psychoanalysis* (*L'ethique de la psychanalyse*), collects seminars delivered during 1959–60. In this Seminar, Lacan rigorously critiques the philosophical tradition of ethical discourse as found in works by Aristotle, Kant and Marquis de Sade, among others. The Seminar also engages with a number of relevant texts by Freud including *Civilization and Its Discontents* (1930) and formulates the psychoanalytic take on the question of ethics. According to Freud, 'civilised morality' is posited as the root cause of nervous illness, and the feeling of guilt has been described as the effect of internalising this morality in the form of the super-ego, which acts against the subject's unconscious desire (Evans 56). Taking his cue from Freud, Lacan states in this Seminar that, 'From an analytic point of view, the only thing of which one can be guilty is of having given ground relative to one's desire' (319).

Although the task of the analyst, in such a situation, is to find out the precise historical point(s) in the life of the subject when she has given ground to her desire, the analyst immediately faces some crucial questions. Should the analyst help the analysand in freeing herself from these internal/external moral agencies and pursue the desire that is in her? Or, should the analyst suggest to the analysand that she sacrifice her desire and adopt the problematic 'civilised morality' in some way or the other? What would be the best kind of 'good' for the subject from the perspective of the psychoanalyst? The way the analyst answers these ethical questions influences the method, direction and goal of treatment (Evans 56–57). In the end, one of Lacan's propositions in *Seminar Book VII* is the following: 'There is no other good than that which may serve to pay the price for access to desire . . .' (321). Lacan illustrates the situation through an exhaustive analysis of Sophocles's tragedy, *Antigone* (c. 441 BC), in which the female protagonist pursues her pure and absolute 'death wish' and tragically ends her life. For Lacan, the essence of the Sophoclean tragedy sheds light on the tragic dimension of analytic experience and the paradoxes of ethics as experienced from the analyst's perspective. Related issues discussed in this Seminar include the introduction of *das Ding* (or 'the thing' that belongs to the real), the problem of sublimation, a reading of courtly romance in conjunction with anamorphic art, the paradox of *jouissance* and the notion of death drive.

Seminar Book VIII

Seminar Book VIII, titled *Transference* (*Le transfert*), collects seminars delivered from 1960 to 1961. Transference refers to the complex intersubjective relation between the analysand and the analyst, developed over the course of the analytic treatment and functioning potentially as both an obstacle and a facilitator in *unconcealing* the analysand's unconscious. The scope of this Seminar is much broader, as Lacan states in the very first sentence: 'I announced for this coming year that I would deal with transference, with its subjective oddity (*sa disparite subjective*). It is not a term that was easily chosen. It underlines essentially something which goes further than the simple notion of asymmetry between subjects' ('Book VIII' 16 November 1960).

This Seminar, considered to be Lacan's major work on the idea of love, engages in an exploration of the notion of 'transference love' in conjunction with a detailed analysis of Plato's masterpiece on the subject, *The Symposium* (c. 385–70 BC). Drawing on material from *The Symposium*, Lacan isolates the Greek term *agalma* (meanings of which include gift, image, ornament) and reads it alongside his term 'object *a*'. Over the course of his discussion, which is full of radical insights, Lacan describes love as a 'comic sentiment' and emphasises his idea that to 'love is to give what one does not have' ('Book VIII' 23 November 1960). Some related issues discussed in this Seminar include the question of the symbolic order and how it structures the relationship between the analysand and the analyst, the question of the analyst's desire and his relation to object *a*.

Seminar Book IX

Seminar Book IX, titled *Identification* (*L'identification*), collects seminars delivered during 1961–62. At the outset, Lacan addresses his analyst audience thus:

> Identification – this is my title and my subject for this year . . . I am sure you do not think that it is an operation or a process that is very easy to conceptualize. If it is easy to recognise, it would perhaps nevertheless be preferable . . . for us to make a little effort in order to conceptualize it. It is certain that we have encountered enough of its effects even if we remain . . . at things which are tangible, even to our internal experience, for you to have a certain feeling about what it is. This effort of conceptualization will appear to you, at least this year . . . to be without any doubt justified retrospectively because of the places, the problems to which this effort will lead us. ('Book IX' 15 November 1961)

While offering insight on the notion of identification in psychoanalysis, Lacan returns to a discussion of the Cartesian *cogito* as he conceptualises the formations of the ego – especially the ideal-ego – as the product of the imaginary identification with the mirror image, and the ego-ideal as the product of symbolic identification with the Name-of-the-Father (this is elaborated on in Chapter Two). As he develops the notion of the subject's identification with the signifier, he offers a critique of Ferdinand de Saussure's theories from *Course in General Linguistics* (compiled by Charles Bally and Albert Sechehaye, published in 1916) and redefines 'sign' as that 'which represents something for someone' ('Book IX' 6 December 1961). Additionally, among other things, he turns to the Russian formalists while developing Roman Jakobson's notions of metaphor and metonymy (elaborated on in Chapter Two), discusses the notion of identification in Freud's *Group Psychology and the Analysis of the Ego* (1921) and makes use of ideas from Euclidean geometry, Russell's paradox and Kant's 'transcendental analytic'.

Seminar Book X

Seminar Book X, titled *Anxiety* (*L'angoisse*), collects seminars delivered from 1961 to 1962. In this Seminar, Lacan puts forward a major formulation regarding anxiety:

> I would just like to point out to you that many things can appear which are anomalous, this is not what makes us anxious. But if all of a sudden all norms are lacking, namely what constitutes the lack – because the norm is correlative to the idea of lack – if all of a sudden it is not lacking – and believe me try to apply that to a lot of things – it is at that moment that anxiety begins. ('Book X' 28 November 1962)

If desire is triggered by the lack of an object, anxiety is experienced when the lack itself is lacking. Whereas desire is caused by object *a*, indicative of the primordially lost object, anxiety is caused when something fills the place of object *a* or when the lack related to the object *a* is lacking. Ruling out anxiety as an emotion, Lacan defines it as the only affect that, unlike emotions, does not deceive us. Over the course of his discussion he explores the relation of anxiety to the real, the uncanny and *jouissance*, and develops the ideas of 'acting out' and 'passage to the act' as the last recourse against anxiety. Both these acts, triggered by failure to communicate through speech, are impulsive responses to the Other. But, there is a crucial difference between them. 'Acting out', Evans writes, 'is a symbolic message addressed to the big Other, whereas a passage to the act is a flight from the Other into the dimension of the real. The passage to the act is thus an exit from the symbolic network, a dissolution of the social bond' (140). Alongside critiquing relevant ideas from the works of, among others, Plato, Hegel, Kant and Sade, Lacan, in this Seminar, explicates in detail the implications of Freud's 1926 text *Inhibitions, Symptoms and Anxieties*.

Seminar Book XI

Seminar Book XI, titled *The Four Fundamental Concepts of Psychoanalysis* (*Les quatre concepts fondamentaux de la psychanalyse*), collects seminars delivered in 1964. The Seminar was the first of its kind to be delivered at the ENS, where the audience included Claude Lévi-Strauss and Jacques-Alain Miller. It was also the first Seminar of the so-called second stage of Lacan's teachings and the very first Seminar to be published in French (1973) and translated into English (1978). The four fundamental concepts of psychoanalysis, as elaborated on by Lacan in this Seminar, relate to his take on the four key terms from Freud – unconscious, repetition, transference and drive. Miller, in *Reading Seminar XI* (1995), notes: 'With his four fundamental concepts, it is as if Lacan were presenting the unconscious in four distinct ways. Indeed, there are four distinct representations of analytic experience, four distinct ways of grasping what is going on in an analysis. It is not at all an abstract Seminar; it is a Seminar that is very close to actual analytic practice' (9). The four Lacanian ways of conceiving the unconscious are: the unconscious as subject, the unconscious as repetition, the unconscious as transference and the unconscious as drive. A host of other issues addressed in this Seminar include a discussion of his 'excommunication' from the IPA, 'gaze' as the object *a*, the difference between *tuché* ('encounter with the real') and *automaton* ('insistence of signs'), the idea of logical time, the relation of alienation to aphanisis and the field of the Other.

Seminar Book XII

Seminar Book XII, titled *Crucial Problems for Psychoanalysis* (*Problèmes cruciaux pour la psychanalyse*), collects seminars delivered between 1964 and 1965. Lacan begins the Seminar in a provocative way by critiquing Noam Chomsky's *Syntactic Structures* (1957) and refuting the claim that Chomsky's expression 'colourless green ideas sleep furiously' is a sentence which is grammatically correct but devoid of meaning. Engaging in an intriguing analysis of English expressions used in British poetry, from Andrew Marvell to Alfred Tennyson, and comically drawing attention to the nature of the unconscious as hidden from the so-called 'consciousness' and thus 'sleeping furiously', Lacan remarks that 'any signifying chain whatsoever, provided it is grammatical, always generates a meaning'. In relation to the discourse of the unconscious, however, Lacan problematises the very notion of meaning and says, 'The unconscious has nothing to do with these metaphorical meanings, however far we may push them' ('Book XII' 2 December 1964). Even then, the 'relationship of sense to the signifier' remains central to the psychoanalytic experience, and the crucial problems for psychoanalysis include investigating the unique way the unconscious is structured by the knots of language. Consequently, over the course of his discussion Lacan returns to a critique of the Cartesian notion of the *cogito* and its inevitable relation to the 'split subject', a renewed critique of Saussurean linguistics which includes Lacan's redefinition of signifier as 'that which represents the subject for another signifier', the 'non-sense' in Lewis Carroll and a formulation of the problems of psychoanalysis vis-à-vis the topology of torsion and the structures of a Moebius strip and a Klein bottle.

It may be mentioned in passing that the topological figures used in this Seminar redefine the concept of space. For instance, a Moebius strip, as Evans puts it, is a topological three-dimensional figure which 'can be formed by taking a long rectangle of paper and twisting it once before joining its ends together'. It subverts the normal Euclidean conception of space 'for it seems to have two sides but in fact has only one (and only one edge)'. 'Locally, at any one point,' Evans continues, 'two sides can be clearly distinguished, but when the whole strip is traversed it becomes clear that they are in fact continuous. The two sides are only distinguished by the dimension of time, the time it takes to traverse the whole strip' (119). Lacan uses this topological figure in many ways. For instance, he explains that the notion of the unconscious as something 'inside' the human subject and some conscious or empirical reality 'outside' of the human subject does not make sense. He describes the unconscious as the discourse of the Other, thus involving the interventions of language and intersubjectivity. The basic point here is that an opposition between inside and outside (or even below versus above with the unconscious as below, the conscious as above) cannot be made. Rather, the outside/above is, like a Moebius strip, 'continuous with' the inside/below.

Figure 1: Moebius Strip

Seminar Book XIII

Seminar Book XIII, titled *The Object of Psychoanalysis* (*L'objet de la psychanalyse*), collects the seminars of 1965–66. In this Seminar, Lacan is concerned with the function of 'object relations' in psychoanalysis, especially how the object dominates the subject's relation to the real. Four objects corresponding to four drives are isolated – breast as the object of the oral drive, faeces as the object of the anal drive, gaze as the object of the scopic drive and voice as the object of the invocatory drive. Lacan states that the first two objects have been promoted in psychoanalysis at the cost of the latter two, whose statuses have remained uncertain. The oral and anal objects relate to the notion of demand while gaze and voice relate to the notion of desire, which is why the latter two require a more complex theory. Over the course of the Seminar, Lacan is compelled to bring himself to 'a rectification of deviations in practice, to the necessary self-criticism of the position of the analyst, a self-criticism which is directed at the risk attached to his own subjectification, if he wants to respond honestly, even simply, to the demand' ('Book XIII' 25 May 1966). The major strands of thought found in this Seminar include: a provocative discussion of the object *a* in relation to Blaise Pascal's theory of 'wager' (on the probability of God's existence and the stance a rational person should take), as developed in his text *Pensées* (1670); a critical discussion of the notion of gaze in relation to Michel Foucault's *The Order of Things* (1966); fresh insight into Diego Velázquez's historic painting *Las Meninas* (1656); and a reappraisal of the mirror stage, *jouissance* and castration.

Seminar Book XIV

Seminar Book XIV, titled *The Logic of Fantasy* (*La logique du fantasme*), collects seminars delivered from 1966 to 1967. Freud had considered fantasy as that which stages the unconscious desire, and in his early teachings Lacan had described fantasy as that which the subject uses as a veil or a defence against the truth of castration or the lack in the mother (Evans 61). Even though the very notion of fantasy is analogous to the images on the cinematic screen and hence to the notion of the imaginary (or identification with images), unlike the Klein group of psychoanalysts, Lacan refuses to reduce fantasy to the imaginary. In this Seminar, Lacan conceptualises the structure of fantasy vis-à-vis the structure of the signifier, or the symbolic register which is the domain of law, logic and language. The logic of fantasy, articulated in terms of the relation of the barred subject to the object *a,* is presented as predominantly a signifying structure. Over the course of his discussion, Lacan restates the Cartesian principle of *cogito ergo sum* ('I think therefore I am') as *cogito ergo es* ('I think therefore you are', or 'I think therefore Id is', where *es* is Latin for 'you are' and German for 'Id'), engages with the idea of sexual difference, sexual non-rapport and sexual act, formulates the notion of *jouissance* – with propositions like, 'There is no *jouissance* except that of the body' ('Book XIV' 31 May 1967) – and returns to notions of alienation, repetition, 'passage to the act' and 'acting out'.

Seminar Book XV

Seminar Book XV, titled *The Psychoanalytic Act* (*L'acte psychanalytique*), collects seminars delivered during 1967–68. In the Lacanian sense, an 'act' as opposed to 'behaviour' (as in 'animal behaviour') belongs to the domain of the symbolic and is something for which the subject assumes responsibility (Evans 1–2). 'The psychoanalytic act,' states Lacan, 'neither seen nor heard of before me, namely, never mapped out, much less put in question, we suppose here to be something belonging to the elective moment when psychoanalysand passes to psychoanalyst' ('Book XV' Annex 3). The mapping of the psychoanalytic act, in this Seminar, includes a consideration of the 'acts' of the analyst, analysand and of the unconscious as subject. Thus, a series of 'acts', including the following, are critiqued: the 'founding acts' of psychoanalysis – in the sense of the laws pertaining to the establishment of Lacan's psychoanalytic schools; the profession and commitment of the analyst; the role played by the analyst in setting the unconscious of the analysand in motion and in helping the analysand reach the 'end of analysis'; the entry of the analysand into analysis; the role played by the 'subject supposed to know', the pathological acts derived from the unconscious as subject; the notion of 'passage to the act' and 'acting out'; the implications of transference and counter-transference and the act of becoming a psychoanalyst. The psychoanalytic act is described as tragic in that the 'end of analysis' is what leads to a sort of subjective destitution, derived from a realisation of naked truths about one's being: 'The end of psychoanalysis supposes a certain realization of truth operation. Namely, that if in effect it ought to constitute this sort of journey, which, from the subject installed in his false-being makes him realize something about a thinking which includes the "I am not"' ('Book XV' 10 January 1968). Related issues addressed in this Seminar include an analysis of the difference between Pavlovian experimentation and psychoanalytic mechanism, a critique of Winnicott's ideas on counter-transference and readings of Socratic dialogues. It may be noted here that this Seminar was interrupted due to the 1968 student movements, street violence and strikes regarding which Lacan, later, on 3 December 1969, in a talk known as 'Impromptu at Vincennes', made the famous statement: 'What you, as revolutionaries, aspire to is a Master. You will have one' (*Television* 126).

Seminar Book XVI

Seminar Book XVI, titled *From an Other to the other* (*D'un Autre à l'autre*), collects seminars delivered between 1968 and 1969. Lacan begins the Seminar with the following words:

> We find ourselves here again this year for a Seminar for which I chose the title *From an Other to the other* to indicate the major reference points around which my discourse ought, properly speaking, to turn. That is why this discourse is crucial at the moment of time that we are at. It is so in as much as it defines what is involved in this discourse called the psychoanalytic discourse, whose introduction, whose coming into play at this time brings so many consequences with it. ('Book XVI' 13 November 1968)

In Lacan, the Other with an uppercase 'O' refers to the symbolic Other and other with a lowercase 'o' (or 'a' as in *autre*) refers to the imaginary other. In this Seminar, however, the emphasis is on the definite article 'the' in 'the other', and the purpose is to move away from the universal to the particular or the singular. As such, the theme of the Seminar perfectly represents the thrust of Lacan's second stage of teaching which is described as follows: 'In this stage Lacan looked at the universal in conjunction with the singular: While the signifier is shared with others, the object small a belongs to the subject; while the big Other is universal, the object small a is singular' (Biswas). Among a host of issues addressed in this Seminar, special mention may be made of the notion of 'surplus *jouissance*' and a reappraisal of Pascal's wager.

Seminar Book XVII

Seminar Book XVII, titled *The Other Side of Psychoanalysis* (*L'Envers de la Psychanalyse*), collects seminars delivered during 1969–70. This was the first Seminar to be delivered at the new venue – the Faculté de Droit at the Pantheon. This Seminar contains a stimulating discussion of Lacan's notion of four discourses: the master's discourse, the university discourse, the hysteric's discourse and the analyst's discourse. These are understood to be the 'four possible types of social bond, four possible articulations of the symbolic network which regulates intersubjective relations' (Evans 45). At the risk of simplifying Lacan's ideas, the following could be stated about Lacan's four discourses. The master's discourse is marked by the master's imperatives and must be obeyed, not because these imperatives have any inherent justification but because they represent the master's will. The master is not interested in knowledge; his interest is power which he must maintain without showing any weakness. According to Fink's *The Lacanian Subject* (1995), in university discourse, 'systematic knowledge' becomes 'the ultimate authority' and, under the guise of reason, largely renders its service to the master (132). The hysteric's discourse is a constant questioning of the master, particularly the epistemic basis of the master's discourse since, ironically, knowledge remains inaccessible to the master. In the analyst's discourse, the analyst surrenders all notions of authority and domination since he has to reduce himself to an object – the object *a,* that is, the 'object cause' of the analysand's desire. In one sense, the title of the Seminar indicates a kind of structural opposition between the master's discourse and the analyst's discourse. Lacan develops four mathemes to represent his four discourses. These mathemes comprise four algebraic symbols – S1, S2, *a*, $\$$ – which, in accordance with the specificity of the discourse, occupy four positions – agent, other, product, truth (*Book XVII* 31).

It may be noted here that the term 'matheme' was coined by Lacan and derived from the combination of the words 'mathematics' and 'mytheme'. Mytheme, a term taken from the works of Claude Lévi-Strauss, stands for the minimal unit of every mythological system and is analogous to 'phoneme', the unit of sound of a specified language. Lévi-Strauss's structural analysis of myths was inspired by Saussure's theorisation of language as a system of signs. Lacan's theorisation of psychoanalysis was influenced by the structuralist ideas formulated by both Saussure and Lévi-Strauss. Lacan uses mathemes to formalise psychoanalytic concepts. Mathemes constitute a language which resists being reduced to imaginary and intuitive understanding and which helps transmit psychoanalytic theories 'integrally' (Evans 111–12). For example, the matheme or formula of the neurotic fantasy is ($\$ \lozenge a$). The concept of fantasy, thus, may be explained as the barred subject's relation to the little object of desire. The rhomboid (◊) stands for the relations of envelopment, development, conjunction and disjunction (Evans 111).

Seminar Book XVIII

Seminar Book XVIII, titled *On a Discourse That Might Not be a Semblance* (*D'un discours qui ne serait pas du semblant*), collects seminars delivered in 1971. The term 'semblance' is central to this Seminar, with reference to which Lacan formulates a number of concepts – including truth, sexual non-relationship, writing and hysteria – while developing his thesis that 'there is no discourse that is not a semblance'. Here, truth is described not as something opposed to semblance/appearance but as 'continuous with' semblance. The relation of truth and semblance is similar to the two sides of the Moebius band, which actually constitute one side since there is only one edge. Some of the related issues discussed in this Seminar, as isolated by Gallagher, include the formulae of sexuation, the idea of sexual relationship as something not inscribable, the notion of the phallus as semblance, 'the woman does not exist', the psychoanalytic significance of the 'writing effects' of Japanese and Chinese languages, a rereading of Poe's 'The Purloined Letter' and a reappraisal of the hysteric's clinical structure ('On a Discourse').

Seminar Book XIX

Seminar Book XIX, titled *. . . Or Worse* (*. . . Ou pire*), collects seminars delivered from 1971 to 1972. One of the elided words of the title is *père*, or father, and in one sense the title could be read as *père ou pire*, meaning, 'father or worse'. The main thrust of this Seminar is the idea that in the absence of the paternal function or 'Name-of-the-Father', which represents the symbolic, the subject's condition would worsen and he would turn into a psychotic. As Fink states in *A Clinical Introduction to Lacanian Psychoanalysis* (1999), 'Lacan does not assert that the father should be propped up in our society. Rather, he issues a warning: to reject the father's role, to undermine the father's current symbolic function, will lead to no good; its consequences are likely to be worse than those of the father function itself, increasing the incidence of psychosis' (111).

Intriguingly, in this Seminar, Lacan moves from 'there is no sexual relationship' to 'there is no second sex'. In this context, it may be mentioned that in this academic year (1971–72), Lacan also delivered additional talks which he called 'the knowledge of the psychoanalyst'. In one such talk, which is necessary to understand this Seminar as well as *Seminar Book XX*, he makes a reference to Simone de Beauvoir. Beauvoir telephoned Lacan while writing *The Second Sex* (1949) to clarify points that would constitute the 'psychoanalytic contribution' to her work. Lacan in reply told her that he would need at least five or six months to disentangle the question of 'second sex' so that he could present to her what he had been speaking of for over twenty years. Beauvoir could not afford more than three or four conversations due to her publishing deadlines, and upon hearing this, Lacan 'declined the honour', as quoted in Gallagher's 'Where was Jacques Lacan in 1971–72?' In this Seminar, Lacan adds his take on the notion of the 'second sex' by saying: '[the] foundation of what I am . . . in the process of bringing forward to you . . . is very precisely the fact that there is no second sex. There is no second sex from the moment that language comes into function' ('Where was Jacques Lacan in 1971–72?'). One implication of this claim would be that the second sex, or the woman, does not exist in the symbolic order (the order of language and discourse), but rather ek-sists it. In the next Seminar, Lacan would discuss this idea whereby a link would be developed between the real and femininity. The major themes of *Seminar Book XIX*, as isolated by Gallagher in 'Where was Jacques Lacan in 1971-1972?', include developments on the formulae of sexuation, the conceptualising of 'matheme' and *lalangue* and the introduction of the Borromean knot.

SHORT TAKES

Borromean Knot

The term 'Borromean knot' is derived from a fourteenth-century aristoctratic and influential family in Italy who carried the name Borromeo and bore a coat of arms which was of three intertwined rings. The rings of the knot were intertwined in such a way that if one was cut, the others would fall apart. Lacan uses the concept of a Borromean knot in two ways. First, he uses the knot to illustrate the interdependence of the three orders – the imaginary, the symbolic and the real. These orders, like the rings of the Borromean knot, are intimately linked in the case of a neurotic. For the psychotic, however, these rings remain separate and Lacan talks about a fourth ring, *sinthome*, which helps the psychotic tie these three orders together. In his later teachings, however, Lacan offers another formulation: for every subject, he seems to suggest, these rings remain separate until a fourth ring ties them together. In this sense, both the neurotic and the psychotic, albeit differently, need the *sinthome*. Thus, while the Borromean knot defines the essential structure of the subject, the construction of *sinthome* at the end of analysis is considered one of the goals of psychoanalysis.

Figure 2: Borromean Knot

Seminar Book XX

Seminar Book XX, titled *Encore* (the original French title is kept untranslated, but the English title is accompanied by the phrase *On Feminine Sexuality: The Limits of Love and Knowledge*), collects seminars delivered during 1972–73. This is perhaps Lacan's best known Seminar in the English-speaking world. The term 'encore' literally means 'once again' or 'still here', as explained by Lacan in his opening address to his audience: 'with the passage of time, I am still (*encore*) here, and you are too' (9). Véronique Voruz and Bogdan Woolf, in *The Later Lacan: An Introduction*, argue that this Seminar initiates the third stage of Lacan's teachings where the emphasis is explicitly on the register of the real. They draw attention to the opening lines of the Seminar – 'with the passage of time, I learned that I could say a little more about it. And then I realized that what constituted my course was a sort of "I don't want to know anything about it"' – and state that the expressions 'could say a little more about it' or 'don't want to know anything about it' are references to the real which ek-sists the symbolic or exists outside but insists on the order of language (ix). The 'beyond of language' is also related, in this Seminar, to the notion of 'feminine *jouissance*'. Lacan describes feminine *jouissance* as:

> There is a *jouissance* . . . 'beyond the phallus'. There is a *jouissance* that is hers, that belongs to that 'she' that doesn't exist and doesn't signify anything. There is a *jouissance* that is hers about which she herself perhaps knows nothing if not that she experiences it – that much she knows. She knows it, of course, when it comes. It does not happen to all of them. (74)

For Lacan, feminine *jouissance* can be experienced but cannot be articulated since articulation necessitates the use of language which is always already phallicised. As such, feminine *jouissance* poses a limit to knowledge. In this context, Lacan refers to Gian Lorenzo Bernini's famous sculpture, *The Ecstasy of St. Teresa,* to develop a parallel between feminine *jouissance* and the mystical experience. As he formulates the idea of femininity, Lacan elaborates on his statement, 'The woman does not exist', where the emphasis is on 'The' (7). One implication of the statement is that *the* woman (or femininity as a definable category) does not exist because existence implies existence in the symbolic, that is, in the phallic domain of law, logic and language. For Lacan, femininity in its purest form resists such categorisation and places a limit on the symbolic. Lacan places the notion of the 'real of femininity' in opposition to the idea of the phallus understood as the 'myth of masculinity'.

With reference to the phallus, which functions as the third term between man and woman in the 'man-woman relationship' – analogous to the bar in the Saussurean formula of signified and signifier, Lacan states that sexual rapport does not exist. It must be noted here that for Lacan, 'man' and 'woman' are not biological categories but 'psychical' structures determined by a specific kind of *jouissance*. Some of the related issues addressed in this Seminar include the notion of love in its relation to language, the relation between knowledge and truth and the major formulations about the concept of *jouissance*. Chapter Four of this book offers further explanations of the notions of phallic myth and femininity.

Seminar Book XXI

Seminar Book XXI, wittily titled *The Non-dupes Err* (*les non-dupes errent*), collects seminars delivered from 1973 to 1974. In French, *nom* ('name') and *non* ('no') share the same pronunciation, and Lacan here plays with the expressions *les non-dupes errent* and *les noms du père* (names of the father). Lacan alludes to his 1963 Seminar (*The Non-existent Seminar*) on the 'Name-of-the-Father', which was cut short after just one session due to his elimination from the IPA's list of training analysts. After ten long years, during which time his reputation grew, Lacan describes his former associates who supported his suspension as 'non-dupes' who erred by rejecting him and, as reported in Gallagher's 'Lacan's Viator and the *Time Traveller's Wife*', those 'whom he refuses even to acknowledge as analysts' (8). This is one of Lacan's most complex Seminars, and Gallagher, who was one of the seven- or eight-hundred people who attended this Seminar, says that he doubts if even ten people understood what Lacan said. One of the explicit reasons for this apparent obscurity is Lacan's claim that he, as a psychoanalyst, was not conveying knowledge but directing his saying to the unconscious. Gallagher isolates five major themes of the Seminar which are as follows: 'Dupes and non-dupes', 'saying versus what is said', 'the unconscious and the psychoanalyst', 'love as contingent' and 'sexed identity and non-relationship' ('Lacan's Viator').

Seminar Book XXII

Seminar Book XXII, titled *RSI* (for both English and French versions), collects seminars delivered during 1974–75. Although the Seminar engages in an analysis of the three registers explained in terms of the Borromean knot – which, as Luke Thurston puts it, is rendered as the 'essential structure of the subject' (qtd. in Evans 192) – Lacan's emphasis is clearly on the notion of the real. Among other things, the imaginary, the real and the symbolic are respectively harmonised with the notions of consistence, ek-sistence and hole.

He also reads the three registers vis-à-vis three Freudian terms – inhibition, symptom and anxiety. It may be noted that, on another level, the terms love, desire and *jouissance* respectively correspond to the imaginary, the symbolic and the real. Related issues discussed in the Seminar include consideration of the notions of the phallus, the ek-sistence of the woman, the names of the father and the phobia of Little Hans.

Seminar Book XXIII

Seminar Book XXIII, titled *Sinthome* (*Le Sinthome*), collects seminars delivered between 1975 and 1976. This Seminar is famous for Lacan's reading of James Joyce's works in conjunction with the notion of psychosis and *sinthome*. '*Sinthome*', Lacan states, 'is an old way of spelling what has more recently been spelt symptom' ('Book XXIII' 18 November 1975). In this Seminar, as Luke Thurston neatly explains, Lacan 'redefines the psychoanalytic symptom in terms of his final topology of the subject' by 'bringing together mathematical theory and the intricate weave of the Joycean text' (qtd. in Evans 191). To the triadic structure of the Borromean knot, corresponding to his conception of the RSI, Lacan adds *sinthome* as the fourth knot that ties together the three rings which otherwise, especially for the psychotic subject, remain separate. In this Seminar, the end of analysis is described as identification with the *sinthome* (or a new symptom, for the neurotic) and construction of the *sinthome* (the fourth ring, for the psychotic). As far as his reading of Joyce is concerned, Lacan draws attention to the 'radical non-function' of the 'Name-of-the-Father' in Joyce's childhood. He suggests this could have led to an incidence of psychosis had Joyce not been so involved in his idiosyncratic writing which, as Thurston puts it, became 'a supplementary chord in his subjective knot'(qtd. in Evans 192). Lacan explains Joyce's epiphanies as examples of 'radical foreclosure' in the sense that 'the real forecloses meaning'. According to him, Thurston continues, the 'Joycean text – from the epiphany to *Finnegans Wake* – entailed a special relation to language; a "destructive" refashioning of it as *sinthome,* the invasion of the symbolic order by the subject's private *jouissance*' (192). In the final analysis, 'Joyce becomes an exemplary *saint homme* who, by refusing any imaginary solution, was able to invent a new way of using language to organise enjoyment' (192). This Seminar is discussed in detail in Chapter Three of this book.

Seminar Book XXIV

Seminar Book XXIV, titled *L'insu que sait de l'une-bévue s'aile à mourre*, collects seminars delivered from 1976 to 1977. As already noted, according to Jacques-Alain Miller, this Seminar initiates the fourth stage of Lacan's teachings. The French title is marked by witty wordplay which render its translation difficult. The word *une-bévue* is a French translation of the German word for the unconscious – *unbewusste*. Literally, *une-bévue* means a blunder or a mistake, but in relation to the German word it means the unconscious. The title could thus be translated as 'Thc unknown that knows about the one-blunder, chances love'. However, on the phonemic level, the title could be spoken as *L'insuccès de l'une-bévue, c'est l'amour*, which would mean 'Love is the failure of one-blunder' (Sédat 1584). The title shows Lacan's manipulation of language to the extreme, in the same vein as James Joyce's methods as used in *Finnegans Wake* (1939) and as talked about by Lacan in the previous Seminar. Lacan describes the Freudian unconscious as 'blunder' and goes beyond the Freudian conception of psychoanalysis by emphasising that the human mind is not topographical nor structural but topological. In this fourth stage of Lacan's teachings, there is a clear shift not only from linguistics to mathematics but also from Euclidean conception of space to topology. Even though he has talked about topology before, in this Seminar Lacan places renewed emphasis on the centrality of topology – especially the 'torus' – in psychoanalytic theory and practice. Torus, in Evans's words, is 'a ring, a three-dimensional object formed by taking a cylinder and joining the two ends together' (211). Lacan describes the essential structure of the human subject as 'toric': 'Man goes round in circles if what I say about his structure is true, because the structure, the structure of man is toric' ('Book XXIV' 14 December 1976). Lacan problematises the notion of the unconscious as 'below' and consciousness as 'above'. Like the torus, which has 'its centre of gravity' outside its volume, the human subject is 'outside himself' or decentred/ex-centric. Like the torus, which has its 'peripheral exteriority and central exteriority' (qtd. in Evans 211) constituted in a single region, the unconscious is both inside as well as outside of the human subject. This idea has its parallel in Lacan's conception of a Moebius band and his notion of unconscious as 'extimate' (not intimate to the human subject but both outside as well as inside the subject, that is, the unconscious as constituted in terms of intersubjectivity). During this period, Lacan exchanged letters and worked with a number of young mathematicians like Michel Thomé and Jean-Michel Vappereau, as he was formulating the topological conception of psychoanalysis (Hewitson).

Seminar Book XXV

Seminar Book XXV, titled *The Moment to Conclude* (*Le moment de conclure*), collects seminars delivered between 1977 and 1978. In this Seminar, Lacan continues his elaboration of topology. He invites the mathematician Pierre Soury to demonstrate topological figures, including variations of a torus and Borromean knot, and engages in conversations with him about the implications of such variations. Mathematics and psychoanalysis are intertwined in an unprecedented manner as is obvious from one of Lacan's remarks: 'There is no sexual relationship, certainly, except between phantasies and the phantasy is to be noted with the accent that I gave it when I remarked that geometry, '*l'âge et haut-maître hie*' [a play on *la géométrie*], that geometry [sic] is woven by phantasies and in the same way the whole of science' ('Book XXV' 20 December 1977).

Seminar Book XXVI

Seminar Book XXVI, titled *Topology and Time* (*La topologie et le temps*), collects seminars delivered during 1978–79. This Seminar opens thus: '*Il y une correspondance entre la toplogique et la pratique. Cette correspondance consiste en les temps. La topologie résiste, c'est en cela que la correspondance existe*' ('Book XXVI' 21 November 1978). This can be translated as: 'There is a correspondence between topology and practice. This correspondence consists in time. Topology resists – it is in this that the correspondence exists' (Johnston 51). For a long time Lacan had been developing the topological conception of analytic practice and in this Seminar he offers a new dimension – time. Freud and Lacan address the relation of the unconscious to time differently. According to Freud, the unconscious is 'timeless' and the notion of temporality is marked by an emphasis on the powerful impact of the past upon the present. According to Lacan, the unconscious has a sort of 'temporal logic' and the notion of temporality is defined by a 'vacillating, dialectical dynamic between past, present, and future' (Johnston 57). As such, Lacan's thrust in this Seminar is on how to formulate the question of time in the topological understanding of the psychoanalytic praxis and he 'puts back into question whether or not topology should be situated in a synchronic, atemporal register, or a diachronic, temporal one' (Johnston 55). It may be noted here that the notion of time has been addressed by Lacan earlier as well, including in *Seminar Book XI* and his 1946 text, 'Logical Time and the Assertion of Anticipated Certainty: A New Sophism'.

Seminar Book XXVII

Seminar Book XXVII, titled *Dissolution* (in both the French and English versions), collects Lacan's addresses, letters and other documents from 1979 to 1980 pertaining to the dissolution of his school École Freudienne de Paris (EFP). Lacan announced the dissolution of his school in January 1980, in a letter published in the magazine *Le Monde*. By this time his health was deteriorating and he found it difficult to speak. Lacan was mostly absent during these seminars, and when he was present he often read from his documents. The texts constituting this Seminar record Lacan's dissolution of the EFP due to violent dissension among the EFP members. This dissension had been growing over the past few years. Lacan declared that the school did not have any function anymore and directed those who were willing to follow him to his new school to state so in writing. Over 1000 letters were sent in response and in February 1980, he announced the founding of the Freudian Cause (*La Cause freudienne*). In July 1980, in his address at the international conference of Lacanian analysts held in Caracas, Lacan stated: 'I have come here before launching my *Cause freudienne*. It is up to you to be Lacanians if you wish; I am Freudian' ('Chronology').

The establishment of the ECF took place in 1981 and J. A. Miller was made its authority. On 9 September 1981, Lacan died after an abdominal operation in the Hartmann Clinic, Paris. His final words were: 'I am obstinate . . . I am dying' (qtd. in Roudinesco 407).

ÉCRITS, AUTRES ÉCRITS AND OTHER TEXTS

Lacan's psychoanalytic lessons are mostly restricted to his seminars. He did, however, also write articles and deliver lectures. Many of these articles and lectures had their roots in his seminars, which in turn, informed his subsequent teaching. Around thirty-five texts, produced by Lacan up to the mid-1960s, were put together and published in 1966, in a single volume called *Écrits*. *Écrits* is notoriously obscure for anyone reading it for the first time. It has been described as written in a radically-new language that is not French but 'Lacanese'. Such was Lacan's popularity as an 'intellectual superstar' that over 5000 copies of the book were sold in the first three days of its publication (Clark 'Biography').

Écrits is an apparently simple title, literally meaning 'writings', but it carries the connotations of (a) writing as different from but related to Lacan's oral teachings and (b) writing as 'rebus'. Jane Gallop writes, 'A rebus is a sort of picture-puzzle which looks like nonsense, but when separated into elements and interpreted, yields sense; it is a sort of writing that cannot be read and yet which becomes intelligible through painstaking interpretation, through another sort of reading' (37). The following is an 'escort card' from around 1865 which is prepared in the rebus-style:

Figure 3: Escort card as rebus

The card looks rather nonsensical, but a more engaged approach would reveal the meaning, 'May I see you home my dear?' Pictures represent words in this puzzle: An eye conveys the letter 'I', the drawing of a house represents 'home', and the image of a deer implies 'dear'. There is also a play on sounds: 'see' becomes 'c'. But before deciphering the line on the escort card, which is pictorially inscribed, the text remains complete nonsense. The precise problem with the text is not the content per se but the very style in which it is presented – its unique, subjective and situational aspects. In a rebus, the subject matter is not only presented, it is mimicked, wherein lies the puzzle.

Following Gallop's discussion, it may be said that Freud described dream as a rebus because, in terms of the processes of displacement and condensation, dream disguises the latent thought beyond recognition. If Lacan's *Écrits* appears obscure then the reason for this might be found in what John P. Muller and William J. Richardson have called the rebus of his writings – 'For the style [of Lacan's writings] mimics the subject matter. Lacan not only explicates the unconscious but strives to imitate it' (qtd. in Gallop 37). Lacan's *Écrits*, similar to his seminars but far more complex by virtue of the difference between writing and speaking, is a discourse on the unconscious striving to mimic the discourse of the unconscious. These complex connotations explain the so-called 'obscurity' of the *Écrits* which Lacan notoriously described as texts 'not to be read', implying, among other things, that his *écrits* needed to be approached differently, needed to be unpacked the way the analyst analyses the dream. In other words, his *écrits*, like his seminars, were meant for the 'experts or cognoscenti' (Miller).

In 1977, Alan Sheridan's English translation, containing nine entries from *Écrits*, was published with the title *Écrits: A Selection* (1977). Obviously, the original French title was kept untranslated to convey its complex connotations. Sheridan's translation, however, has been criticised for being flawed. The Lacanian analyst Bruce Fink re-translated these articles, and translated the rest of the original collection, which he then published as a collection in 2006 with the title *Écrits: The First Complete English Translation*. Some of the oft-cited texts from *Écrits* (in Fink's translation) include 'Seminar on "The Purloined Letter"', 'Mirror Stage as Formative of the *I* Function as Revealed in Psychoanalytic Experience', 'Logical

Time and Assertion of Anticipated Certainty', 'The Function and Field of Speech and Language in Psychoanalysis' (known also as the famous 'Rome Discourse'), 'The Freudian Thing, or the Meaning of Return to Freud in Psychoanalysis', 'The Instance of the Letter in the Unconscious, or Reason since Freud', 'On a Question Prior to Any Possible Treatment of Psychosis', 'The Signification of the Phallus', 'Guiding Remarks on a Convention of Feminine Sexuality', 'Kant with Sade', 'The Subversion of the Subject and the Dialectic of Desire in the Freudian Unconscious' and 'Science and Truth'. Some of these essays are discussed in detail in the subsequent chapters.

The 1966 *Écrits* obviously does not contain all of Lacan's writings and lectures. Even some of the texts which were written or presented before 1966 were not included in this collection. For instance, Lacan's 'The Family Complex' was not included in *Écrits* due to its great length, while his doctoral thesis – his only book-length work to have been published – was published as a separate volume. Lacan's articles and lectures after 1966 were not put together in a single volume for a long time. It was only in 2001 – twenty long years after his death – that another collection of Lacan's writings was published with the title *Autres écrits* (*Autres*, in French, means 'other'). This collection contains forty-four articles spread across eight sections. Some of these articles are taken from the pre-seminar days, including the already cited articles on the family complex (*Les complexes familiaux dans la formation de l'individu*) and on British psychiatry (*La psychiatrie anglaise et la guerre*). Some of the most famous articles from this collection include the four texts originally published in the 1970s: *Radiophonie* (1970), which was based on Lacan's radio interviews; 'Lituraterre' (1971), which is the opening entry of the *Autres écrits* and which contains Lacan's invaluable insight on the interface between psychoanalysis and literary studies; *L'étourdit* (1973), which is a notoriously obscure text described by Christian Fierens as the 'primary form that diverts us from our conscious semantics, it is the apparition of the unconscious in its dimension of non-sense, and it opens up a beyond of common meaning' (20); and *Television* (1974), the text of which was based on a film of Lacan's teachings and broadcast by the Office de la

Radiodiffusion-Télévision Francaise (ORTF), in which Lacan answered questions posed by Jacques-Alain Miller. In *Television,* Lacan made some famous claims like, 'He who interrogates me also knows how to read me' (1) and 'Ten years is enough for everything I write to become clear to everyone' (45). Although some of the texts included in this collection have separately been translated, *Autres écrits* as a whole has not yet been translated into English. Some of the articles from this collection are also discussed in detail in the following chapters.

The texts of Lacan, apart from his seminars and *écrits*, include his case reports or case presentations, letters, interviews, invited talks, discussions, occasional notes, occasional remarks, conference addresses and miscellaneous lectures. Many of these texts were published individually in psychiatric, psychoanalytic and other journals including *Evolution Psychiatrique*, *La Psychanalyse*, *Cahiers du Art*, *Minotaure*, *Ornicar?* and *Scilicet*. An anthology of three lectures delivered by Lacan in 1967 was published in 2005 as *Mon Enseignement*, and its English translation, *My Teaching*, was published in 2008. Lacan's letters – which were addressed to psychoanalysts, mathematicians and public intellectuals and have been separately published and translated – remain uncollected. The rest of his works share the same fate.

One could not agree more with Russell Grigg when he says (as quoted in the epigraph) that compared to the case of Freud, one feels the absence of a 'standard edition of the complete works of Jacques Lacan' and the absence of a translator like James Strachey. Michael Clark, in his annotated bibliography on Lacan, has listed a total of 299 texts spoken or written by Lacan, the list being incomplete. However, by and large, Lacan's texts remain unpublished, uncollected and untranslated. Questions have been raised regarding the authenticity and editorial policy of many of those works which have been officially published or translated. It may be noted that Lacan had elevated the status of Jacques-Alain Miller, who established his seminars, to the level of a 'co-author' (Roudinesco 415–17). Miller must be credited for the Herculean task of transforming Lacan's impromptu speeches, which were meant for listening and were addressed to a particular audience in a given context, into readable, punctuated texts accessible to a reading public comprising analysts as well as non-experts. However, Miller's editorial policies regarding the Seminars are not beyond criticism. For instance, while establishing the Seminars, Miller did not consider all the extant versions and did not provide the reader with scholarly notes, annotations or other critical apparatuses (416). Eventually, Miller married Lacan's daughter and was appointed by Lacan as the literary 'executor' of his published and unpublished works (404). However, thirty-five years after Lacan's death, the unavailability and inauthenticity of Lacan's texts remain a hindrance to Lacanian studies. It is not for nothing that Miller has been blamed for not being pro-active.

NOTES

[1] In this context, I am indebted to Dr Santanu Biswas's formal and informal discussions of *Hamlet* in my postgraduate days (2008–10).

REFERENCES

Biswas, Santanu. 'Locating and Annotating the Expression "The Later Teaching of Lacan."' *Psychoanalysis Lacan*. Web. 20 September 2017. <http://psychoanalysislacan.com/wp-content/uploads/2015/11/Biswas_ed_Alves.pdf>.

'Chronology.' *Lacan dot com*. Web. 20 September 2017. <http://www.lacan.com/rolleyes.htm>.

Clark, Michael. *Jacques Lacan: An Annotated Bibliography Volume I*. London: Routledge, 2014. Kindle File.

Evans, Dylan. *An Introductory Dictionary of Lacanian Psychoanalysis*. London: Routledge, 1996. Print.

Feldstein, Richard, Bruce Fink and Maire Jaanus, eds. *Reading Seminar XI: Lacan's Four Fundamental Concepts*. New York: SUNY Press, 1995. Print.

Fierens, Christian. 'Reading *L'étourdit*.' *Lacan in Ireland*. Trans. Cormac Gallagher. Web. 20 September 2017. <http://www.lacaninireland.com/web/wp-content/uploads/2010/06/CF-CG-Trans-Letter-411.pdf>.

Fink, Bruce. *A Clinical Introduction to Lacanian Psychoanalysis: Theory and Technique*. Cambridge: Harvard UP, 1999. Print.

---. *The Lacanian Subject: Between Language and Jouissance*. New Jersey: Princeton UP, 1995. Print.

Gallagher, Cormac. 'Lacan's Viator and *The Time Traveller's Wife*.' *Lacan in Ireland*. Web. 20 September 2017. <http://www.lacaninireland.com/web/wp-content/uploads/2010/06/S-WIFE-Cormac-Gallagher.pdf>.

---. 'On a Discourse that Might Not Be a Semblance: Book XVIII, 1971: A Collage.' *Lacan in Ireland*. Web. 20 September 2017. <http://www.lacaninireland.com/web/wp-content/uploads/2010/06/CG-27.pdf >.

---. 'Where was Jacques Lacan in 1971–72?: . . . *ou pire* and the Knowledge of the Psychoanalyst.' *Lacan in Ireland*. 20 September 2017. <http://www.lacaninireland.com/web/wp-content/uploads/2010/06/Spring_2004-WHERE-WAS-JACQUES-LACAN-IN-1971-72.pdf>.

Gallop, Jane. *Reading Lacan*. Ithaca: Cornell UP, 1985. Print.

Grigg, Russell. 'Lacan in Translation.' *World Association of Psychoanalysis*. Web. 20 September 2017. <http://wapol.org/ornicar/articles/ggg0155.htm>.

Hewitson, Owen. 'From the Bridges of Königsberg – Why Topology Matters in Psychoanalysis.' *Lacan Online*. Web. 20 September 2017. <http://www.lacanonline.com/index/2015/01/from-the-bridges-of-konigsberg-why-topology-matters-in-psychoanalysis/>.

Johnston, Adrian. *Time Driven: Metapsychology and the Splitting of the Drive*. Illinois: Northwestern UP, 2005. Print.

Lacan, Jacques. *Écrits: The First Complete Edition in English*. Trans. Bruce Fink. New York: W. W. Norton & Co., 2006. Print.

---. 'Le séminaire livre XXVI: La topologie et le temps, 1978–79.' *Patrick Valas*. Web. 20 September 2017. <http://www.valas.fr/IMG/pdf/la_topologie_et_le_temps_1978_1979.pdf>.

---. *Television: A Challenge to the Psychoanalytic Establishment*. Trans. Denis Hollier, Rosalind Krauss, Annette Michelson, Jeffrey Mehlman and Bruce Fink. London: W. W. Norton & Co., 1990. Print.

---. *The Seminar of Jacques Lacan Book I: Freud's Papers on Technique, 1953–54*. Trans. John Forrester. London: W. W. Norton & Co., 1991. Print.

---. *The Seminar of Jacques Lacan Book II: The Ego in Freud's Theory and in the Technique of Psychoanalysis, 1954–55*. Trans. Sylvana Tomaselli. London: W. W. Norton & Co., 1991. Print.

---. *The Seminar of Jacques Lacan Book III: The Psychoses, 1955–56*. Trans. Russell Grigg. London: Norton, 1997. Print.

---. 'The Seminar of Jacques Lacan Book IV: The Object Relation, 1956–57.' *Scribd*. Trans (unofficial). L. V. A. Roche. Web. 20 September 2017. <https://www.scribd.com/doc/143580546/The-Seminar-of-Jacques-Lacan-Book-4-The-Object-Relation>.

---. 'The Seminar of Jacques Lacan Book V: The Formations of the Unconscious, 1957–58.' *Lacan in Ireland*. Trans (unofficial). Cormac Gallagher. Web. 20 September 2017. <http://www.lacaninireland.com/web/wp-content/uploads/2010/06/Book-05-the-formations-of-the-unconscious.pdf>.

---. 'The Seminar of Jacques Lacan Book VI: Desire and Its Interpretation, 1958–59.' *Lacan in Ireland*. Trans (unofficial). Cormac Gallagher. Web. 20 September 2017. <http://www.lacaninireland.com/web/wp-content/uploads/2010/06/Book-06-Desire-and-its-interpretation.pdf>.

---. *The Seminar of Jacques Lacan Book VII: Ethics of Psychoanalysis, 1959–60*. Trans. Dennis Porter. London: W. W. Norton & Co., 1997. Print.

---. 'The Seminar of Jacques Lacan Book VIII: Transference, 1960–61.' *Lacan in Ireland*. Trans (unofficial). Cormac Gallagher. Web. 20 September 2017. <http://www.lacaninireland.com/web/wp-content/uploads/2010/06/THE-SEMINAR-OF-JACQUES-LACAN-VIII-Draft-21.pdf>.

---. 'The Seminar of Jacques Lacan Book IX: Identification, 1961–62.' *Lacan in Ireland*. Trans (unofficial). Cormac Gallagher. Web. 20 September 2017. <http://www.lacaninireland.com/web/wp content/uploads/2010/06/Seminar-IX-Amended-Iby-MCL-7 NOV_.20111.pdf>.

---. 'The Seminar of Jacques Lacan Book X: Anxiety, 1962–63.' *Lacan in Ireland*. Trans (unofficial). Cormac Gallagher. Web. 20 September 2017. <http://www.lacaninireland.com/web/wp-content/uploads/2010/06/Seminar-X-Revised-by-Mary-Cherou-Lagreze.pdf>.

---. *The Seminar of Jacques Lacan Book XI: The Four Fundamental Concepts of Psychoanalysis, 1964*. Trans. Alan Sheridan. New York: W. W. Norton & Co., 1998. Print.

---. 'The Seminar of Jacques Lacan Book XII: Crucial Problems for Psychoanalysis, 1964–65.' *Lacan in Ireland*. Trans (unofficial). Cormac Gallagher. Web. 20 September 2017. <http://www.lacaninireland.com/web/wp-content/uploads/2010/06/12-Crucial-problems-for-psychoanalysis.pdf>.

---. 'The Seminar of Jacques Lacan Book XIII: The Object of Psychoanalysis, 1965–66.' *Lacan in Ireland*. Trans (unofficial). Cormac Gallagher. Web. 20 September 2017. <http://www.lacaninireland.com/web/wp-content/uploads/2010/06/13-The-Object-of-Psychoanalysis1.pdf>.

---. 'The Seminar of Jacques Lacan Book XIV: The Logic of Phantasy, 1966–67.' *Lacan in Ireland*. Trans (unofficial). Cormac Gallagher. Web. 20 September 2017. <http://www.lacaninireland.com/web/wp-content/uploads/2010/06/14-Logic-of-Phantasy-Complete.pdf>.

---. 'The Seminar of Jacques Lacan Book XV: The Psychoanalytic Act, 1967–68.' *Lacan in Ireland*. Trans (unofficial). Cormac Gallagher. Web. 20 September 2017. <http://www.lacaninireland.com/web/wp-content/uploads/2010/06/Book-15-The-Psychoanalytical-Act.pdf>.

---. 'The Seminar of Jacques Lacan Book XVI: From an Other to the other, 1968–69.' *Lacan in Ireland*. Trans (unofficial). Cormac Gallagher. Web. 20 September 2017. <http://www.lacaninireland.com/web/wp-content/uploads/2010/06/Book-16-from-an-Other-to-the-other.pdf>.

---. *The Seminar of Jacques Lacan Book XX (Encore): On Feminine Sexuality, Limits of Love and Knowledge, 1972–73*. Trans. Bruce Fink. London: W. W. Norton & Co., 1998. Print.

---. 'The Seminar of Jacques Lacan Book XXIII: Le Sinthome, 1975–76.' *Lacan Online*. Trans (unofficial). Luke Thurston. Web. 20 September 2017. <http://www.lacanonline.com/index/wp-content/uploads/2014/11/Seminar-XXIII-The-Sinthome-Jacques-Lacan-Thurston-translation.pdf>.

---. 'The Seminar of Jacques Lacan Book XXIV: L'insu que sait de l'une-bévue s'aile à mourre, 1976–77.' *Lacan in Ireland*. Trans (unofficial). Cormac Gallagher. Web. 20 September 2017. <http://www.lacaninireland.com/web/wp-content/uploads/2010/06/insu-Seminar-XXIV-Final-Sessions-1-12-1976-1977.pdf>.

---. 'The Seminar of Jacques Lacan Book XXV: The Moment to Conclude, 1977–78.' *Lacan in Ireland*. Trans (unofficial). Cormac Gallagher. Web. 20 September 2017. <http://www.lacaninireland.com/web/wp-content/uploads/2014/03/Book-25-The-Moment-to-Conclude.pdf>.

Miller, Jacques-Alain. 'Lacan's Later Teaching.' *Lacanian Ink*. Trans. Barbara P. Fulks. Web. 5 September 2017. <http://www.lacan.com/frameXXI2.htm>.

Muller, John P., and William J. Richardson. *Lacan and Language: A Reader's Guide to Écrits*. New York: International UP, 1982. Print.

Nobus, Dany, ed. *Key Concepts of Lacanian Psychoanalysis*. New York: Other Press, 1998. Print.

Rabaté, Jean-Michel, ed. *The Cambridge Companion to Lacan*. Cambridge: CUP, 2003. Print.

Roudinesco, Elisabeth. *Jacques Lacan*. Trans. Barbara Bray. New York: Columbia UP, 1997. Print.

Sédat, Jacques. 'Seminar, Lacan's.' *International Dictionary of Psychoanalysis*. Vol. 3. Ed. Alain de Mijolla et al. Detroit: Thomson/Gale, 2005. Print.

Voruz, Véronique, and Bogdan Woolf, eds. *The Later Lacan: An Introduction*. Albany: SUNY Press, 2007. Print.

Chapter Two

The Subject in Lacan

> The subject is nothing other than what slides in a chain of signifiers, whether he knows which signifier he is the effect of or not.
>
> Jacques Lacan, *Seminar Book XX*

> Okay, between what and what is the subject divided? . . . It's not between this and that for Lacan; it's not that you have a conscious part and then a stupid iceberg beneath the unconscious . . . the subject is divided between something and nothing.
>
> Slavoj Žižek, 'On Jacques-Alain Miller'

The word 'individual' is derived from the Latin root *individuus*, which literally means 'indivisible'. The rise of individualism in early modern Europe promoted an idea of human subjectivity characterised by unity, autonomy and omnipotence. The general worldview shifted from medieval theocentrism (God as the ultimate cause of all the happenings in the world) to a modern anthropocentrism (man as the centre of the world, man as all-powerful, man as a challenge to God as embodied, for instance, in the figure of Christopher Marlowe's Dr Faustus). Feudalism was challenged by capitalism, which enabled the rich from the lower class to undergo upward mobility. In theology, Protestantism (particularly Calvinism) promoted a form of individualism whereby the economic prosperity in this world was considered to be a sign of salvation – a thesis proposed in Max Weber's *The Protestant Ethic and the Spirit of Capitalism* (1905). The discoveries of the new territories glorified the European man's sense of supremacy. In literature, the new genre of the novel, unlike the earlier genres of epic and romance, chronicled the journey of one particular individual from rags to riches. In modern Western philosophy, especially in Descartes, a new conception of subjectivity emerged captured in the dictum *cogito ergo sum* or 'I think therefore I am'. The existence of the individual was confirmed not with reference to an external, abstract, non-negotiable agent like God but with reference to the individual's own consciousness of being. However, the myth of the autonomy, unity and omnipotence of the individual human being was challenged in a number of ways in nineteenth-century Europe. In Marxian, Darwinian and Freudian thought, various discourses on 'determinism' surfaced (Douglass 142). A complex notion of 'economic determinism' posited how the economic class an individual was born to determined her view of the world and the self. The concept of 'biological determinism' assigned the behavioural patterns of an individual to her genes. The idea of 'psychic determinism' explained the mental make-up of an individual as being determined by unconscious mental processes. This does not mean these new trends of thought were entirely pessimistic about human freedom (for surely Marxian thought promoted the ideologies of revolution which would bring about a future socialist state where the proletariat would no longer be exploited). Rather, the discourse on determinism seriously questioned the idea of the 'absolute' agency of man, his sense of 'complete' command over himself and over the world at large.

Drawing on Freud's psychoanalytic writings, Lacan dismisses the notions of being, self and consciousness which promote the human individual as a form of autonomous and undivided agency. Describing Freud's discovery of the unconscious as a Copernican revolution (which reversed the flawed theory that the earth is still and the sun is moving around it), Lacan discards the idea that the 'conscious I' is what determines human thoughts and behaviours. It is the unconscious that plays a determining role in the construction of human subjectivity. Lacan assigns an 'agency' to the unconscious, that is, considers the unconscious to be not a passive entity but an active subjectivity, and renames it the 'subject of the unconscious' which is defined as 'an effect of the signifier' or 'sliding in a chain of signifiers' (*Book XX* 50; Evans 197–98). This is the predominant notion of subjectivity in Lacan. Related to this is the concept of the 'divided subject'. Broadly speaking, for Lacan, the 'I' of a human is split between being and thinking. The 'being I' (the Cartesian 'I am') is not the same as the 'thinking I' (the Cartesian 'I think'). Being is the domain of the imaginary 'I' or the ego, while thinking is the domain of the symbolic 'I' or the subject of the unconscious. The opposition between the ego and the subject of the unconscious constitutes just one implication of the divided subject. There is, however, another implication. As mentioned in the epigraph, this division involves a split between 'something' and 'nothing' – between the imaginary and symbolic identifications which the subject develops over the course of his familial and social life and the experience of nothingness ('encountering the real') that occurs during the moments of disillusionment with the imaginary and symbolic identifications. In a successful clinical analysis, the analysand is said to have a glimpse of the real at the end of the analysis. It should be noted that Lacan uses the algebraic symbol $\$$ – the letter 'S' struck through, standing for the term 'subject' (*sujet*, in French) – to represent the divided nature of the subject. The subject, according to Lacan, has at least two more connotations. The first involves the conception of masculinity and femininity. Lacan defines masculine and feminine subjectivities not as biological entities but as 'logical structures'. Developing the notion of sexual difference, or more precisely 'sexuation', Lacan defines masculinity as the enjoyment of the phallic *jouissance* and femininity as that of both the phallic and the feminine *jouissance*. Obviously, the crucial term that defines the subject here is *jouissance*, which is in opposition to the conception of the subject as an effect of the signifier. The second connotation is that in Lacanian nosography, human beings are broadly divided into three clinical categories (with respective sub-categories) – the psychotics, the neurotics and the perverts. These categories are also called 'clinical structures' and are ruled by specific mechanisms. With reference to the event of castration, the neurotic is the one who represses it, the psychotic forecloses it and the pervert disavows it.

Lacan's broader conception of the subject is discussed in this chapter and is further elaborated on in Chapter Three, which specifically deals with the three clinical structures. The discussion which follows focuses on the following threads: (a) the formation of the ego and the imaginary order of subjectivity; (b) the advent of the subject of the unconscious and the symbolic order of subjectivity; (c) the linguistic aspects of the subject of the unconscious; (d) the real order of subjectivity – *lalangue*, *jouissance*, sexuation; and (e) the status of the subject at the end of the analysis.

THE FORMATION OF THE EGO AND THE IMAGINARY ORDER OF SUBJECTIVITY

In a number of texts from the early stages of his career, Lacan develops the idea that the ego (*Ich* in Freud, *moi* in Lacan), as understood in the school of ego psychology, is predominantly in the order of the imaginary and thereby in opposition to the subject of the unconscious. Lacan conceptualises the three formations of the ego as the ideal-ego (*ideal Ich* in Freud, *moi idéal* in Lacan), the ego-ideal (*Ich-ideal* in Freud, *idéal du moi* in Lacan) and the super-ego (*Über-Ich* in Freud, *surmoi* in Lacan). These distinctions are not always clear in Freud and Lacan formulates them systematically. Simply put, for Lacan, the ideal-ego is formed through identification with the specular or semblable image which is obviously external to the subject and leads to the imaginary 'projection' of the 'I' outside of the subject; the ego-ideal is formed through identification with the law of the father and leads to the subject's 'introjection' or unconscious adoption of the symbolic order constituted by reason, language and law; and the super-ego (via which the subject's incarnation of morality occurs) is explained as not only having its roots in symbolic identification with the father but as having some 'maternal origins' as well and additionally functioning as the categorical imperative for 'enjoyment' by obscenely imposing an 'anti-legal morality' on the subject (qtd. in Evans 91–92, 154, 202–03). The texts where these concepts are elaborated on include, but are not limited to, Lacan's essays on the family complex, the mirror stage and his Seminars on the ego and the formations of the unconscious.

The formation of the ego takes place at the 'mirror stage' when the human child is caught in her own specular image. In his 1949 paper titled 'The Mirror Stage as Formative of the *I* Function as Revealed in Psychoanalytic Experience', included in *Écrits*, Lacan asserts that the mirror stage occurs between the ages of six and eighteen months. During this period a child is not capable of physical coordination but 'its visual system is relatively advanced, which means that it can recognise itself in the mirror before attaining control over its bodily movements' (Evans 118). The human child, unlike animal offspring, recognises its own image as well as that of its surroundings in the mirror. In this regard, the mirror stage stands in sharp contrast to the child's prior undifferentiated experiences. As Lacan elaborates on in his paper, recognition at the mirror stage is indicated by an 'illuminative mimicry' or, more elaborately, by a series of gestures in which the child 'playfully experiences the relationship between the movements made in the image and the reflected environment, and between this virtual complex and the reality it duplicates' (*Écrits* 75), that is, the child's own body, persons and things around him. 'The function of the mirror stage thus turns out', in Lacan's view, 'to be a particular case of the function of imagos, which is to establish a relationship between an organism and its reality . . . or . . . between the *Innenwelt* [inner world] and the *Umwelt* [surroundings]' (78).

The consequence of the mirror stage is the paradoxical formation of the ego through the processes of identification, *méconnaissance* and alienation. On the part of the subject, who is 'still trapped in his motor impotence and nursling dependence', the unified specular image stands in contrast to the uncoordinated, fragmented body (*Écrits* 76). This contrast generates a sense of rivalry, tension and aggression between the subject and its own image and 'the wholeness of the image threatens the subject with fragmentation' (118). This tension is resolved through identification with the specular image and this 'primary identification' of the subject with its counterpart is what leads to the constitution of the ego. Identification with the specular image is an example of *méconnaissance* or 'imaginary' self-knowledge related to an illusory sense of unified selfhood and self-mastery, where the term 'illusion' stands for 'a necessary illusion'. The recognition of the specular image thus leads to an essential misrecognition of the selfhood as unified. The 'jubilant assumption' of the specular image on the part of the subject additionally causes alienation, since the 'I' is literally located outside the subject. This is why Lacan states in *Écrits*:

> The mirror stage is a drama whose internal pressure pushes precipitously from insufficiency to anticipation – and, for the subject caught up in the lure of spatial identification, turns out fantasies that proceed from a fragmented image of the body to what I will call an 'orthopaedic' form of its totality – and to the finally donned armor of an alienating identity that will mark his entire mental development with its rigid structure. Thus, the shattering of the *Innenwelt* to *Umwelt* circle gives rise to an inexhaustible squaring of the ego's audits. (78)

The '*I* function', as Lacan states in the significantly titled 'The Mirror Stage as Formative of the *I* Function as Revealed in Psychoanalytic Experience', is thus a 'function of misrecognition'. It is this *méconnaissance* which characterises the 'I' or the ego 'in all its defensive structures'.

The mirror stage, however, is just one stage in the psychic development of the child and is linked to what Lacan, in his 1938 text titled 'Family Complexes in the Formation of the Individual', calls the 'intrusion complex'. The intrusion complex, together with the weaning complex which precedes it and the Oedipus complex and castration complex which succeed it, constitute what Lacan has termed the 'family complexes', which play a pivotal role in the 'formation of the individual'. Lacan defines the 'human family' as 'the original order of reality where social relations are constituted', and defines 'complex' as 'a specific form of reality that was objectified at a given stage of time' whose function is 'to repeat this organization of reality in the subject's subsequent experience' (qtd. in Clark C45). Although 'weaning' refers to the physical separation from the mother's breast as the child consumes 'foreign' food and drink, and 'weaning complex' is generated by the anxiety of this separation, Lacan carefully points out that this is less a biological matter and more a cultural and psychological issue. This physical crisis, established during birth and culminating at the weaning stage, is conditioned by cultural habits which influence the timing of weaning and is intensified by the resultant mental crisis in the form of trauma. At the weaning stage, the breast of the mother functions as the imago – the internalised image from which the separation at stake has taken place and the retrieval of which might restore the child's sense of unity with the mother. The weaning complex is also called the 'separation complex' as it separates the child from the mother and thus contributes to the gradual disintegration of the mother-child dyad. What follows the weaning complex is the intrusion complex, which is identified with the mirror stage. The intrusion complex is marked here by both (a) the child's recognition of itself in the mirror and (b) the child's recognition of its semblances, or doubles, in the form of siblings. Both the sibling and the specular image, Lacan says, are considered as the rival 'other' that exposes the insufficiency of the infant's self, thereby rousing jealousy. However, the identification which resolves the situation is ambivalent since it not only involves 'specular satisfaction' but also 'alienation'. The identification at the mirror stage, in any case, comes as a rescue from the separation complex. The joy derived from identification with the specular image is also the root of narcissism.

The imaginary register, rooted in the mirror stage and the ideal-ego, is thus characterised by duality, rivalry, jealousy, identification, *méconnaissance*, semblance, narcissism and alienation. Evans's remarks are conclusive when he says: 'The imaginary is the realm of image and imagination, deception and lure. The principal illusions of the imaginary are those of wholeness, synthesis, autonomy, duality and, above all, similarity' (84).

It must be noted that the imaginary, in terms of the mirror stage, is not confined to a 'historical' moment in the life of a child. This is because the mirror stage has a 'structural' value and it 'typifies an essential libidinal relationship with the body-image' as it also 'illustrates the conflictual nature of the dual relationship' (qtd. in Evans 118). The ego as the imaginary has to be understood as such.

THE ADVENT OF THE SUBJECT OF THE UNCONSCIOUS AND THE SYMBOLIC ORDER OF SUBJECTIVITY

While the imaginary – which predominantly constitutes the ego – has its roots in the mirror stage, the symbolic – which largely constitutes the unconscious – has its roots in the Oedipal stage. In Lacan's 'Family Complexes in the Formation of the Individual', the Oedipus complex is said to occur 'around four years of age and involves a fantasy of castration, the sublimation of reality, and the repression of sexuality, all of which help situate the individual within the social order' (Clark C45). The Oedipal stage is marked by the recognition of sexual difference and is in this regard remarkably different from the earlier two stages. Weaning and intrusion complexes are dominated by a duality in the form of the child and its mother, or the child and its siblings, or the child and its specular image. What dominates the Oedipus complex, however, is a triad in which, apart from the mother and the child, a third term emerges. That being said, Lacan problematises such a neatly made differentiation between the family complexes later on, in his Seminar on the formations of the unconscious for instance, when he talks about 'three moments' of the Oedipus complex. In the first moment, the triad involves the child, the mother and the 'imaginary phallus'; the second moment comprises the child, the mother and the 'imaginary father'; and the third moment pertains to the child, the mother and the 'real father'. Lacan elaborates by stating that in the first moment of the Oedipus complex, otherwise called the pre-Oedipal phase, 'the child seeks . . . to be able to satisfy his mother's desire . . . to be . . . the satisfying object for the mother' ('Book V' 22 January 1958).

This moment is described as the 'primitive phallic stage' since, at this stage, 'it is in a way in a mirror that the subject identifies himself with what is the object of desire of the mother' ('Book V' 22 January 1958). In other words, at this stage the child sees the mother and himself as lacking something. He realises that the mother must be lacking something which is why she desires something beyond herself. And he too is lacking something since he is not sufficiently able to fulfil the mother's desire. An imaginary object is posited in place of the lack, namely the 'phallus', which the child tries to embody so as to be complete in himself and complete the mother. Why this imaginary object should be called 'phallus' and not something else is debatable, but Lacan is, in a way, preserving Freudian legacy. In this instance 'phallus' is thus not anything biological because it is an imaginary object. The mother's desire, at this first stage, is elevated to the status of law, and as such, the child's sole target remains to obey that law. The difference from Freud's formulation of the Oedipus complex is clear here – the child does not desire the mother but desires to be the sole object *of* the mother's desire, and by positing the phallus as the imaginary object that he thinks the mother desires, he moulds his desire in the fashion of the mother's desire. This is one of the reasons why Lacan later states that man's desire is the desire of the Other (or of the mother, as the first big Other for the child).

According to Lacan, the following happens in the second moment of the Oedipus complex:

> On the imaginary plane, the father intervenes well and truly as one who deprives the mother, namely that what is here addressed as a demand to the Other is referred on to a higher court . . . because in some ways that about which we question the other, always encounters in the other this other of the other, namely her own law in so far as it traverses every part of her. ('Book V' 22 January 1958)

In other words, what pops up between the mother and the child is not an imaginary object but the imaginary father, who controls the desire of the mother by prohibiting the imaginary phallus as an object of desire and by being the source of the law which the mother herself obeys. What appears at this stage is 'the law of the father in so far as it is conceived imaginarily by the subject as depriving the mother' ('Book V' 22 January 1958) of the symbolic phallus. The symbolic phallus, as different from the imaginary phallus, stands for the law of the father. By implication:

> [This stage also] detaches the subject from his identification [and] attaches him at the same time to the first appearance of the law in the shape of this fact: that the mother is dependent on it, dependent on an object, on an object which is no longer

> simply the object of her desire, but an object that the other has or does not have. ('Book V' 22 January 1958)

It is not the father with whom the mother is shown to have a relationship at this stage, it is rather 'the word of the father'. It is also when, by being deprived of the imaginary object, the mother is described as undergoing castration. The key to the Oedipus complex, hence, is 'the close liaison between this reference by the mother to a law that is not her own with the fact that in reality the object of her desire is sovereignly possessed by that same other [imaginary father] to whose law she refers' ('Book V' 22 January 1958).

The third moment of the Oedipus complex, Lacan says, 'is as important as the second, because it is on it that the outcome of the Oedipus complex depends' ('Book V' 22 January 1958). The third moment is marked by the intervention of the 'real father' who can give the mother what the mother desires because the father is now revealed as a 'potent father'. As far as paternal agency is concerned, Lacan contrasts the third moment with the first two moments of the Oedipus complex. In the first moment, the father existed in 'the realities of the world' in a 'veiled form', as far as 'in the world, the law of the symbol reigns' and 'already the question of the phallus is posed somewhere else in the mother, where the child must locate it'. In the second moment, the father existed through 'his privative presence in that he is the one who supports the law, and this occurs no longer in a veiled fashion but in a fashion mediated by the mother, who is the one who put forward as the one who, for her, lays down the law' ('Book V' 22 January 1958). But in the third moment, the father is marked as having the phallus (the potent organ). This is precisely why the child must put an end to the desire to become the phallus or the desire to fulfil the desire of the mother. Anxieties, deriving from his lack of ability to fill the lack in the mother, come to an end since the phallus, which he posited as the means to fill that lack, cannot be embodied by him because the father, who is responsible for causing the lack in the mother and who is the bearer of the law, *has* it. Thus, 'the father can give the mother what she desires' and hence, for the child, there takes place 'the restitution . . . of the relation of the mother to the father on the real plane'. These revelations offer the child a 'favourable' way out from the Oedipus complex, and the anxieties associated with it, in terms of 'identification with the father' ('Book V' 22 January 1958). The father, as possessor of the phallus and bearer of the law, represents the ego-ideal for the subject, and identification with the father involves a symbolic introjection of the ego-ideal. Lacan describes the ego-ideal as:

> [That] which appears at this level in the symbolic triangle, precisely there, at the pole where the child is, and in the measure that it is at the maternal pole that everything that from now on will be reality begins to be constituted. And it is at the level of the father that everything that from now on will be the 'super-ego' begins to be constituted. ('Book V' 22 January 1958)

Hence, Lacan concludes:

> It is in so far as the father intervenes as real and as a potent father in a third moment, that which succeeds the privation or the castration inflicted on the mother [that is, the mother's lack of the symbolic phallus], on the mother as imagined at the level of the subject, in her own imaginary position of dependency, it is in so far as he intervenes at the third moment as the one who, for his part, has it, that he is interiorized as ego-ideal in the subject and that, as I might say, let us not forget, at that very moment the Oedipus complex dissolves. ('Book V' 22 January 1958)

Furthermore, the third moment of the Oedipus complex is related to castration of the subject. Lacan talks about two kinds of castration. In the second moment of the Oedipus complex, the mother is deprived of the imaginary phallus as the imaginary father appears as the bearer of the law that prohibits oneness with the mother; what happens here is the negation of the verb 'to have'. That is the first kind of castration. The second kind of castration takes place when the subject realises he cannot *be* the object of the mother's desire; the verb negated here is 'to be' (Evans 23). The castration of the subject is directly related to the renunciation of *jouissance*. The outcome of the castration is symbolic identification, that is, identification with the father or with logic, language and law. This is also called secondary identification, as primary identification involves imaginary identification with the specular image. As has been noted, the primary identification constitutive of the ideal-ego – involving the formation of the ego – is also called imaginary projection, whereas the secondary identification constitutive of the ego-ideal – involving the formation of the super-ego – is called symbolic introjection.

What happens in the Oedipus complex is the metaphorical substitution of one term by another – the desire of the mother is substituted by the Name-of-the-Father. The Name-of-the-Father not only represents the name of the biological father but, most importantly, includes the 'names' and 'no' of the father – the language which constructs the subject and the prohibition which makes the subject sacrifice/repress his desire to be the object of the mother's desire. The 'name' and the 'no' of the father together constitute the symbolic domain. The metaphorical substitution at the Oedipus phase is what leads to the socialisation of the neurotic subject who gets caught up in phallic signification. In the case of the psychotic subject, however, no such substitution takes place as the subject 'forecloses' the Name-of-the-Father. The psychotic, like Norman in Hitchcock's *Psycho* (further discussed in Chapters Three and Five), cannot really break away from the mother-child dyad. The Oedipus complex, considered to be the 'fundamental metaphor' (Evans 115), is what triggers the phallic signification for the subject. Since the Oedipus complex is the basis, or anchoring or quilting point of all other significations (Name-of-the-Father is first signifier), all significations, in this sense, are phallic, that is, involve the Name-of-the-Father (141). In his paper 'On a Question Prior to Any Possible Treatment of Psychosis', which is based on his Seminar on the theme of psychoses (1955–66), Lacan draws the following schema regarding paternal metaphor:

$$\frac{\textit{Name of the Father}}{\textit{Desire of the Mother}} \cdot \frac{\textit{Desire of the Mother}}{\textit{Signified to the subject}} \rightarrow \textit{Name of the Father}\left(\frac{A}{\textit{Phallus}}\right)$$

Figure 4: Paternal metaphor (*Écrits* 465)

In this diagram, the 'Name-of-the-Father' substitutes the 'Desire of the Mother', and 'Desire of the Mother' substitutes the 'Signified of the subject'. The product of these two substitutions is the phallic signification. Some of the relevant remarks made by Lacan in this context are:

- 'In the subjective economy, commanded as it is by the unconscious, it is, in effect, a signification that is evoked only by what I call a metaphor – to be precise, the paternal metaphor' (*Écrits* 463). In other words, the paternal metaphor is what triggers the signification pertaining to the unconscious and the subject.
- 'The signification of the phallus, as I said, must be evoked in the subject's imaginary by the paternal metaphor' (464).
- 'It is an accident in this register and in what occurs in it – namely, the foreclosure of the Name-of-the-Father in the place of the Other – and the failure of the paternal metaphor that I designate as the defect that gives psychosis its essential condition, along with the structure that separates it from neurosis' (479). In other words, whereas the neurotic undergoes phallic signification, the psychotic forecloses it.

It is through the renunciation of *jouissance* and the substitution of the desire of the mother with the Name-of-the-Father that the unconscious, as the subject or the subject of the unconscious, comes into existence. The combination of the imaginary identification (with the small other) and symbolic identification (with the big Other that includes the unconscious itself, among other things) is what leads to the emergence of the divided subject. One of the differences between the ego and the subject of the unconscious may be explained in relation to the notion of knowledge. Lacan differentiates between two kinds of knowledge – *connaissance* ('imaginary knowledge') and *savoir* ('symbolic knowledge'). 'Symbolic knowledge is the knowledge of the truth about one's unconscious desire' and is related to the subject of the unconscious, whereas imaginary knowledge, misrecognition (*méconnaissance*) of oneself, is 'an obstacle which hinders the subject's access to symbolic knowledge' (Evans 97). Obviously, the imaginary knowledge is related to the ego. The next section discusses the various aspects of the subject of the unconscious.

THE LINGUISTIC ASPECTS OF THE SUBJECT OF THE UNCONSCIOUS

According to Lacan, the unconscious and the subject of the unconscious are predominantly located in the order of the symbolic, that is, the order of language. A discussion of Lacan's conception of the mechanisms of the unconscious would be helpful to understand the issue. The crucial texts in this context are 'The Function and Field of Speech and Language in Psychoanalysis' (1953), 'The Instance of the Letter in the Unconscious, or Reason since Freud' (1957), 'Subversion of the Subject and the Dialectic of Desire' (1960), *Seminar Book XI* (1964) and *Seminar Book XX* (1972–73). The following is an attempt to explain some of the important points made in these texts.

1. Formations of the Unconscious are Linguistic

In his essay 'The Function and Field of Speech and Language in Psychoanalysis', included in *Écrits*, Lacan argues that the unconscious is structured like a language because the formations of the unconscious – namely, dream, parapraxes, jokes and symptoms – are all linguistic formations. These formations are originally Freud's discoveries and are to be found in some of Freud's early texts like *The Interpretation of Dreams* (1900), *Psychopathology of Everyday Life* (1904), *Jokes and Their Relation to the Unconscious* (1905) and various case histories. In Freud, the linguistic nature of these formations is implicit, not pronounced. Lacan foregrounds their linguistic dimension and shows how they are structured by and like a language. These formations are indicative of the agency of the unconscious and as such constitute the subject of the unconscious.

Lacan states that in *The Interpretation of Dreams*, dream is described as having 'the structure of a sentence'. Furthermore, the version of the dream which is 'given in the telling of the dream' is rhetorical (*Écrits* 221). The displacement and condensation which predominantly define the so-called 'dream-work' are in fact 'syntactical displacements' and 'semantic condensations' out of which the implicit intentions of the 'oneiric discourse', or the discourse of dream, has to be deciphered. In Lacan's more elaborate description:

> Ellipsis and pleonasm, hyperbaton or syllepsis, regression, repetition, apposition – these are the syntactical displacements; metaphor, catachresis, antonomasia, allegory, metonymy, and synecdoche – these are the semantic condensations; Freud teaches us to read in them the intentions – whether ostentatious or demonstrative, dissimulating or persuasive, retaliatory or seductive – with which the subject modulates his oneiric discourse. (*Écrits* 221–22)

Such verbal dynamics are found in the case of parapraxes as well, including slips of the tongue, bungled actions, unmotivated choices and involuntary forgetting, all of which Freud talks about in another of his seminal texts, *The Psychopathology of Everyday Life*. In all of these instances, Freud places confidence in symbols and linguistic codes. For example, every bungled action is described as 'a successful, even "well-phrased", discourse', and every slip of the tongue is 'the gag that turns against speech' (*Écrits* 222).

Turning to the discussion of jokes, Lacan states that '*Jokes and Their Relation to the Unconscious* remains the most unchallengeable of his [Freud's] works because it is the most transparent; in it, the effect of the unconscious is demonstrated in all its subtlety'. The witty dimension of jokes is derived from 'the ambiguity conferred on it by language' (223). Playing on the words *l'esprit* and *esprit libre*, Lacan defines wit (*l'esprit*) or witticism (*pointe*) as that 'in which language's creative activity unveils its absolute gratuitousness, in which its domination of reality . . . is expressed in the challenge of nonmeaning, and in which the humour, in the malicious grace of the free spirit [*esprit libre*], symbolizes a truth that does not say its last word' (223). The crucial fact about a joke is that it is 'always about something else'. Lacan notes: '"A joke [*esprit*] in fact entails such a subjective conditionality . . . a joke is only what I accept as such," continues Freud, who knows what he is talking about'. A joke is what reveals how the intent of the subject of the unconscious surpasses that of the ego: 'Nowhere is the individual's intent more evidently surpassed by the subject's find . . . since not only must there have been something foreign to me in my find for me to take pleasure in it, but some of it must remain foreign for this find to hit home' (224). The subject here is the 'third person' evoked by the joke (and different from the analysand's ego and the analyst). Since this subject cannot be grasped as such in the consciousness in which it erupts, it must be 'presupposed'. This subject appears to be a foreign element, an antibody located outside of the individual and emerging from the place of the Other.

While discussing symptom, another formation of the unconscious, Lacan similarly highlights its fundamental linguistic basis. He states in *Écrits* that a symptom of neurosis or of any other clinical structure involves an 'overdetermination constituted by a double meaning', understood as the 'symbol of a defunct conflict beyond its function in a *no less symbolic* present conflict' (222). Lacan states that Freud further insists that the analyst needs to 'follow the ascending ramification of the symbolic lineage [of the symptom] in the text of the patient's free associations, in order to detect the nodal points [*noeuds*] of its structure at the places where its verbal forms intersect' (223). The concepts of double meaning, symbolic lineage, 'text' of free association and nodal points of verbal manifestations all refer to symptom being structured like a language. Lacan brings in terminology used by the structural linguist Saussure and further states that a symptom is 'the signifier of a signified that has been repressed from the subject's consciousness' (232). This repression is what he would elsewhere describe as metaphor – in the sense that here takes place a sliding or substitution of one signifier by another – and symptom as such manipulates the semantic ambiguity central to language. The deciphering of symptoms as speech is what led Freud to rediscover 'the first language of symbols, still alive in the sufferings of civilized man' (232). Indeed, Lacan points out in *Écrits* the linguistic structures of symptoms as isolated by Freud:

> Hieroglyphics of hysteria, blazons of phobia, and labyrinths of *Zwangsneurose* [obsessive neurosis]; charms of impotence, enigmas of inhibition, and oracles of anxiety; talking arms of character, seals of self-punishment, and disguises of perversion: these are the hermetic elements that our exegesis resolves, the equivocations that our invocation dissolves, and the artifices that our dialectic absolves, by delivering the imprisoned meaning in ways that run the gamut from revealing the palimpsest to providing the solution [*mot*] of the mystery and to pardoning speech. (232)

Given its linguistic basis, the articulation of symptom in the clinical context leads to its very removal. This is due to the fact that such articulation makes the analysand see the truth of her unconscious desire. Lacan hence states in *Écrits*, 'it is already quite clear that symptoms can be entirely resolved in an analysis of language, because a symptom is itself structured like a language: a symptom is language from which speech must be delivered' (223).

2. Speech is the Medium to 'Refind' the Unconscious

In the same text, 'The Function and Field of Speech and Language in Psychoanalysis', Lacan argues that though the unconscious is structured like a language, its reconstruction takes place in analysis only through the speech (free association) of the analysand. The function and field of speech in psychoanalysis are crucial to understanding the unconscious. 'Whether it wishes to be an agent of healing, training, or sounding the depths, psychoanalysis has but one medium: the patient's speech', states Lacan. He adds, 'The obviousness of this fact is no excuse for ignoring it' (*Écrits* 206), and the psychoanalyst needs to be aware of how speech functions. In the analytic context, two kinds of speech are encountered, namely, the 'empty speech' and the 'full speech'. These are instrumental in the (re)construction of the unconscious in psychoanalysis (reconstruction, or even construction itself, because the nature and mechanism of one's unconscious is discovered during, and not prior to, the analysis). The key to the notion of speech is that 'all speech calls for a response' (206). Empty speech is that which, in the analytic chamber, meets with silence. Silence or what is not said by the analysand, in analysis, is what indicates 'a reality beyond speech', and the task of the analyst would be to make the subject speak that which he fails to speak, to thus face 'the perceived echo of his own nothingness' (206). Thereafter, the task of the analyst is 'to figure out to which "part" of this discourse [the analysand's discourse] the significant term is relegated' and then punctuate 'propitiously' the discourse of the analysand (209). And for this purpose the analyst, Lacan claims, has to consider the analysand's 'description of an everyday event as a fable addressed as a word to the wise, a long prosopopoeia as a direct interjection, and, contrariwise, a simple slip of the tongue as a highly complex statement, and even the rest of a silence as the whole lyrical development it stands in for' (209).

The task of punctuating the discourse of the subject must be 'propitious', and that is why Lacan emphasises the very notion of variable-length session; meaning, the length of the analytic session cannot be predetermined but follows the logic of the analysand's discourse and the analyst's appropriate punctuation of the same. Lacan, here, is obviously challenging the IPA's standard forty-five minute sessions when he says:

> It is, therefore, a propitious punctuation that gives meaning to the subject's discourse. This is why the ending of the session – which current technique makes into an interruption that is determined purely by the clock and, as such, takes no account of the thread of the subject's discourse – plays the part of a scansion which has the full value of an intervention by the analyst that is designed to precipitate concluding moments. Thus we must free the ending from its routine framework and employ it for all the useful aims of analytic technique. (*Écrits* 209)

Lacan elaborates on the question of 'full speech' and its relation to the unconscious in the following manner. The origin of psychoanalysis was the discovery of the hysteric symptoms, the cause of which was assigned to the traumatic event in the life of Josef Breuer's patient, Anna O. The very method of 'talking cure', as introduced by Freud and Breuer, had this at its heart – the traumatic event which triggered the symptom was discovered and ascertained only by 'putting the event into word (in the patient's "stories")' which thereby 'led to the removal of the symptom' (*Écrits* 211). In this sense, the effect of the so-called 'full speech' in psychoanalysis is 'to reorder past contingencies by conferring onto them the sense of necessities to come' (213). Such reordering is possible only through a speech that functions as intersubjective interlocution where 'the subject's act of addressing brings with it an addressee' and as such 'the speaker is constituted in it as intersubjectivity' (214). The history of the subject is constituted in an intersubjective discourse to the extent that the constitution of the unconscious takes place through language that comes from outside, that is, from the Other. The interlocution during analysis, including the intersubjective discourse of the analysand and the analyst, is thus rendered as instrumental in the restoration and reconstitution of the intersubjectively constituted history of the subject as well as the 'restoration of continuity in the subject's motivations' (214).

Because of its intersubjective or transindividual dimension, the unconscious in Freud, according to Lacan, has the position of a 'third term' vis-à-vis the analyst and the analysand. Lacan formulates this status of the unconscious as: 'The unconscious is that part of concrete discourse qua transindividual, which is not at the subject's disposal in re-establishing the continuity of his conscious discourse' (214). The unconscious, as a third term, is not at the subject's disposal because the whole fabric of Freud's work shows that it is a 'censored chapter' in the history of the subject. Psychoanalysis shows that the unconscious is etched in the 'monuments', 'archival documents', 'semantic evolution', 'traditions' and other 'traces' pertaining to the subject. Lacan precisely summarises this point when he says:

> The unconscious is the chapter of my history that is marked by a blank or occupied by a lie: it is the censored chapter. But the truth can be refound; most often it has already been written elsewhere. Namely, in monuments: this is my body, in other words, the hysterical core of neurosis in which the hysterical symptom manifests the structure of a language, and is deciphered like an inscription which, once recovered, can be destroyed without serious loss; in archival documents too: these are my childhood memories, just as impenetrable as such documents are when I do not know their provenance; in semantic evolution: this corresponds to the stock of words and acceptations of my own particular vocabulary, as it does to my style of life and my character; in traditions, too, and even in the legends which, in a heroicized form, convey my history; and, lastly, in its traces that are inevitably preserved in the distortions necessitated by the insertion of the adulterated chapter into the chapters surrounding it, and whose meaning will be re-established by my exegesis. (*Écrits* 215)

The task of psychoanalysis is to teach the subject to recognise the unconscious as his history which is 'refound' through analysis. Through such recognition, the subject is helped to 'complete the current historicisation of the facts that have already determined a certain number of the historical "turning points" in his existence' (*Écrits* 217). Psychoanalysis, functioning as historicisation, reveals the stigmas and the pages of shame and glory which mark the history of the subject.

It may be noted that, on a similar line, in his 1964 Seminar (*Book XI*), Lacan discusses the notion of the subject of the unconscious as 'a failure of speech'. The foremost concern in psychoanalysis is the 'phenomenon of talking' (Miller 9). The task is to make sense of the subject which talks or fails to talk, and says what it intends to, or does not intend to. Lacan privileges the gaps in the discourse of the analysand rather than the discourse itself; the unconscious is viewed by him, as an 'impediment, failure, split':

> Impediment, failure, split. In a spoken or written sentence something stumbles. Freud is attracted by these phenomena, and it is there that he seeks the unconscious. There, something other demands to be realized which appears as intentional, of course, but of a strange temporality. What occurs, what is *produced*, in this gap, is presented as *the discovery*. It is in this way that the Freudian exploration first encounters what occurs in the unconscious. (*Book XI* 25)

The unconscious as subject is the failure in speech – that which interrupts the speech and is usually designated as 'unintentional'. The unconscious, as stumbling, appears to be without substance since it appears only to disappear the next moment. This is why the subject of the unconscious is also defined by Lacan as a 'fading subject'. However, such stumbling evokes an alien aspect of our being as its fading involves 'a modality of nothingness'. As Miller notes, Lacan 'tries to present the unconscious as something that is both a modality of nothingness and a modality of being. It is a strange kind of being that appears when it ought not to: precisely when a strange intention is being realized' (10).

3. The Subject of the Unconscious is Marked by its 'Signifierness'

In his 'The Instance of the Letter in the Unconscious, or Reason since Freud', included in *Écrits*, Lacan brings out the linguistic structure of the unconscious, making an exhaustive use of the structuralist theory of the signifier. 'Right from the outset,' Lacan states, 'people failed to recognise the constitutive role of the signifier in the status Freud immediately assigned to the unconscious in the most precise and explicit ways' (*Écrits* 426). Freud's discovery of the unconscious took place way ahead of the formalisation of linguistics by Saussure and Jakobson and thus, according to Lacan, paved the way to their discoveries. In a 1960 paper, titled 'The Subversion of the Subject and Dialectic of Desire' and included in *Écrits*, he reiterates the issue by stating that though the notions of signifier and signified and metaphor and metonymy, which ground structuralist linguistics, are present in Freud – the unconscious is nothing but these linguistic elements, these operations – this terminology could not directly be used by Freud for obvious historical reasons. Lacan notes, 'Geneva 1910 and Petrograd 1920 suffice to explain why Freud did not have this particular instrument [structuralist linguistics] at his disposal'. 'But', argues Lacan:

> [This] historically motivated lacuna makes all the more instructive the fact that the mechanisms described by Freud as those of the primary process, by which the unconscious is governed, correspond exactly to the functions this school of linguistics believes determine the most radical axes of the effects of language, namely metaphor and metonymy – in other words, the effects of the substitution and combination of signifiers in the synchronic and diachronic dimensions, respectively, in which they appear in discourse. (*Écrits* 676–77)

That mechanisms of the unconscious truly correspond to the functions of language is established by the fact that Freud discovered this truth even though he could not take advantage of the linguistic discoveries of Saussure and Jakobson.

According to Lacan, Freud's writings are replete with references to language, philology and linguistic analysis. 'In Freud's complete works', says Lacan, 'one out of three pages presents us with philological references, one out of two pages with logical inferences, and everywhere we see a dialectical apprehension of experience, linguistic analysis becoming still more prevalent the more directly the unconscious is involved' (*Écrits* 424).

More specifically, Freud's discovery of the dream-formation is a linguistic discovery as far as dream, the 'royal road to the unconscious', is described by Freud as 'a rebus . . . quite literally'. Dream is a rebus because (a) it has a phonemic structure, (b) the value of the dream-images, like 'unnatural figures of the boat on the roof, or the man with a comma for a head', are that of the signifiers because 'they allow us to spell out the "proverb" presented by the oneiric rebus' and (c) 'The linguistic structure that enables us to read dreams is at the crux of the "signifierness of dreams"' (424), that is, at the crux of the dream-interpretation. Value of a dream-image 'has nothing to do with its signification', and this is explained by Freud in terms of 'Egyptian hieroglyphics in which it would be ridiculous to deduce from the frequency in a text of a vulture (which is an aleph) or a chick (which is a vau) – indicating a form of the verb "to be" and plurals – that the text has anything whatsoever to do with these ornithological specimens'. The case of these hieroglyphs is an extreme one since here 'we are dealing with writing where even the supposed "ideogram" is a letter' (424).

Lacan claims that the dream-work and indeed the logic of the unconscious formations in general are marked by a number of characteristics which are fundamentally linguistic. Most crucial of these include: transposition, condensation and displacement. According to Freud, dream-work is the mechanism through which latent thought is converted into the manifest content of a dream. All of the three above-mentioned processes contribute to the dream-work. 'Transposition', literally, involves the exchange of something for something else. A dream, for Freud, is always something other than what it appears to be. This implies that the chain of signifiers that surfaces in a dream replaces or disguises another chain. Another feature of the dream-work is that it disguises the original repressed wishes on which the dream is constituted. Not all elements/characters from the latent content are brought into the domain of the dream – some elements are selected at the cost of others. Again, some of the selected elements may be highlighted at the cost of others. Such selection, selective foregrounding and even merging of the different figures so as to hide the true wish behind the dream constitute the mechanism of 'condensation'. The third feature of the dream-work is defined as 'displacement', which may be explained as a transformation of the latent content into the manifest content of dream in terms of a change in emphasis, location, and time.[1] Lacan links the idea of displacement to the notion of metonymy.

To elaborate, transposition (*Entstellung*) is what constitutes the 'general precondition for the functioning of the dream' (*Écrits* 425). Lacan designates transposition 'as the sliding of the signified under the signifier, which is always happening (unconsciously, let us note) in discourse'. He claims that Saussurean linguistics is grounded by the algorithm S/s, which reads as 'signifier over signified, "over" corresponding to the bar separating the two levels' (415). The algorithm is noted as follows:

$$\frac{S}{s}$$

Figure 5: Saussurean algorithm (*Écrits* 414)

Here however, Lacan has radically modified Saussurean theory in order to not only show its flaws but to also reveal the psychoanalytic implications of the same. In *Course in General Linguistics*, Saussure had drawn the following diagram to represent the concept (signified) and the sound-image (signifier) – the two elements which constitute the linguistic sign.

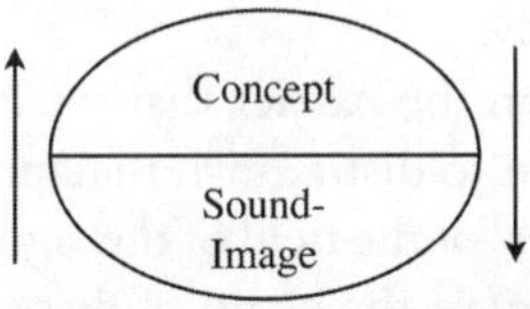

Figure 6: Saussure's drawing of the linguistic sign (Saussure 66)

Obviously, in Saussure's diagram, the signified is over the signifier and there are also two arrows which indicate the reciprocal relation between the two. Saussure argues that the two elements of the linguistic sign are as inseparable as the two sides of a paper, and their togetherness or union is represented by the circle. Through his conception of the 'Saussurean algorithm' – which, let it be noted, is not Saussure's but is Saussurean – Lacan modifies Saussure's diagram on a number of levels. First, he inverts the positions of the signifier and signified to establish the 'primacy of the signifier' over signified – he represents signifier with an uppercase 'S' and signified with a lowercase 's' (Evans 187). Second, he removes the circle and the arrows to indicate that there is no reciprocation or union between the signifier and the signified, which share a rather unstable relation, especially in the context of unconscious formations like slips of the tongue. Third, he keeps the line between the signifier and the signified to designate it as the 'bar' that separates the two – one is barred from the other, evoking the idea of the barred subject, that is, the subject as barred from knowing her unconscious desire; this bar is also indicative of the 'resistance inherent in signification' (187). Fourth, he dismisses the prevalent idea of the sign by talking about the domain of 'pure signifiers', that is, the domain of the unconscious where the signifier exists prior to the signified. In this way, Lacan's Saussurean algorithm defines his topography of the unconscious. Furthermore, Lacan's consideration of language as comprising signifiers alone amounts to 'abolishing' the Saussurean sign (187). Fifth, meaning, for Lacan, 'insists' in the chain of the signifier whereas 'none of the chain's elements *consists* in the signification it can provide at that very moment'. The chain of signification involves 'an incessant sliding of the signified under the signifier' (*Écrits* 419). Lacan notes that in dreams as well as in discourse, in general, such sliding of the signified under signifier happens unconsciously.

Lacan's emphasis on the barrier that separates the signifier from the signified leads him to distinguish metaphor from metonymy as the two sides or 'slopes' of the field of the signifier. Saussure stressed the horizontal linearity of the chain of discourse, but Lacan argues there is in fact a 'polyphony' of discourse that also aligns it vertically along the several staves of the musical score. These two vectors are derived from Jakobson's distinction between the metonymic (the 'linear') and the metaphoric (the 'vertical') poles of language. These two aspects of the signifier's impact on the signified are also to be found in condensation (metaphor) and displacement (metonymy). Condensation (*Verdichtung*), states Lacan, 'is the superimposed structure of signifiers in which metaphor finds its field; its name, condensing in itself the word *Dichtung*, shows the mechanism's connaturality with poetry, to the extent that it envelops poetry's own properly traditional function' (*Écrits* 425). Indeed, for Lacan, the very notion of the poetic is constituted by metaphor. The following formula was used by Lacan to represent the idea of metaphor:

$$f\left(\frac{S'}{S}\right) S \cong S(+)s$$

Figure 7: Lacan, formula of metaphor (*Écrits* 429)

Relying on Evans's explanation of the formula, it may be stated that the 'f . . . S', on the left side of the equation, stands for the 'effect of signification'. The parenthetical 'S'/S' symbolises 'the substitution of one signifier for another'. The 'S' and the 's' on the right side of the equation respectively stand for the signifier and the signified. The symbol (+) represents the 'crossing of the bar (–)' (referencing the Saussurean algorithm). The sign ≅ means 'is congruent with'. The formula of metaphor thus implies that 'the signifying function of the substitution of one signifier for another is congruent with the crossing of the bar' (Evans 115).

According to Lacan, displacement (*Verschiebung*), the best means for the unconscious 'by which to foil censorship [of repression and of the super-ego]', is the 'transfer of signification that metonymy displays' (*Écrits* 425). Lacan offers the following formula for metonymy:

$$f\left(S \ldots S'\right) S \cong S(-)s$$

Figure 8: Lacan, formula of metonymy (*Écrits* 428)

Once again relying on Evans's explanation of the formula, it may be said that while 'f . . . S' stands for the function or effect of signification, the parenthetical 'S . . . S'' stands for 'the link between one signifier and another in a signifying chain'. On the right side the bar is not crossed this time between the signifier and the signified. The formula of metonymy thus implies that the

'the signifying function of the connection of the signifier with the signifier is congruent with maintenance of the bar'. Put differently, 'in metonymy, the resistance of signification is maintained, the bar is not crossed, no new signified is produced' (Evans 117).

SHORT TAKES

Metaphor and Metonymy

In language, metaphor and metonymy are figures of speech. A metaphor describes or explains an idea, object, action or situation by comparing it to something else. Think, for instance, of the sentence 'Religion is the opiate of the masses' by Karl Marx. For Marx, religion is used as a tool to make people concentrate on the 'there and then' (their well-being in heaven) while they are exploited in the 'here and now'. His statement asserts that religion is like an opiate in that it offers some quick relief and illusory happiness, thereby rendering people oblivious and inert to the harsh realities of their lives. Metonymy involves signification through association. Think, for instance, of Shakespeare's famous line from the play *Julius Caesar*, 'Friends, Romans, countrymen, lend me your ears.' Here, 'ears' are not literally to be lent – the word 'ears' stands for the concept of 'attentive listening'. The relation between 'ears' and 'attentive listening' is one of close association. Lacan's usage of the two terms, however, is very technical. The terms metaphor and metonymy, as Evans explains in *A Dictionary of Lacanian Psychoanalysis*, are derived from the theories of language formulated by Ferdinand de Saussure and Roman Jakobson. Language operates through two opposite axes: one which combines words in a given sentence, the other which selects words for the sentence at the cost of not selecting some other words (to choose some words while speaking is also to not choose some other words). The first is the horizontal axis while the second is the vertical axis. The first is a process that takes place *in praesentia,* the second is that which takes place *in absentia*. According to Saussure, the first is called the syntagmatic axis which, according to Jakobson, is called metonymy, while the second is called the paradigmatic axis which Jakobson calls metaphor. Metaphor thus is the 'substitutive' axis of language and Lacan uses Jakobson's definition to formulate ideas like the paternal metaphor, in which the substitution of one signifier (desire of the mother) by another (Name-of-the-Father) takes place. Furthermore, Lacan talks about the metaphorical and metonymic processes of signification and how they impact the question of subjectivity. The two mechanisms of the unconscious, namely condensation and displacement, are also understood respectively in terms of metaphor and metonymy.

In this context, Lacan reiterates his description of symptom as metaphor and desire as metonymy – 'For the symptom *is* a metaphor, whether one likes to admit it or not, just as desire *is* a metonymy, even if man scoffs at the idea' (*Écrits* 439). His explanation of symptom as metaphor is precise:

> Metaphor's two-stage mechanism is the very mechanism by which symptoms, in the analytic sense, are determined. Between the enigmatic signifier of sexual trauma and the term it comes to replace in a current signifying chain, a spark flies that fixes in a symptom – a metaphor in which flesh or function is taken as a signifying element – the signification, that is inaccessible to the conscious subject, by which the symptom may be dissolved. (431)

The notion of metonymy is what is most crucial in the 'instating' of the 'lack of being'. For Lacan, what the metonymic structure indicates is 'the signifier-to-signifier connection that allows for the elision by which the signifier instates lack of being [*le manque de l'être*] in the object-relation, using signification's referral [*renvoi*] value to invest it with the desire aiming at the lack that it supports' (428).

The minus sign placed within the parenthesis in the metonymic structure represents this 'lack of being', as it also represents the 'bar' which resists signification between signifier and signified. Furthermore, desire supports the lack of being due to the premise, according to Lacan, that desire is desire for a lack – because the primordial object of desire is always already lost (as in the infant's unconscious desire for/of the mother) and also because the goal of desire, which is linguistic, unlike need, which is biological, is not fulfilment but recognition. It is the metonymic operation of desire which instates the being, yes, but a being as lacking.

The lack of being that emerges from the metaphoric and metonymic operations of the unconscious is what brings out a new notion of the 'subject'. This subject, or more precisely, the subject of the unconscious, is essentially a product of the chain of signifiers and signification and thus belongs to the order of the symbolic. The subject of the unconscious is also excentric to the individual since it is grounded in language, which is situated in the Other. This subject is radically opposed to the conventional notion of 'ego' in ego-psychology, which Lacan considers 'imaginary', and 'cogito' in philosophy, which Lacan dismisses as a misleading notion of subjectivity. This point is reiterated by Lacan on many other occasions as well.

4. The Subject of the Unconscious is the 'Subject of Enunciation'

In his 1960 paper titled 'Subversion of the Subject and the Dialectic of Desire in the Freudian Unconscious', Lacan goes on to theorise the subject of the unconscious in relation to the chain of signification to which the unconscious is inevitably bound. He asks, 'Once the structure of language is recognized in the unconscious, what sort of subject can we conceive of for it?' (*Écrits* 677). He explains, here, the difference or rupture between the grammatical subject of a statement and the unconscious subject of enunciation. The grammatical subject of a statement is not the subject of the unconscious, the latter having a 'fading' existence. Bruce Fink, in his book *The Lacanian Subject*, substantiates this difference. Fink draws on the special use of the English word 'but' in a sentence like, 'I cannot deny but that is a difficult thing', and shows the different agencies at work on 'I' (grammatical 'subject' of the sentence, the enunciated subject) and on 'but' (enunciating subject, or the subject outside this sentence, the subject of the unconscious). While the enunciated subject stands for the 'conscious or ego discourse', the enunciating subject involves the 'non-ego or unconscious discourse'. The latter also interrupts, or says 'no' to the former, the way a slip of the tongue interrupts a conversation. According to Fink, this special 'but', similar to the French '*ne*', announces the unconscious subject of enunciation, 'thereby showing that the subject is split – of two minds, so to speak, for and against, conscious and unconscious' (*The*

Lacanian Subject 40). Furthermore, the eruption of the subject of the unconscious, as in the case of slips of the tongue, is fleeting, as the subject fades immediately after appearing into consciousness.

It may also be mentioned that, in this essay, Lacan elaborates on the subject of the unconscious and dialectic of desire in terms of drawing the 'graph of desire' (*Écrits* 692). Simply put, the graph comprises a horseshoe-shaped line, described as the 'vector of the subject's intentionality' (Evans 76), which is intersected at four different points by two structurally alike horizontal lines. The horizontal vectors represent two diachronic signifying chains: (a) the signifying chain on the upper part is that of the unconscious (level of enunciation) which runs from the point of '*jouissance*' to that of 'castration' (b) the signifying chain on the lower part is that of consciousness (level of statement) which runs from the point of 'signifier' to that of 'voice'. Fink, in 'Knowledge and *Jouissance*', has explained that these two lines represent the two statuses of the subject in Lacan – the subject of the signifier and the subject of *jouissance* (24).

The subject of the unconscious cannot be designated as a subject of statement (signifier to voice), says Lacan, since 'he does not even know that he is speaking' (*Écrits* 692). The subject of the unconscious can be designated via the concept of drive (the subject of *jouissance* or of drive) 'on the basis of a pinpointing that is organic, oral, anal, and so on, which satisfies the requirement that the more he speaks, the further he is from speaking' (692). Thus, the subject of the unconscious is captured in the upper signifying chain which is on the level of enunciation. Lacan describes the signifier as that which represents the subject for another signifier and S(Ⱥ) is described as that signifier, also designated as phallus, for which all other signifiers represent the subject. The movement of an individual's socialisation is from *jouissance* to castration.

THE REAL ORDER OF SUBJECTIVITY: *LALANGUE, JOUISSANCE,* 'SEXUATION'

The real, in Lacan, is linked to core experiences of life and death; it is linked to life by way of *jouissance*. *Jouissance*, literally meaning 'orgasmic bliss', is placed in opposition to the notion of pleasure. *Jouissance*, related to the body, is an enjoyment that is limitless. One of the 'civilising mechanisms' of society is related to the idea that deriving limitless pleasure must be prevented. This is why society sets various 'pleasure principles', that is, laws which regulate and channel sexual pleasure (through marriage, morality, abstinence, etc.). While the idea of pleasure involves enjoyment in accordance with the pleasure principles, the idea of *jouissance* involves enjoyment that transgresses these principles. To be socialised is to learn to sacrifice or control one's *jouissance*. *Jouissance*, instinct, or the body which a human being is born with, must come under the sway of the laws and regulations of civilisation. For Lacan, human sexuality is different from animal sexuality precisely because the so-called 'instinct' that defines the latter has to be curbed and moulded for the former to be in accordance with the norms of civilisation. That is why Lacan replaces the word 'instinct' with the word 'drive' while developing the concept of human sexuality. The human body, which, as a whole, remains a source of *jouissance* immediately after birth, is gradually socialised in terms of concentrating on erogenous zones and even dress codes. In general, *jouissance* is what has a pre-symbolic dimension, and the real in the form of *jouissance*, thus, designates an order of subjectivity which is opposed to the symbolic as law. Lacan goes on to distinguish between two kinds of *jouissance* – the phallic and the feminine. The fundamental difference between them lies in the fact that while phallic *jouissance* can be represented through language (has a place in the domain of the symbolic), feminine *jouissance* resists any such representation (or is located in the domain of the real). Feminine *jouissance* is what exists outside of the domain of the signifier. In this sense, the real qua feminine *jouissance* is opposed to the symbolic qua signifier. The subject of *jouissance* is thus different from the subject of the signifier – though both *jouissance* and the signifier are constitutive elements of the unconscious. It may be noted that Freud put the id, the repressed wishes/desires (structured by signifiers) and parts of the ego and super-ego within the domain of the unconscious. In this regard, if the subject of the unconscious has a symbolic or linguistic dimension, even to some extent an imaginary dimension (the ego in Freud's version partly being within the domain of the unconscious), it also has a real dimension marked by *jouissance*.

The real is also linked to death in the sense that it has the potential to expose the limits of the imaginary and symbolic dimensions of subjectivity in terms of the affect of anxiety or the experience of trauma. Both the imaginary and symbolic orders of subjectivity are respectively constructed through the processes of primary and secondary identifications. Construction of subjectivity through identification with the small other or the big Other is nothing but an emulation of something placed outside the subject. Such a construction is done at the cost of denying or keeping aside the real order. However, the real does unsettle the subject at various moments when the subject suffers disillusionment from experiencing the nothingness of his being. In particular, the encounter with the feminine *jouissance* (the real) may cause the dissolution of the phallic myth (the symbolic constituted by the myth of male supremacy, omnipotence and virility), as is illustrated in the analysis of *The French Lieutenant's Woman* (1969) in Chapter Four. In a sense, feminine *jouissance* is what makes a man-woman relationship impossible, as is shown below through the discussion of 'sexuation' or sexual non-rapport.

The real order of subjectivity, in this regard, involves the subject of *jouissance* (the unconscious as *jouissance* and as structured by *lalangue*), the distinction between masculinity (phallic *jouissance*) and femininity (feminine *jouissance*) and the concept of sexuation. According to Lacan, the unconscious not only comprises signifiers of repressed thoughts but also certain pre-symbolic or extra-symbolic elements. In many ways, Lacan's 1972–73 Seminar (*Book XX*) stands out in this context as far as the exposition of the real order of subjectivity is concerned. In this text, one finds an accentual shift from 'subject of the signifier' to 'subject of *jouissance*', to use Fink's terms ('Knowledge and *Jouissance*' 24–26, 34). The following paragraphs discuss the real order of subjectivity with reference to this Seminar.

One of Lacan's preoccupations in this Seminar is a shift from language to *lalangue*. Here, he defines the unconscious not as structured like a language but as structured like *lalangue*. The term *lalangue* is of Lacan's own coinage. It is related to *jouissance* and thus to the real and is opposed to language and thus to the symbolic. One difference between language and *lalangue* is that where language is used for the purpose of communication, *lalangue* 'serves purposes that are altogether different from that of communication' (*Book XX* 138). If *lalangue* does not serve the purpose of communication, what role does it play? Lacan says *lalangue* 'affects us first of all by everything it brings with it by way of effects that are affects'. *Lalangue* does not communicate meaning/signified but affects the subject – it endows the subject with *jouissance* as well as with affects like anxiety. Language is also described by Lacan as 'the function of' *lalangue* and as 'made up of' *lalangue* (138–39). Evans explains this point: '*Lalangue* is like the primary chaotic substrate of polysemy out of which language is constructed, almost as if language is some ordered superstructure sitting on top of this substrate' (100). In other words, *lalangue* is that substance which lacks symbolic or logical ordering while also serving as the very basis of language (which is marked by order, grammar and logic). It is as if *lalangue* triggers the very functioning of language. While language belongs to the domain of the symbolic and the signifier, *lalangue* verges on the real. To define the unconscious as *lalangue* is to foreground affects and *jouissance* as constitutive elements of the subject of the unconscious (the real order of subjectivity). This is clearly different from the conception of the subject of the unconscious as an effect of the signifier (the symbolic order of subjectivity).

Another major concern in *Seminar Book XX* is the concept of *jouissance* and how it affects subjectivity. As mentioned before, Lacan talks about two kinds of *jouissance* – the phallic *jouissance* and the feminine/Other *jouissance*. Fink points out that the term phallic is to be understood in conjunction with the term fallible ('Knowledge and *Jouissance*' 37). The phallic *jouissance* is what fails to provide complete enjoyment or full satisfaction. Furthermore, phallic *jouissance* is phallic in the sense that it is in the domain of the symbolic – phallus is the bar between the signifier and the signified in Lacan's Saussurean algorithm. It is because of this bar that the signifier cannot reach and always misses the signified. For its connection with the order of law and language, phallic *jouissance* is also called symbolic *jouissance* and semiotic *jouissance*.

As opposed to phallic *jouissance*, the Other *jouissance* is what is described by Lacan as infallible, ineffable and ek-sistent. It is infallible because it supposedly reaches the mark. It is ineffable because it can be experienced but not articulated, since articulation involves the signifier and phallicisation (which lead to the missing of the mark). And it is ek-sistent because it exists outside of the symbolic but impinges on it from the real. As Fink states, the Other *jouissance* is 'the *jouissance* that the Other gets out of us – after all, Lacan says we are duped by *jouissance*, *joués* . . . but then again it could be our enjoyment of the Other, or even our enjoyment as the Other . . . That ambiguity should be kept in mind as we turn to the formulas of sexuation themselves' ('Knowledge and *Jouissance*' 38).

The two kinds of *jouissance* are explained by Lacan with reference to the notion of sexuation. Sexuation is to be understood as the 'logic' of masculine and feminine subjectivities. Men and women, in Lacan's formulation, are not biological entities but logical structures, that is, they are defined in terms of the structure or formula arrived at by Lacan. As Fink puts it, 'sexuation is not biological sex: what Lacan calls masculine structure and feminine structure do not have to do with one's biological organs but rather with the kind of *jouissance* that one is able to obtain' ('Knowledge and *Jouissance*' 36). Sexuation is thus, according to Lacan, to be distinguished from notions of sexual 'identity' or 'orientation'. Lacan presented his famous formulae of sexuation in his seminar dated 13 March 1973 (*Book XX* 78).

The formulae, like any other diagram/formula/graph in Lacan, comprise a number of algebraic symbols and mathemes. A crucial symbol here is *L̸a*, that is, the French article '*la*' ('the') which is crossed. '*La*' is crossed to indicate that no universalisation about women is possible since that would involve the symbolic order in which feminine *jouissance* ek-sists. This is why Lacan, on a number of occasions, states: *la femme n'existe pas* (the woman does not exist), or *Il n'y a pas la femme* (there is no such thing as the woman), placing the emphasis on 'la', which does not exist.

The formulae of sexuation capture Lacan's understanding of the masculine and feminine structures. Fink, in 'Knowledge and *Jouissance*', explains the masculine structure in the following manner: 'All of man's *jouissance* is phallic *jouissance*. Every single one of his satisfactions may come up short . . . Nevertheless, there is the belief in a *jouissance* that could never come up short, the belief in another *jouissance*' (38). Here, the fallibility of phallic *jouissance* is derived from the reduction of the partner to an object. We, the barred subjects, do not desire our partner as a whole; it is only something in the partner (some part of the other [*autre*]) that attracts us – 'our partner's voice or gaze that turns us on, or that body part we enjoy in our partner' (38). Phallic *jouissance* is also what Lacan defines as 'hommosexual' – with a double 'm' – where *homme*, in French, means 'man'. What characterises the masculine structure is the enjoyment involving the reduction of the partner to an object *a*. 'Regardless of whether one is male or female (those are the biological terms) and regardless of whether one's partner is male or female, to enjoy in this way is to enjoy *like* a man' (37).

The feminine structure is explained by Fink in the following words:

> Not all of her *jouissance* is phallic *jouissance* . . . There *is* not any that is not phallic *jouissance* – the emphasis going on the first "is." All the *jouissances* that *do exist* are phallic, but that does not mean there cannot be some *jouissances* that are not phallic – it is just that they do not exist: they ek-sist. The Other *jouissance* can only ek-sist, it cannot exist, for to exist it would have to be spoken. ('Knowledge and *Jouissance*' 39)

Sexuation divides human subjects into two categories – man and woman. A man is defined as someone who, irrespective of biological specificities or chromosomes, can experience either phallic *jouissance* or feminine *jouissance* but not both. A woman is defined as someone who, irrespective of biological specificities or chromosomes, can potentially experience both kinds of *jouissance*. It should be noted that by rendering masculinity and femininity in terms of sexuation, Lacan is not promoting a so-called heterosexual worldview. The structures do not correspond to sexual differences on a biological level. The formulae of sexuation are equally applicable to 'homosexual' partners. 'In female homosexuality', Fink makes clear, 'both partners could come under feminine structure, masculine structure, or one of each; the same goes for male homosexuality' ('Knowledge and *Jouissance*' 41).

The question of sexuation poses limits to the clinical analysis (which is largely dependent upon speech and language) of women. In her article 'What Does the Unconscious Know about Women?', Lacanian analyst Colette Soler addresses this issue. Soler begins by defining the unconscious as 'a kind of knowledge . . . once it is deciphered and interpreted on the basis of what the analysand (male or female) says' (107). While a woman is analysable in the clinic, on the basis of phallic *jouissance* she is 'outside the unconscious' as far as feminine *jouissance* is concerned. Feminine *jouissance* 'is manifest in the experience of the sexual relationship and also in mystical love, but it cannot be translated in terms of unconscious knowledge' (107). For Soler, feminine *jouissance* accordingly cannot be analysed in psychoanalysis which is why 'analysis has led to an emphasis on phallic *jouissance*, for its practice is only concerned with *jouissance* that is filtered through the signifier [*passée au signifiant*]' since 'analysis reveals that there is a remainder, and that the whole of *jouissance* can never be said' (107). The unconscious, according to Soler, 'does not know everything' about women, 'but what it knows is sufficient for us to analyse women' (99).

The idea of sexuation renders impossible the sexual relationship between men and women. This is related to the fact that a relationship between a man and a woman would directly involve the intervention of the feminine *jouissance*. Feminine *jouissance* is what escapes phallic knowledge and ek-sists the symbolic order in which the very notion of 'relationship' is moulded. Feminine *jouissance* qua real is also what disrupts the imaginary and symbolic notions of masculinity or 'phallic myth' (virility, superiority, potency and so on) which men identify with as part of their larger shaping of identity. For Lacan, the relationship between man and woman is always mediated by a third term, the phallus, which functions like the Saussurean bar between the signifier and the signified. Like the bar, which keeps the two terms alienated from one another and constantly makes the signifier 'miss the mark', phallic *jouissance* too, as has been noted, keeps the masculine subject always dissatisfied with his partner. The real of the feminine *jouissance*, on the other hand, challenges and disrupts the symbolic and imaginary identifications on which the very phallic subjectivity stands. Be it the phallus, or the object *a*, or the signifier of the lack in the Other, there is always a third term between man and woman, which is why sexual rapport is rendered impossible. The real of the feminine *jouissance* is what exceeds the notion of the subject caught in the symbolic network of language. The order of the real, as a hole in the symbolic and as that which ek-sists the symbolic, disrupts the imaginary and symbolic dimensions of subjectivity.

THE STATUS OF THE SUBJECT AT THE END OF THE ANALYSIS

Patients suffering from pathological symptoms go to see a psychoanalyst. Theoretically, at the end of a successful psychoanalysis, the status of the subject/patient undergoes substantial change. This change can be understood in at least three ways – the removal of pathological symptoms, identification with the symptoms that 'allow one to live' and construction of the *sinthome*. The first two correspond to both the neurotic and the pervert, whereas the third one specifically corresponds to the psychotic. What does this mean?

A symptom, as has been noted, is a formation of the unconscious. Symptoms, similar to dreams, parapraxes and jokes, are not necessarily pathological. When symptoms become pathological, the subject goes to the analyst to get rid of them. In fact, the very advent of psychoanalysis was caused by Freud's encounter with patients exhibiting pathological symptoms which medicines or hypnotherapy were unable to treat. Every pathological symptom is linked to some unconscious motive derived from some sort of repression in the life of the subject. When the analysand engages in free association of his thoughts, his symptoms are articulated through words. Articulation leads to the knowledge about the symptoms and this knowledge has the potential to lead to the removal of these symptoms. A successful analysis involves the removal of the pathological symptoms.

It must be noted, however, that in his early teachings, Lacan described symptom as a signifier which needs to be deciphered in analysis. In his later teachings, a shift gradually took place towards locating the symptom vis-à-vis *jouissance*. In fact, in *Seminar Book XXII*, Lacan defines a symptom 'as the way in which each subject enjoys [*jouit*] the unconscious, in so far as the unconscious determines him' (qtd. in Evans 191). In this second sense, symptom is not something that the subject must be rid of but something which the subject must learn to identify with at the end of the analysis. This second kind of symptom, being related to *jouissance,* verges on the real. Over the course of a successful analysis, the patient is led to encounter the falsity of his imaginary being, the truth of his unconscious desire and the 'real' of *jouissance*. At the end of the analysis, the subject is not made to continue in a state of 'waste', but rather, as Esthela Solano-Suárez writes, to produce 'an unprecedented bond with the symptom in terms of identification' by promoting an orientation towards the real (95–96). Analysis might involve the removal of one kind of symptom (which belongs to the domain of the symbolic), but it also involves identification with another kind of symptom (which verges on the real qua *jouissance*). This new kind of symptom, related to the 'modality of the subject's *jouissance*', as Luke Thurston puts it in his article on 'Sinthome', is what necessitates the introduction of the term *sinthome* which designates the status of symptom at the end of the analysis. 'Far from calling for some analytic "dissolution",' Thurston continues, 'the *sinthome* is what "allows one to live" by providing a unique organisation of *jouissance*. The task of analysis thus becomes, in one of Lacan's final definitions of the end of analysis, to identify with the *sinthome*' ('Sinthome' 191). In this regard psychoanalysis of the neurotic and even the pervert involves a movement from the symbolic to the real, from the symptom to the *sinthome*.

The concept of *sinthome* has a more specific connotation with regard to the psychotic subject. Psychosis offers the greatest challenge to the psychoanalyst. As has been stated, the psychotic subject is one who forecloses the paternal function and, hence, experiences no substitution of the desire of the mother by the Name-of-the-Father. Since such a substitution, or a successful Oedipus complex (leading to the event of castration), is absent in the case of the psychotic, the crucial question raised is whether psychoanalysis can have anything to do with psychosis. As Jean-Louis Gault explains, for Freud, the psychotic subject has nothing to expect from psychoanalysis since, due to his foreclosure of castration and the paternal function, no 'transference love' is possible vis-à-vis the analyst (77). Lacan, however, radically departs from Freud on the question of psychosis by differentiating between 'treatment' and 'cure' in psychoanalysis. In the case of neurosis, cure is at stake, whereas in the case of psychosis, treatment is what the subject may expect from analysis (73–78). The treatment of psychosis involves assisting the psychotic subject to move from the real to the symbolic – the exact reverse of the neurotic cure – since the problem, for the psychotic, is that he is predominantly exposed to the order of the real because of the absence of the Name-of-the-Father, which, for the neurotic, functions as protection against the real. This is why psychotic symptoms include delusions and hallucinations which indicate the disjunction between the psychotic universe and the reality structured by the symbolic. The psychotic subject is to be treated during analysis by way of assisting in a movement from the real to the symbolic, which would involve the construction of a new symptom or *sinthome*. There is, however, a crucial difference between the *sinthome* of the psychotic and the *sinthome* of the neurotic. The structure of the neurotic subject is marked by the interdependent existence of the real, the symbolic and the imaginary orders, exactly like the rings in a Borromean knot. These rings or orders are knotted in such a way that if one is cut, the entire structure falls apart. In the case of the psychotic, however, these rings are found in an unknotted state. The essential structure of subjectivity demands the knotting of these rings and the *sinthome* of the psychotic is constructed at the end of the analysis to function as a fourth ring which would keep the RSI together.

There is, however, an alternative reading of the notion of *sinthome*. As Russel Grigg indicates in his article 'From the Mechanism of Psychosis to the Universal Condition of Symptom: On Foreclosure', there is a shift in Lacan's conception of the Borromean knot in his Seminar on *sinthome*. While earlier, the three orders or rings (RSI) were considered knotted for the neurotic and separate for the psychotic, in his later teachings Lacan seems to suggest that for every subject the rings are separate. If, or when, the rings are joined, they are joined by the fourth ring or the *sinthome* (66). Thus, construction of the sinthome is not something specific to the psychotic but is necessary for the neurotic as well. There is, of course, a qualitative difference between the *sinthomes* of the psychotic and the neurotic as their structures are different.

Whatever be the variations, the point remains that the end of the analysis brings about some crucial changes in the nature of the analysand's subjectivity. While there takes place a removal of pathological symptoms, there also occurs identification with new symptoms or construction of the *sinthome*. A successful psychoanalysis thus triggers a new order of subjectivity which helps the subject come to terms with himself and the world at large.

NOTES

[1] I am here indebted to Dr Santanu Biswas for his formal and informal discussions on the 'formations of the unconscious' in my postgraduate days (July–December 2008).

REFERENCES

Clark, Michael. *Jacques Lacan: An Annotated Bibilography Volume I.* London: Routledge, 2014. Kindle File.

Douglass, Eric J. *Reading the Bible Ethically: Recovering the Voice in the Text.* Leiden and Boston: Brill, 2014. Print.

Evans, Dylan. *An Introductory Dictionary of Lacanian Psychoanalysis.* London: Routledge, 1996. Print.

Fink, Bruce. 'Knowledge and *Jouissance*.' *Reading Seminar XX: Lacan's Major Work on Love, Knowledge, and Feminine Sexuality*. Eds. Suzanne Barnard and Bruce Fink. Albany: SUNY Press, 2002. Print.

---. *The Lacanian Subject: Between Language and Jouissance*. New Jersey: Princeton UP, 1995. Print.

Gault, Jean-Louis. 'Two Statuses of the Symptom: "Let Us Turn to Finn Again".' *The Later Lacan: An Introduction.* Eds. Véronique Voruz and Bogdan Woolf. Albany: SUNY Press, 2007. Print.

Grigg, Russell. 'From the Mechanism of Psychosis to the Universal Condition of Symptom: On Foreclosure.' *Key Concepts in Lacanian Psychoanalysis.* Ed. Dany Nobus. New York: Other Press, 1998.

Lacan, Jacques. *Écrits: The First Complete Edition in English*. Trans. Bruce Fink. New York: W. W. Norton & Co., 2006. Print.

---. 'The Seminar of Jacques Lacan Book V: The Formations of the Unconscious, 1957–58'. *Lacan in Ireland*. Trans (unofficial). Cormac Gallagher. Web. 20 September 2017. <http://www.lacaninireland.com/web/wp-content/uploads/2010/06/Book-05-the-formations-of-the-unconscious.pdf>.

---. *The Seminar of Jacques Lacan Book XI: The Four Fundamental Concepts of Psychoanalysis, 1964.* Trans. Alan Sheridan. London: W. W. Norton & Co., 1998. Print.

---. *The Seminar of Jacques Lacan Book XX (Encore): On Feminine Sexuality, Limits of Love and Knowledge, 1972–73*. Trans. Bruce Fink. London: W. W. Norton & Co., 1998. Print.

Miller, Jacques-Alain. 'Context and Concepts.' *Reading Seminar XI: Lacan's Four Fundamental Concepts*. Ed. Richard Feldstein et al. Albany: SUNY Press, 1995. Print.

Saussure, Ferdinand de. *Course in General Linguistics.* Trans. Wade Baskin. New York: Columbia UP, 2011. Print.

Solano-Suarez, Esthela. 'Identification with the Symptom at the End of Analysis.' *The Later Lacan: An Introduction*. Eds. Véronique Voruz and Bogdan Woolf. Albany: SUNY Press, 2007. Print.

Soler, Colette. 'What Does the Unconscious Know about Women?' *Reading Seminar XX: Lacan's Major Work on Love, Knowledge, and Feminine Sexuality.* Eds. Suzanne Barnard and Bruce Fink. Albany: SUNY Press, 2002. Print.

Thurston, Luke. 'Sinthome.' *An Introductory Dictionary of Lacanian Psychoanalysis*. Ed. Dylan Evans. London: Routledge, 1996. Print.

Weber, Max. *The Protestant Ethic and the Spirit of Capitalism*. Trans. Talcott Parsons. London: Routledge Classics, 2001. Print.

Žižek, Slavoj. 'Slavoj Žižek on Jacques-Alain Miller.' *YouTube*. Web. 7 March 2017. https://www.youtube.com watch?v=9eMbN7pqNMA .

Chapter Three

The Clinical Structures: Psychosis, Neurosis, Perversion

> A claim against people who are supposedly acting against you is not enough for us to have a psychosis. It may well be an unjustified claim, contributing to a delusion of presumption, this doesn't make it a psychosis . . . for us to have a psychosis, there must be disturbances of language – this at least is the rule of thumb I suggest you adopt provisionally.
>
> Jacques Lacan, *Seminar Book III*

Lacan's take on the psychoanalytic technique is derived from his formulation of the three clinical categories, namely, psychosis, neurosis and perversion. These categories have a number of sub-categories. Psychosis is predominantly of two kinds – paranoia and schizophrenia; neurosis is of three kinds – hysteria, obsessional neurosis and phobia; and perversion comprises sadism, masochism and fetishism. The categories do not receive an equal amount of coverage in Lacan's teachings; arguably, psychosis receives the most. Lacan does not reduce these categories to a collection of symptoms but rather defines them as 'structures'. This implies that a neurotic, for instance, might manifest symptoms of psychosis without having a psychotic structure. Symptoms do not necessarily determine the clinical category in psychotherapy, structures do. The three clinical structures are defined by three mechanisms: *Verwerfung*, or foreclosure which forms psychosis; *Verdrängung*, or repression which constitutes neurosis; and *Verleugnung*, or disavowal which leads to perversion. All these terms are taken from Freud. These three mechanisms can be explained with reference to the concept of paternal function, the internalisation of which leads to the socialisation of the subject. The psychotic forecloses the paternal function, whereas the neurotic represses it and the pervert disavows it. The three structures can also be explained in terms of the desire of the mother. The desire of the mother is never barred for the psychotic, while it is barred for the neurotic and it 'must be barred' for the pervert (Fink 194). Furthermore, these structures are related in different ways to *jouissance*. *Jouissance* uncontrollably invades the psychotic, whereas the neurotic avoids it and the pervert makes it a point to set it limits (Fink 173). That is to say, in the case of the psychotic, the mother-child dyad is not successfully broken since the Name-of-the-Father does not shape his psychical universe. There is no symbolic identification for a psychotic. This is precisely why there is no question of sacrifice of *jouissance* for the psychotic. As discussed in Chapter Five, Norman Bates, in Alfred Hitchcock's film *Psycho,* exemplifies the psychotic structure. In the case of a neurotic, the Oedipus complex and subsequent substitution of the desire of the mother by the Name-of-the-Father happens successfully and the neurotic thereby gets 'socialised'. The neurotic adjusts to the 'pleasure principle' set by society and avoids transgressing into the domain of *jouissance*. In the case of a pervert, the law (Name-of-the-Father) must be brought into being, which is why that which is against the law (continuing with the desire of the mother) must be barred and the original internalisation of the paternal function needs to be disavowed (Fink 193).

The technique of psychoanalysis involves the diagnosis of the clinical structures and the treatment of the subject in accordance with her specific clinical structure. Before moving into the discussion of the clinical categories, however, it must be noted that a theoretical understanding of these categories is far from enough to enable clinical diagnosis. A psychoanalyst, in the Lacanian sense, is one who is imbued with considerable phenomenological experience derived from undergoing psychoanalysis under the supervision of another analyst and engaging in clinical practice for a considerable period of time. It is these experiences which, together, contribute to the analyst's understanding, diagnosis and treatment of a patient.

Lacan's theorisation of the clinical structures has its roots in his own clinical experience, as is obvious from the constant reference in his Seminars to his 'case presentations'. As is often the case with Lacan's theories, this too is marked by a rearticulation of Freud's views. Although Lacan only touches upon these clinical categories in his seminars, *écrits* and other texts, it is possible to isolate a number of his works where they occupy a substantial place. Chronologically, these works would include (a) Lacan's doctoral thesis titled *Paranoiac Psychosis in Its Relation to Personality*, (b) lectures on *Verneinung* which are included in *Écrits* but which originally come from *Seminar Book I*, (c) *Seminar Book III* which is on the subject of psychoses, (d) the article based on *Seminar Book III* – namely, 'On a Question Prior to Any Possible Treatment of Psychosis', which is included in *Écrits*, (e) *Seminar Book IV* and *Seminar Book VIII* – where, among other places, Lacan talks about phobia and perversion, (f) *Seminar Book X* which is on the subject of perversion and anxiety, (g) 'Kant with Sade' (1963) included in *Écrits* and (h) *Seminar Book XXIII* which is on the subject of *sinthome* and the works of James Joyce. A discussion of these texts would help us understand the conceptual development of the three clinical structures in Lacan. The discussion comprises the following sections: the case of Aimée; Lacan's reading of Freud's case history of Wolf Man; Lacan's reading of Freud's case history of Schreber; psychosis and the case of James Joyce; the structural differences between neurosis and psychosis; the three sub-categories of neurosis; and the concept of perversion.

AIMÉE'S SELF-PUNITIVE PARANOIA

This section should begin with the caveat that the case of Aimée was written not by Lacan the psychoanalyst but by Lacan the psychiatrist. His doctoral thesis, which comprises the analysis of this case, was defended and published in 1932, the same year he started his own psychoanalysis under the supervision of Rudolph Loewenstein. At the time, Lacan was not even a member of the Psychoanalytic

Society of Paris. Lacan the psychoanalyst would later discard some of the points made in his thesis, but the case of Aimée offers us some idea of Lacan the psychiatrist and his earliest, though small-scale, use of Freud.

Aimée was a female psychotic whom Lacan treated at the Sainte-Anne Hospital. The original name of the patient was Marguerite Anzieu, whom Lacan, in order to preserve the patient's anonymity, calls Aimée. Lacan did not choose this name randomly; this is the name of the female protagonist in the first of two novels written by the patient. In 'The Case of Aimée, or Self-Punitive Paranoia', Lacan asserts that Aimée suffered from paranoia – a form of psychosis (214). Her attempt to kill a theatre actress she alleged as 'instigating "scandal" against her' were the headlines of many newspapers. According to her, the actress had been 'mocking and menacing her' for a number of years. Aimée also alleged that there was a second party, a famous writer, involved in this plan to persecute her. She claimed that in his novels he 'disclosed various incidents of her personal life' (214). While describing the 'patient's life situation', Lacan tells us she was born to a peasant family hailing from Dordogne, a region located in South West France. Her siblings included three brothers and two sisters. She was thirty-eight years old at the time of the incident, and was working in the capacity of an administrator for a railway company. She had been employed there since she was eighteen and had, eventually, married one of her co-workers. They lived together for six years, during which time they had a son, before she started living by herself. She regularly kept in touch with her son, who stayed with his father.

Aimée had a history of being reprimanded by the police and being admitted to psychiatric hospitals. As Lacan indicates, her medical history contained instances of disorder, like her thinking that the 'people in the street make insulting remarks, accuse her of extraordinary vices; people around her say all sorts of evil things about her; the whole town of Melun knows about her behavior and regards her as depraved' ('The Case of Aimée' 214). She exhibited signs of 'delusion of persecution and jealousy, illusions, misinterpretations, grandiose ideas, hallucinations, excitement, incoherence' (214). Aimée's attack on the actress also paralleled events in her medical history. Earlier, she had pursued a communist journalist for allegedly writing but not publishing an article about her grievances, and she had also assaulted an employee of a publishing house for rejecting her manuscript.

Aimée's delusions and other symptoms did not continuously show up; sometimes they disappeared. This was the case during her admission to Sainte-Anne's asylum, when she 'was well orientated, had no intellectual impairment, showed no evidence of thought disorder and her attention was unimpaired'. However, even though 'her delusions had lost their intellectual appeal, some of them still evoked emotion' (214). Sometimes she felt ashamed of the way she thought of things, whereas sometimes she would state that she did those things precisely because she believed someone wanted to kill her child. Over the course of her treatment, Lacan discovered that her delusions comprised a range of manifestations of paranoia. Her jealousy and her prejudices gave birth to delusions of persecution. She also manifested delusions of grandeur which involved 'dreams of escaping to a better life and notions of having a grand mission to accomplish' (214). Such delusions also generated erotomania or a delusory belief that a royal personage (the Prince of Wales) was in love with her.

Lacan states that Aimée's pathological condition first manifested at the age of twenty-eight when she was working in an office where her husband also worked. At this stage, she had been married for four years and was pregnant. She started to believe that her colleagues, the people on the streets and the newspaper journalists were criticising her, condemning her and conspiring against her. She could not identify any reason for such condemnation and concluded that they were behaving in such a way because they wanted the child inside her to die. Her depression led to arguments with her husband, who had earlier accused her of being with another man before marriage. Sometimes she reacted violently, as Lacan notes: 'One day she slashed the tyres of a colleague's bicycle. One night she threw a jug of water at her husband's head; another time she threw an iron at him' ('The Case of Aimée' 216).

Aimée's child was born dead and this led to an intensification of her delusions. A woman she had known for three years called to find out how she was doing post-delivery, but Aimée thought this woman had planned the death of her child. Aimée's second pregnancy and childbirth happened without any problems, and she bore a healthy son whom she breastfed for fourteen months. She started misinterpreting things, however. For instance, she 'provoked a scene with the driver of a car which she considered had passed too close to the child's pram' (216). After a while, she planned in secret to go to America to try her luck as a novelist. When her husband found out, she stated that she wanted to abandon the child but then said she wanted to go to America not at the expense of their son but for his benefit. It is at this point that she stayed in a psychiatric hospital for the first time. She was eventually discharged, though not actually cured. She applied for a transfer and came to stay in Paris. It was in Paris where she heard the name of the theatre actress – vaguely referred to by her colleagues during the course of a conversation – and immediately considered her to be the source of her fear, that is, the person seeking to murder her child. Lacan notes that the patient did not know the actress at all; she did not even know the kinds of plays or films in which the actress performed. She saw the actress only twice, once onstage and once on-screen, before she attempted to kill her.

But her fear wasn't limited to just that particular theatre actress. Aimée also made up a number of imagined persecutors including actresses, writers, etc. Over the course of time she actually developed an extreme hatred of female performers, considering them to be nothing but high-class prostitutes who wanted to destroy her and her son. This hatred is clearly expressed in her two autobiographical novels. Lacan states that both the novels were well written, but in terms of literary quality the first was better than the second. Translators of Lacan's text have described the plot of the first novel as follows:

> In the first chapter, titled 'Spring', she is pictured in an idyllic setting, as a country girl in the age of chivalry, dreaming of marriage. In the second chapter, 'Summer', two strangers make their appearance. One is a 'courtesan' who destroys the innocent atmosphere and causes Aimée to feels intense jealousy. In the third chapter, 'Autumn', disaster strikes as Aimée and her fiancé become the subject of gossip and

> scandal in the town. She responds by thinking purer and purer thoughts. In the last chapter, 'Winter', she dies just after the strangers go away.
>
> ('The Case of Aimée' 217–18)

In the second novel, her revulsion towards 'women of the theatre' is very explicit, as she is quoted as saying in Lacan's 'The Case of Aimée, or Self-Punitive Paranoia': 'High class prostitutes are the scum of society. They undermine it and destroy it. They make other women the slaves of society and ruin their reputation' (218).

'The most striking aspect of the whole case', Lacan remarks, 'is the delusional state. It was systematised, and its two main features were the accompanying emotion (predominantly anxiety), and the peculiar way in which it developed, particularly with regard to the seemingly casual choice of victim' ('The Case of Aimée' 218). In his analysis of the case, Lacan first raises the question, 'Does Aimée's psychosis represent an organic process?' (219). He says that the psychosis at stake cannot be explained in terms of organic factors – related to 'the puerperium, thyroid dysfunction, abuse of thyroid medication, the menstrual cycle' (220) – even though some of these could be found in and had an effect on, Aimée. Nor can the organisation of Aimée's delusional system be explained in terms of the 'primitive or elementary' phenomena like oneiroid states, which are states of altered consciousness resembling dreams (219). Lacan asserts that these phenomena 'cannot explain how a delusional system can become established or account for its particular organisation' (220). Rather, in the case of Aimée, 'the crucial factor lies in the personality of the subject.' However, could Aimée be explained as a case of 'paranoid personality' (223)? Lacan investigates Aimée's childhood, her adulthood, her love affairs and her marriage and discards the possibility. This is because paranoid personalities, according to Lacan, are marked by pride, vanity, distrust, false judgement and so on. Aimée's personality, on the other hand, was marked by self-consciousness, moral uncertainty, intermittent anxiety and morbid conscience.

For Lacan, Aimée's psychosis does not have a biological or organic origin; it is psychogenic or has a psychological origin. More crucially, Aimée's is not any general kind of paranoia but rather illustrates an entirely new category of psychosis which he identified and called 'self-punitive' paranoia ('The Case of Aimée' 224). In this context, Lacan isolates two striking features of the case.

First, he notes that on the twentieth day of her imprisonment, 'her symptoms disappeared abruptly' ('The Case of Aimée' 224). The rapid evaporation of her delusional system (the absence of her symptoms was noticeable in the one-and-a-half years she spent in the Sainte-Anne hospital afterwards) was remarkably opposed to the 'organic, schizophrenic, depressive or manic conditions' which 'resolve slowly, with frequent oscillations, and then only partially'. Instead, Aimée's case was somewhat comparable to 'one set of circumstances – in subjects with delusional states based on passion who have accomplished the murder of the person who was the object of the delusion' (224). By killing the person, the subject feels relieved and their delusional system thereby evaporates immediately. Obviously, in Aimée's case no such killing took place and, moreover, she failed in her attempt(s). Furthermore, her 'aggressive act against the actress did not result in immediate relief; she obtained no satisfaction in contemplating her victim's plight' (224). Additionally, the evaporation of Aimée's delusional system did not take place immediately – it took twenty days of her staying in prison for it to happen. What, then, explains Aimée's relief as well as her delay in relief? Lacan explains that 'something had changed as a result of her attack [that is, the assassination attempt]' (224). She had to live in prison in the company of criminals, some of whom passed cynical remarks on her current situation. She was also scorned by people she knew. It is only when she realised she had been made to undergo some amount of 'punishment' that she felt relief. Following this line of analysis, Lacan concludes: 'Aimée's psychosis is based on self-punitive mechanisms which dominate her personality structure' (223). This (hypo)thesis explains, Lacan adds, the other contents of Aimée's delusional system. 'Her persecutors', for instance, 'were trying to harm her child "in order to punish the mother". On one occasion when asked why she had believed her child was being threatened, she replied: "To punish me, because I did not accomplish what I set out to do"' (225).

Second, Aimée had a peculiar notion regarding her persecutors.

There were several in number and she had no real-life connection with any of them; they constituted a 'prototype' for her on both emotional and representational levels. Aimée had an elder sister who, following the death of her husband, came to live with Aimée. This sister, considered 'morally superior' ('The Case of Aimée' 222), exerted immense influence on Aimée in terms of offering her advice. Aimée was also very close to a female colleague whose social airs and domineering attitude overwhelmed her. Both these women impacted Aimée on an emotional level as she considered herself to be morally and socially inferior.

With reference to the representational value of Aimée's persecutors, Lacan further clarifies her self-punitive paranoia. Her desire to persecute writers, actresses and other 'women of the world' is derived from her aspiration to be like them – to experience freedom and social ease. They thus embodied something she would have loved to be but in reality could not be. 'In striking the actress', Lacan writes, 'Aimée struck her externalized ideal, in the same way as someone driven by passion strikes the unique object of their hate and their love' ('The Case of Aimée' 225). The assassination attempt, however, did not bring any relief to her because by striking the actress she had symbolically struck herself, and also because she was legally proved guilty. Her time in prison allowed her to comprehend the entire situation, and the sense of being punished brought her relief. As if 'she experienced the satisfaction of a desire accomplished', her 'delusions, rendered ineffective by this realisation, vanished' (225).

Lacan, in this way, explains the psychogenic dimension of Aimée's psychosis. But there are two significant points to be noted in this context. First, the relation between organic and psychogenic dimensions of psychosis needs to be clearly understood. According to Lacan, Aimée's psychosis had its roots in a pre-existing personality disorder which was aggravated by organic insults and life events she experienced. Second, at this stage in his career, when he was yet to rigorously engage with Freud and turn to psychoanalysis as the fundamental technique to treat mental cases, Lacan the psychiatrist states that the use of psychoanalysis to analyse psychosis is 'justifiable' ('The Case of Aimée' 224).

He refers to the notion of 'personality' or 'personality functions', which he argues must take into account the Freudian discovery of the unconscious. However, Lacan arrived at his conclusions about Aimée's case by closely observing her psychosis itself and not by directly or substantially applying psychoanalytic techniques. In fact, emphasis on the psychogenic origin of psychosis in Lacan's thesis is supported not by Freud but by theories put forward by Pierre Janet and Ernst Kretschmer. Even though psychoanalysis is not the predominant analytic technique in his doctoral thesis, Lacan draws on Freud and psychoanalysis in his thesis in different ways, for instance by referring to Freud's text 'Some Neurotic Mechanisms in Jealousy, Paranoia and Homosexuality' (which Lacan translated from German into French in 1932) and 'The Ego and the Id'. These texts explore crucial concepts like homosexuality, ego, id and super-ego, mental personality, identification, jealousy and paranoia. Additionally, Lacan was influenced by the surrealistic interpretation and representation of psychical reality, with surrealism being an offshoot of the Freudian discovery of the unconscious. Olga Cox-Cameron, in her article 'Lacan's Doctoral Thesis: Turbulent Preface or Founding Legend' (2000), has rightly stated:

> It is only by way of the psychoanalytic texts which he invokes to delineate Aimée's self-punishing paranoia, and also by way of certain Dalinian concepts imported into this psychoanalytic discussion that this thesis [Lacan's doctoral thesis] to some extent opens onto the literary preoccupations of his own era, and carries within itself germs of his important future thinking on identity, representation and writing. (44)

It may be noted here that in his final teachings, Lacan rejected some of the issues raised in his doctoral thesis. One of the objections he raised was against the title 'Paranoiac Psychosis and its Relation to Personality'. Paranoia cannot have a 'relation' to personality since the very notion of personality, itself, is paranoiac. In *Seminar Book XXIII*, for instance, Lacan states: 'If I have been opposed to the republication of this book [his doctoral thesis] for so long, this is due to something simple: there is no relation between paranoiac psychosis and the personality. Because it's the same thing' (16 December 1975).

WOLF MAN'S HALLUCINATION

In 1954, Lacan delivered two lectures on the concept of *Verneinung*, or negation, in response to Jean Hyppolite's commentary on Freud's 1925 text on the very same subject. These lectures are titled 'Introduction to Jean Hyppolite's Commentary on Freud's "Verneinung"' and 'Response to Jean Hyppolite's Commentary on Freud's "Verneinung"' (1956), and constitute Chapters 15 and 16 of *Écrits: The First Complete Edition in English*. Here, Lacan theorises the function of hallucination (as a psychotic symptom) by delving into the case history of 'Wolf Man' elaborated on by Freud in 'From the History of an Infantile Neurosis' (1918).

Wolf Man was the name Freud gave to his patient Sergei Pankejeff (1886–1979), who had developed a fear of wolves in his childhood and whose most significant dreams involved white wolves. Wolf Man's treatment with Freud began in the year 1910. A crucial detail in Feud's case history is that the patient could recall a hallucination involving a mutilation experience from childhood. One day, when he was in his fifth year, he was playing next to his maid in a garden of walnut trees. As he was cutting notches into the bark of one such tree, he suddenly noticed, to his horror, that he had sliced his little finger, which was now hanging by a thread of skin. He experienced not pain but a lot of anxiety. He said nothing to the maid but sat on a bench nearby and stayed there without looking at his finger. After some time he calmed down and, upon carefully inspecting his finger, discovered it was in fact unwounded. It may be noted that the walnut tree is part of another memory of a hallucination in which he found blood seeping from the tree itself. Freud adds a crucial piece of information to these hallucinations, as highlighted by Lacan: 'the subject had recounted several times an episode in which his uncle bought him a pocketknife at his request while his sister received a book' (*Écrits* 326). Both of the incidents – hallucinating a mutilation and the repetition of the narrative of receiving a knife from an uncle – relate to the event of castration which, for the patient, has apparently not been included in the symbolic register. Wolf Man's hallucinations, for Lacan, are indicative of the return of castration in the order of the real. What is at stake, in the case of a hallucination, is not repression (*Verdrängung*); a hallucination is not the return of the repressed the way, for instance, a dream is. Repression is linked to the successful completion of the Oedipus complex by way of castration. This is the trajectory of the neurotic subject. Wolf Man, on the other hand, did not want to know anything about castration and this attitude towards castration is what Freud described as *Verwerfung,* which Lacan translates as 'excision' and 'foreclosure'. The effect of foreclosure, observable in psychotic tendencies, is a 'symbolic abolition' since the substitution of desire of the mother by Name-of-the-Father is foreclosed in the case of the psychotic. Wolf Man 'excised' castration; he behaved as if it never existed. Lacan explains that even though the term foreclosure has not been highlighted by Freudians, it occupies a crucial place in Freudian theory. Foreclosure is opposed to *Bejahung*, the latter understood as the primal affirmation or inclusion of something in the symbolic register. This also relates to the difference between existence and ek-sistence. Existence involves inclusion in the symbolic order, whereas ek-sistence involves exclusion from the symbolic and surfacing in the real. In this regard, negation or repression of castration can take place if and only if the experience of castration has been included and affirmed in the symbolic register in the first place.

Unlike primal affirmation, foreclosure constitutes what is primordially 'expelled' from the symbolic. In fact, the latter is what cuts short the former. What is excised cannot be refound in the subject's history. The subject, moreover, according to Lacan, is not able to know anything about that which is excised, since 'to be able to know it . . . it would have had to come in some way to light in the primordial symbolization' (*Écrits* 324). In this sense, that which is excised is that which is *not* repressed, *not* negated and *not* present in the primal affirmation. However, that which is excised does not get abolished because 'what did not come to the light in the symbolic appears in the real' (324). Here, Lacan explains the real as 'the domain of that which subsists outside of symbolization'. In other words, if it is castration that is expelled from the symbolic order, it stages a return in the form of hallucination, for example, in the real order. In the case of Wolf Man, castration is what is 'excised' by the subject 'from the very limits of what is possible, but which is also thereby withdrawn from the possibilities of speech' and this is why it appears in the real erratically (324). Furthermore, Lacan describes the real as that which is always already there, meaning, it is always there even though it is excluded from primordial symbolisation. It is a well-known formula in Freudian theory that what is repressed or negated from consciousness always returns in the case of the neurotics, albeit in the guise of unconscious formations. We now have another formula – what is expelled from the symbolic also returns, but in this case the return is a return to the real. Hallucinations are what exemplify the return of the expelled in the real, for in hallucinations a person finds things which do not exist in reality.

Returning to the analysis of Wolf Man's hallucinations, Lacan states that the symbols of mutilation and blood seeping from a tree/finger are what ek-sist the subject, or exist in the real against the background of its absence in reality. He thus states, 'The content of the hallucination, which is so massively symbolic, owes its appearance in the real to the fact that it does not exist for the subject. Everything indicates, indeed, that the subject remains fixated in his unconscious in an imaginary feminine position that evacuates all meaning from his hallucinatory mutilation' (*Écrits* 327).

It is through this connection that Lacan makes a distinction between schizophrenia and paranoia – the two forms of psychosis. For the schizophrenic, 'all of the symbolic is real' since the symbolic is marked by emptiness. The paranoiac, on the other hand – as in the case of Aimée, whom Lacan refers to here – partially lives in a delusional universe and her 'retroaction in a cyclical time' makes the anamnesis or recollection of her troubles very difficult. For the paranoiac, the 'discursive organization' of her universe, is 'long and painful to establish and continue' (327).

It may be noted that one year later, in *Seminar Book III*, Lacan briefly returns to the case of Wolf Man and clarifies that, though Wolf Man exhibited psychotic tendencies he was not, in strict clinical terms, a psychotic. (One can manifest psychotic symptoms without being a psychotic.) However, through his symptoms, like hallucination, he bore testimony to the very process of foreclosure. Since foreclosure is key to psychosis, Wolf Man's hallucinations are crucial to make sense of the experiences of the psychotic subject.

The psychotic is one who has rejected castration and its symbolic function. The hallucination involving the mutilation of a finger is linked to the impossibility of symbolising castration. This impossibility is indicated by the suspension of the symbolic qua speech during a hallucination. As Lacan writes, Wolf Man does not share his experience with the nurse, his usual confidant, because his speech is suspended – there is, for him, an abyss, 'a temporal submersion, a rupture in experience, following which it turns out that he has nothing at all wrong with him, it's all over, let's drop the subject' (*Book III* 13).

SCHREBER'S DELUSIONS

It is Lacan's analysis in *Seminar Book III* of the case of Daniel Paul Schreber – whose memoir Freud used as the basis for his ideas on paranoia – that contains the most substantial commentary on psychosis. Between 1884 and 1885, Schreber, who occupied an important position in the German judiciary at the time, suffered from hypochondriacal delusions. He was admitted to, and after a while discharged from, the psychiatric clinic of Professor Paul Emil Flechsig, and it was assumed that he was completely cured. He spent quite a 'normal' and happy life for the next eight years, during which time he had only one major regret – not having a child. In 1893, he was promoted to the prestigious post of the Presiding Judge for Leipzig's Court of Appeal. He was overwhelmed by the responsibilities of the position and this event caused great mental crises. He was fifty-one years old, which was considered a young age for such a post. His colleagues were far more experienced and accustomed to the work than he was. For a month he overworked himself and felt a little unhinged. Under pressure, he started suffering from disturbing thoughts, flight of ideas (abrupt and rapid shifts from one idea to another disconnected idea) and insomnia. It was at this time that he was, once again, taken to psychiatric clinics. He was first taken to Flechsig's clinic, then to Dr Pierson's mental home in Dresden and finally to the Sonnenstein Asylum where he was kept till 1901. It was during the last few months of his confinement that, as Lacan states, 'his delusion went through an entire series of phases of which he gives us an account that is, it seems, extremely trustworthy and extraordinarily composed' (*Book III* 25). Schreber's written account of his illness was published in the form of a book in 1903, after his release from the asylum. The book was titled *Memoirs of My Nervous Illness*. Based on this memoir, Freud wrote his paper 'Psycho-Analytic Notes upon an Autobiographical Account of a Case of Paranoia' (1911).

Lacan's analysis of the Schreber case comprises three overlapping strands. First, Lacan explains what Schreber actually meant by his thoughts of being a woman, and of being the wife of God. Second, Lacan talks about Schreber's relation to the imaginary other, or the little other, and the symbolic Other, or the big Other. Third, Lacan comments on the psychotic's relation to the symbolic order qua language and paternal function.

Between his first psychotic attack and his second confinement, Schreber had the following fantasy, as quoted in Lacan's *Seminar Book III*: 'it really must be rather pleasant to be a woman succumbing to intercourse' (61). This thought, Schreber writes, took him by surprise. This is something he imagined but to which he reacted with indignation. Schreber's fantasy of feminisation gives reason to describe the paranoiac as someone whose unconscious sexual drive is marked by homosexual tendencies. The homosexual dimension of Schreber's personality thus occupies a place in Freud's analysis of the case. Lacan, however, more critically investigates this feminisation and the homosexual tendencies to find out the mechanism that is at stake in psychosis.

Lacan questions Freud on at least two levels. First, is the connection between latent homosexuality and feminisation qua the fantasy of 'fertilising impregnation' self-evident and absolute? Does every acceptance of feminisation imply homosexuality in the way it is developed in Schreber's delusion in which he is God's wife? Second, 'Freud's theory', Lacan states, 'is that the only way for Schreber to avoid what results from the fear of castration is *Entmannung,* unmanning, or simply emasculation, transformation into a woman' (*Book III* 307–08). But such an argument is problematic since Schreber himself observes at one point that it would be better 'to be a spirited woman than a poor unfortunate man, oppressed, or even castrated' (qtd. in *Book III* 308).

The crucial point is that virility, or upholding the role of a man, did signify something for Schreber initially, which is what explains his indignation at the thought of engaging in intercourse as a woman. This very fantasy, which disrupts his virility, is what eventually triggers the delusion of him becoming the wife of God. According to Lacan, this implies that 'for him there is no other way of realizing himself, of affirming himself as sexual, than through admitting he is a woman, transformed into a woman' (*Book III* 252). 'The signifier *being a father*', Lacan further clarifies, 'is what creates the highway in sexual relations with a woman. If the highway doesn't exist, one finds oneself faced with a number of elementary minor paths, copulation and then the woman's pregnancy' (293). Schreber lacks this fundamental signifier (that is, the Name-of-the-Father) which structures the universe of the neurotic. He could not access the highway. Hence, he had to take the minor path of imagining himself as a woman and as being impregnated by God who, being a father, is what he exalts on an unprecedented level in his memoir. In order for this process to take place, his entire world had to be reconstructed. Indeed, 'the course of the delusion reveals the need to reconstruct the cosmos – the world's entire organisation – around the fact that there is a man who can only be the wife of a universal god' (252). The trajectory of the delusion thus extends from 'the first hint of identification with and capture by the feminine image, to the blossoming of a world system in which the subject is completely absorbed in his imagination by a feminine identification'(63).

What is at stake in this trajectory is a thread that runs through the imaginary other and the symbolic Other – in which the former is affirmed and the latter is excluded. Schreber is related to the imaginary other in terms of a mirror relationship involving rivalry, which leads to the dissolution of the other's identity. There are two kinds of protagonists with whom he has an imaginary relationship. Lacan claims that on the one hand there are 'those who are apparently alive and who are free to move about, his guards and his nurses, and who are the *fleeting-improvised-men*', and on the other hand, 'there are the more important protagonists, who invade Schreber's body, who are the souls, the majority of souls, and the longer this goes on, the more they are ultimately corpses' (*Book III* 97). In other words, some of the protagonists are living beings in his universe, the rest are dead, existing either in the form of souls or in the form of corpses. Schreber himself largely belongs to the second category – 'At a particular moment he has the revelation that the previous year his own death had occurred and that it was announced in the newspapers' (97). But alongside this memory of death, he remembers his colleague being very much alive and being more gifted than him. Thus, the subject himself is fragmented between the living and the dead. This fragmentation shapes Schreber's construction of the other who, too, is fragmented. In fact, Schreber's account reveals that the imaginary identity of the other is subject to fragmentation, segmentation, divisibility and multiplicity. The protagonists, who are dead in Schreber's world, have 'ascended to where only souls exist, insofar as they are human, in a beyond where they are assimilated bit by bit into the grand divine unity, not without having gradually lost their individual characters' (97). Before this assimilation into the divine unity, they have undergone a purification of desire, after which their identity has been completely fragmented to the point of annihilation. This is noticeable, for instance, in his reconstruction of Flechsig, his first doctor. As Lacan notes: 'so we see, throughout this entire history, a fragmented Flechsig, a superior Flechsig, the luminous Flechsig, and an inferior part that ends up fragmented into between forty and sixty little souls'. There is not only the occurrence of 'multiple identities of the one same character', but there are also 'little enigmatic identities, variously piercing and harmful inside him [Schreber]', whom he calls 'little men' (97–98). The imaginary other, with multiple identities, penetrates and fragments Schreber.

In Schreber's universe, the idea of God too is not symbolic but imaginary. Schreber's God is not an Other who is beyond understanding, or the bearer of law, or one whom Schreber addresses or shares a language with, but is imagined as seductive and Schreber's own shadow. According to Lacan's notes, this God is 'tainted by an imaginary degradation of otherness, and as a result he is, like Schreber, stricken with a sort of feminization' (*Book III* 101). The God is also imaginary in the sense that there takes place no communication (or intervention of language or the symbolic) between them.

Schreber's exclusion of the symbolic Other from his delusional universe involves his problematic relation with language and with the paternal function. For a neurotic, the completion of the Oedipus complex is triggered by the occurrence of castration in the form of the paternal metaphor, that is, the substitution of the desire of the mother by the Name-of-the-Father. To exclude the symbolic Other is to make the occurrence of the 'name', 'no' and law of the father impossible.

Lacan notes that at the point in Schreber's life when his psychosis declared itself, he was more than once 'in the situation of expecting to become a father' (*Book III* 320), though he did not actually become a father. On the other hand, by being selected for the most prestigious post in the judiciary – involving the most eminent function in the domain of law – he was 'admitted to the top of the legislative hierarchy, among men who make laws and are all twenty years older than he is'. This 'disturbance in the order of generations', as Lacan puts it, was preceded by 'an explicit call from the ministers' to make him assume the new position (321). Here, once again, Schreber confronts the paternal function, in the form of the law-maker, and this encounter is what leads to his mental crisis and psychotic break.

It is the inability to perform the paternal function in the symbolic order that leads to Schreber's exaltation of the father in the imaginary order – an exaltation which constitutes the basis of his delusion. Paternal metaphor is what determines the neurotic subject's relation to language. And unlike the neurotic, the psychotic who does not undergo a successful Oedipus complex cannot speak in metaphorical language. A psychotic cannot be a poet since poetry involves the introduction of a new dimension of experience or the creation of a symbolic relation with the world through metaphor. This is why Lacan states that Schreber is not a poet, since metaphor is what characterises poetry. For Lacan, 'Poetry is the creation of a subject adopting a new order of symbolic relations to the world. There is nothing like any of this in Schreber's *Memoirs*' (*Book III* 78). Furthermore, metaphor is what involves the occurrence of two sets of terms referring to one another and the substitution of the signified by the signifier. Without such substitution, without the mutual evocation of signifier and the signified, meaning is not generated. Schreber uses words like 'soul murder' and 'nerve contact', which have no meaning. The psychotic is one who creates a signifier without the signified; he is the one who coins words, but words which, as Lacan would state with reference to *Finnegans Wake*, are not 'letter' but 'litter' ('Lituraterre').

In fact, Lacan develops the relation of the psychotic to language in a most insightful way and argues that the psychotic structure can be discerned only through its peculiar organisation of language and discourse. The language of the psychotic or the 'delusional discourse', unlike the normative neurotic discourse, is marked by two levels – the level of signifier and the level of meaning. At the level of signifier, delusional discourse is characterised by neologism, while at the level of meaning it is characterised by the fact that the meaning 'essentially refers to nothing but itself' and as such 'remains irreducible' (*Book III* 33).

PSYCHOSIS, *SINTHOME* AND THE CASE OF JAMES JOYCE

Seminar Book XXIII (1975–76) belongs to the final phase of Lacan's teaching and comprises some of Lacan's last pronouncements on the clinical structures. In this Seminar, he approaches the issue of clinical categories, especially that of psychoses, in terms of the concept of the Borromean rings of the real, the symbolic and the imaginary, and the notion of *sinthome* which, for the psychotic, works as the fourth ring which knots together the RSI. Lacan talks about the 'triplicity' of the three terms which he characterises as 'a consistence which is only feigned by the imaginary, a foundational hole which emerges in the symbolic, and an ek-sistence which belongs to the real' ('Book XXIII' 13 January 1976). These three terms, constituting the three Borromean rings, are not actually knotted for the psychotic and as such threaten to come undone. To avoid the pathological attack of psychosis, the psychotic either develops a *sinthome* on his own or is helped to develop one during psychoanalysis. Lacan illustrates this idea through an analysis of the life and works of James Joyce. Joyce, Lacan claims, was a psychotic who avoided any possible pathological attack by creating a literary universe of his own. It was Joyce's eccentric writings, culminating in *Finnegans Wake*, which functioned as a *sinthome* for Joyce and which thereby kept the three registers of his psychical experience knotted together.

Some pertinent observations Lacan made about Joyce include (1) Joyce's resistance to psychoanalysis, (2) the question of Joyce's madness/psychosis and his relation to language, (3) Joyce's relation to the Name-of-the-Father, (4) sexual non-rapport as Joyce's central symptom and (5) Joyce's works having the structure of a Borromean knot.

1. Joyce's Resistance to Psychoanalysis

Lacan regretted the fact that he did not have the opportunity to analyse Joyce in person and that he could only comment on him by reading his books. In any case, Joyce was not inclined to psychoanalysis; he made fun of Freud and Carl Jung, referring to them as 'Tweedledum' and 'Tweedledee' (qtd. in 'Book XXIII' 10 February 1976). Moreover, Joyce completely refuted the diagnosis that his daughter Lucia was a schizophrenic. Lacan mentions that when he was delivering this Seminar, Lucia was still alive and was undergoing treatment in a hospital in England. Joyce, however, who died in 1941, 'fiercely defended the daughter . . . against the control of the doctors' and 'had only one thing to say about her: my daughter is telepathic'. In his letters, Joyce notes that his daughter 'is far more intelligent than everyone else, that she informs him in a way that is miraculous . . . about everything that happens to a certain number of people, and that these people have no secrets from her' (17 February 1976). Lacan says that even though Joyce resists the doctor's interpretation, he claims she is telepathic 'on the basis of certain signs, declarations which he understands in a special way'. This defence and analysis of his daughter, Lacan says, reveals more about Joyce than his daughter. Joyce's use of the term 'miraculous telepathy', in place of the doctor's term 'schizophrenia', is perhaps derived from his problematic relation to language and the Name-of-the-Father. His interpretation of Lucia is an extension of his own symptom: 'something was imposed on him at the locus of speech' and 'something Joyce bears witness to . . . [that is,] the absence . . . of the father' (17 February 1976).

2. The Question of Joyce's Madness/Psychosis and His Relation to Language

Regarding Joyce's clinical orientation, Lacan asks the following overlapping questions: 'At what point is one mad?', 'Was Joyce mad?', 'What was it that inspired his writings?' ('Book XXIII' 10 February 1976). Lacan says these questions are worth asking even though there may not be any satisfactory answers. These questions crop up when one confronts Joyce's writings, which seem to have been inspired by a kind of psychotic relation to language (somewhat Schreberian). Joyce's works are, for instance, full of neologisms including the word 'scribbledehobble', which happens to be the title of one of his manuscripts. Furthermore, Joyce 'disarticulates' the English language and 'has a peculiar way of breaking up phrases, notably in *Ulysses* [1922] indeed, it's a process aiming to give language another use – and one which is far from being ordinary' (20 January 1976). It is as if 'a certain relation to language is imposed on him' throughout his works. This 'relation to language' is what makes him write, break and dislocate speech (*parole*), to the extent that at the end of *Finnegans Wake*, Joyce 'ends up breaking or dissolving language itself by decomposing it, going beyond phonetic identity' (17 February 1976).

3. Joyce's Relation to the Name-of-the-Father

Lacan says that 'Joyce has a symptom whose origin is this: that his father was lacking, radically lacking – he speaks of nothing but this' ('Book XXIII' 17 February 1976). It was through his writings, which would bring him a 'name', that Joyce compensated for the lacking father or the lacking Name-of-the-Father. This issue is illustrated in a number of ways.

First, through Stephen Dedalus, Joyce undertakes the mission to create, as phrased at the end of *A Portrait of the Artist as a Young Man*

(1916), 'the uncreated conscience of my race' (225), implying such a conscience is lacking. However, the belief 'that there is a race which has an uncreated conscience', for Lacan, 'is a great illusion' ('Book XXIII' 13 January 1976).

Second, throughout *Ulysses* Stephen is in search of a lacking father. Lacan says he searches for the father 'in settings where he has no chance of finding him'. Leopold Bloom is clearly a father-figure, 'a father in search of a son', but not the father Stephen is in search of. But then, 'throughout the novel, there is a gravitational attraction between the thoughts of Bloom and Stephen'. This is what constitutes Joyce's symptom; *Ulysses* bears witness that he 'remains rooted in his father, even as he denies him' (13 January 1976).

Third, Joyce's denial or rejection of the father takes place on many levels, and this is what truly constitutes his foreclosure or *Verwerfung*. For instance, Joyce in *Stephen Hero* (1944) and in *Portrait* indicates that his father taught him nothing and neglected everything except the Jesuit church. This is why Joyce was compelled to fall back upon Jesuit fathers. Even though his father considered the Jesuit church a 'very good institution', Joyce considered it 'diplomatic'. Lacan states that to compensate for a father whom he denied, Joyce felt 'imperiously called' to valorise his own name at the expense of his father's (17 February 1976).

Fourth, Stephen tells his friend Cranly that he has lost faith in the teachings of the church, though he does not elaborate on this matter. Instead, at the end of Joyce's *Portrait*, he subscribes to the motto 'silence, exile, and cunning' (219). But where does this motto take him, or for that matter, Joyce? What does the rejection of the father, or of the church – considered as the representative of the law of the father – actually lead to? Lacan says it leads to Joyce imagining himself as a kind of a 'redeemer' and as the only artist to have ever lived. Indeed, Joyce thinks he is *the* artist. That is what is implied by the title *A Portrait of the Artist as a Young Man*. Lacan states: 'A portrait of the artist – the stress should be placed on the "the", which in English is not of course quite our own definite article, but one can have confidence in Joyce – if he says the, it is because he thinks that of artists he is the only one, that there he is singular' (18 November 1975).

4. Sexual Non-rapport as Joyce's Central Symptom

Apart from the lack of the father, there is another lack in Joyce – 'the lack of the sexual relation', which constitutes, Lacan says, Joyce's 'central symptom' and which is located in his 1918 play *Exiles* ('Book XXIII' 13 January 1976). According to Lacan, the word 'exile' expresses best the notion of sexual non-rapport or sexuation (this concept has been described in Chapter Two). For Joyce, it is this exile that binds him to his wife Nora. The non-relation in question is thus very specific. This non-relation, as manifested in Joyce's play, is explained by Lacan in the following words:

> Non-relation means that there is no reason why he should take a woman among others to be his. A woman among others is also one who has a relation to some other man, and this 'some other man' is the character he imagines and for whom he opens the choice of 'a woman' in question, who as it happens is none other than Nora. (13 January 1976)

Indeed, the female protagonist in *Exiles* is an open choice for a man other than her husband. However, Lacan also adds that Nora is Joyce's 'inside-out glove', which is precisely Joyce's thoughts about Nora: 'she fit him like a glove' (10 February 1976). What does this imply? Here is Lacan's explanation:

> For Joyce, there is only one woman, she is always modelled the same, and he only puts on his glove with the most intense revulsion. It is palpably only with the greatest of depreciations that he makes Nora into a chosen woman. Not only must she fit him like a glove, but she must be tight as a glove. She has absolutely no use. (10 February 1976)

There is no relation between Joyce and Nora except for the fact that she is his *sinthome* and he is her 'devastation', which is 'an affliction worse than a *sinthome*' (17 February 1976). It is through Nora functioning as a *sinthome*, as Joyce's 'glove', that he can avoid the attack of clinical psychosis. She is, in this sense, the fourth ring of the Borromean knot.

5. Joyce's Works Having the Structure of a Borromean Knot

Lacan describes Joyce's epiphanies as the sites where the unconscious and the real are knotted together, and *Finnegans Wake* as that which partly constitutes Joyce's *sinthome*. At every turn in Joyce's writings, one encounters an epiphany. In Lacan's words:

> Please note this, when he gives a list of his epiphanies: that they are always distinguished by the same thing, that they are the result of a mistake, namely that the unconscious is linked to the real. It's an amazing thing, which Joyce himself does not describe otherwise. It is absolutely legible in Joyce that the epiphany is where, due to a mistake, the unconscious and the real are knotted together. ('Book XXIII' 11 May 1976)

In *Finnegans Wake,* a number of incredible things happen. Even though Joyce has great contempt for history – Stephen in *Ulysses* describes history as a nightmare which unleashes the greatest of evils, which harms humanity and from which he is trying to awake – he ironically uses the form of the dream as well as Giambattista Vico's conception of history (as cyclical) in the construction of *Finnegans Wake* (*Ulysses* 42).[1] According to Vico, the cycle of history involves the recurrence of three ages – that of the gods, that of the heroes and that of the humans. This notion of cyclical recurrence is not only thematically but structurally evoked in *Finnegans Wake.* For instance, the last word of Joyce's book – 'the' (628) – is actually the missing first word of the opening line – 'riverrun, past Eve and Adam's, from swerve of shore to bend of bay, brings us by a commodius vicus of recirculation back to Howth Castle and Environs' (3).[2] The opening line also refers to Vico ('vicus') and the concept of 'recirculation'. The idea of history as a nightmare is thus not the only form of historiography in Joyce. Additionally, for Lacan, it is ironic that Joyce would use the form of a dream to construct this text even though it had quite solely been the subject matter of psychoanalytic investigation at that point of time (and Joyce had a problematic take on psychoanalysis) and even though dream is, in the final analysis, a nightmare (one from which he attempted to awake). In Lacan's words, Joyce wrote *Finnegans Wake*, 'albeit as a dream, which like every dream is a nightmare, even if it be a mild nightmare' ('Book XXIII' 16 March 1976). Though Joyce implies that in this dream-narrative 'the dreamer is no particular character, it is the dream itself' (16 March 1976), he cannot escape the fact that he is thus sliding 'towards the collective unconscious'. Lacan states 'There is no better proof that the collective unconscious is a *sinthome* than Joyce, for one cannot say that, in his imagination, *Finnegans Wake* does not form part of this *sinthome*' (16 March 1976). Being the type of enigma which would keep scholars busy for two or three hundred years, as Joyce himself claims, this text is 'made exactly like a Borromean knot' (11 May 1976). Obviously, *sinthome* is rendered key to the understanding of this Joycean knot.

PSYCHOSIS AND NEUROSIS: STRUCTURAL DIFFERENCES

In *Seminar Book III*, Lacan formulates the clinical categories of psychosis and neurosis on the basis of a solid distinction between four Freudian terms – *Bejahung* (primal affirmation), *Verneinung* (negation), *Verwerfung* (foreclosure) and *Verdrängung* (repression). It is at the end of this Seminar that Lacan offers the term foreclosure as the best possible translation of *Verwerfung*. It may be noted that the terms excision, rejection and exclusion had previously been used in the place of foreclosure.

Foreclosure is what characterises the psychotic. Simply put, it involves the impossibility of accessing the signifier of the Name-of-the-Father, which involves castration on the part of the subject. In *Seminar Book III*, Lacan brings up Freud's paper on negation, where Freud states that 'something that has been rejected [from within] returns from without' (46). This non-symbolised 'something' is what has been foreclosed and what constitutes the core of psychosis. The foreclosed that belongs to the domain of the real is not the repressed, since both the repressed and the return of the repressed are linguistic formations existing in the symbolic order. Foreclosure thus precedes the 'entire neurotic dialectic' which begins with affirmation or inclusion of things in the symbolic order. Lacan describes that which is foreclosed as 'something primordial regarding the subject's being' that 'does not enter into symbolization and is not repressed, but rejected' (81). The notion of the rejected, or foreclosed, or non-symbolised is what implies the very order of the real. In this regard, it is inevitable introducing the real order, even though Freud does not do so. This is because it is with reference to the real order alone that the psychotic phenomenon can be explained. 'In the beginning, then', Lacan adds, 'there is either *Bejahung*, which is the affirmation of what is, or *Verwerfung*' (82). The dichotomy of *Bejahung* (affirmation of the primordial signifier) and *Verwerfung* (rejection of the primordial signifier) is what determines the destiny of the subject.

Lacan clarifies how foreclosure is different from repression. He draws attention to Freud's statement that in the case of foreclosure, 'the subject did not want to know anything about castration, even in the sense of repression' (*Book III* 149). Repression involves the repression of the knowledge of castration, and the neurotic subject behaves as if castration has not happened. Castration is something that the neurotic does not want to know but is something that is known to his unconscious. The task of psychoanalysis is to show the neurotic that he does indeed know about castration. The mechanism of foreclosure is different from that of repression in the sense that the subject does not know anything at all about castration. The signifier of the Name-of-the-Father does not figure in the vocabulary of the subject who has undergone foreclosure. The primordial signifier is what is excluded from the body of signifiers that constitute the paranoiac subject.

Regarding negation, Lacan states that it is only once primal affirmation has taken place that negation can occur. It is to be noted that there is no opposition between primal affirmation and negation, but between primal affirmation and primal rejection. Negation, Lacan states, 'belongs to the order of discourse and concerns what we are capable of bringing to the light of day in an articulated form' (*Book III* 84). Negation operates in close conformity with the circumstances in which the subject is placed in reality and thus involves the intervention of the 'reality principle'. It 'concerns the attribution, not of the value of symbols, *Bejahung,* but of the value of existence' and 'it always concerns the refinding of an object' (84). The 'judgement of existence' is what constitutes the subject's 'initial apprehension of reality'. Such judgement consists in the subject's saying: 'This is not my dream or my hallucination or my representation but an object' (150). What is this object and what does its re-finding involve in the process of negation? Negation is 'a matter of testing the external by the internal', which causes the rejection of a primal signifier (150). This involves the constitution of reality in terms of re-finding the object.

Obviously, negation can only take place provided primal affirmation has taken place. Moreover, negation proves itself an inadequate response in the case of psychosis. That is why Lacan notes that '*Verwerfung* is not at the same level as *Verneinung*. When, at the beginning of a psychosis, the non-symbolized reappears in the real, there are responses made from the side of the mechanism of *Verneinung*, but they prove inadequate' (*Book III* 86).

The difference between neurosis and psychosis is elaborated on by Lacan beyond the fundamental opposition between primal affirmation and foreclosure. This extended difference can be explained on at least four levels.

First, on the level of symptoms, the difference between psychosis and two kinds of neurosis (hysteria and obsession) has been explained by Freud in what Lacan calls 'a striking summary' in a passage occurring in *The Interpretation of Dreams*. Lacan discusses how Freud says that different subjects would express differently the 'wish to become pregnant which have been repressed into the unconscious', or the subject's 'defensive reaction against that wish' (*Book III* 248). According to Freud, a hysteric would express this wish or reaction against it by vomiting, an obsessional by 'painstaking protective measures against infection', and a paraphrenic or psychotic by being 'led to complaints or suspicions that he is being poisoned' (248). In this regard, the same signified may be referred to by these three subjects by three different sets of signifiers: vomiting, infection, poison. These signifiers may be instrumental in determining the clinical structure of a given subject.

Second, unlike the neurotic, the psychotic's unconscious is marked by malfunction. Lacan says that, in the case of the psychotic, 'the unconscious is present but not functioning. Contrary to what has been thought, the fact that it's present doesn't imply a solution but, on the contrary, a very special inertia' (*Book III* 143–44). The neurotic, on the other hand, is marked by having undergone the processes of primal affirmation, negation, and repression. The unconscious and formations of the unconscious, and the repressed and the return of the repressed together constitute the psychical register of the neurotic. The unconscious qua the repressed is what forms the symbolic order for the neurotic, since repression is linked to language. Repression is linked to language not only because the repressed is a set of wishes structured by language but also because the 'return of the repressed' (which indicates in the first place that repression had taken place) is a new kind of language as is evident in the linguistic nature of symptoms and other formations of the unconscious.

Third, referring to two articles by Freud – 'The Loss of Reality in Neurosis and Psychosis' (1924) and 'Neurosis and Psychosis' (1924) – Lacan formulates that the fundamental distinction between neurosis and psychosis is based on disturbances in the subject's relation to reality. In the psychotic's case, the issue is one of a 'profoundly perverted relation to reality known as a delusion' (*Book III* 44). In the case of the neurotic, a certain role is ascribed 'to flight, to avoidance, in which conflict with reality plays a part'. Reality is not synonymous with external reality, Lacan points out, drawing on Freud's ideas, and what is at stake in the incidence of neurosis is the sacrifice of 'psychical reality' (44). The flight from psychical reality occurs in the neurotic subject at a phase when it gets very difficult to articulate 'a hole, a rupture, a rent, a gap, with respect to external reality'. Confronting the gap in the external reality, the subject elides his own psychical reality. For the neurotic, the gap is not there from the beginning. 'In psychosis, on the contrary', Lacan says, 'reality itself initially contains a hole that the world of fantasy will subsequently fill' (45). It is due to this always and already-existing hole in reality – reality in the sense of the symbolic body of signifiers – that it becomes very difficult for the psychotic to make any symbolic mediation between himself and what emerges as new for him in the external reality, between himself and the Other. This is the cause of his exaltation of the imaginary, fantasy and delusion.

Fourth, the difference between psychosis and neurosis is derived from the differences in their respective relation to desire. Lacan says that 'the desire that is to be recognised in delusion is situated on a completely different level from the desire that has to make itself recognised in neurosis' (*Book III* 104). 'In neurosis', Lacan continues, 'one always remains inside the symbolic order, with this duality of signifier and signified that Freud translates as the neurotic compromise' (104–05). Delusions are outside the symbolic order; they belong to the imaginary register. The desire that is repressed or manifested in psychosis accordingly belongs to the imaginary register. Desire, in the sense of the repressed, reappears *in loco* in the case of neurosis, but reappears *in altero* in the case of psychosis. Here, *in loco* refers to reappearance (in disguise, as in, a dream) of the repressed in the very midst of symbols or in the order of the symbolic, whereas *in altero* involves the re-appearance (without disguise, as in, a delusion) of the repressed, not in the symbolic but in the imaginary.

THE THREE SUB-CATEGORIES OF NEUROSIS

Apart from discussing psychosis, *Seminar Book III* also considers the structure of neurosis, particularly two of its sub-categories – hysteria and obsessional neurosis. 'The structure of a neurosis', Lacan says, 'is essentially a question' (174). The obsessional neurotic encounters a question like, 'To be or not to be?' or 'Am I or what am I (dead or alive)?' or 'Why do I exist?' Lacan states that whatever be the qualities, nature or material from which they are borrowed, the symptoms of the obsessional have 'the value of being a formulation, a reformulation, or even an insistence, of this question'. The question of existence and death is what functions as the 'fundamental signifier' for the obsessional (170).

The hysteric's universe is centred around the questions, 'Am I a man, or am I a woman? What is a woman? What is it to be a woman?' Thus, the fundamental question for the hysteric – both male and female – is the question concerning his or her sexuality or sexual identity. Both men and women, in hysteria, wonder about 'what it is to be a woman'. Moreover, to be a woman does not necessarily mean possessing the hysteric structure; to be a woman and to wonder what a woman is are two completely different things.

That being said, Lacan states that clinical experience offers evidence that there are 'many more women hysterics than men hysterics' (*Book III* 178).

In this context, Lacan offers an analysis of the case history of Dora, as elaborated on by Freud in 'Fragment of an Analysis of a Case of Hysteria' (1905). The real name of Dora, Freud's patient, was Ida Bauer (1882–1945), and she was diagnosed as a hysteric. Dora was first brought to Freud when she was sixteen years old and then a second time when she was eighteen years old. Her symptoms included the development of a cough and aphonia (loss of voice). There are four characters involved in Dora's case – Dora, Dora's father and the couple Herr K and Frau K; Dora's mother is conspicuously absent from her psychical universe. Dora's father had a relationship with Frau K. It was Dora's complaints that Herr K had allegedly made sexual advances towards her (something her father disbelieved) and that she had slapped him (something Herr K denied), and her insistence that her father must end contact with Herr K, that made her father bring her to Freud. Additionally, over the course of her sessions with Freud, Dora claimed that her father wanted her to be with Herr K. In his case history, Freud is visibly dissatisfied with his treatment of Dora, considering it a failure in therapy. Lacan discusses how Freud attributes this failure to Dora's 'unusual object relationships' (*Book III* 90). Dora's object of love was not, as Freud thought for a long time, her father or Herr K but instead her father's mistress, Frau K. As Lacan highlights, this love interest manifested itself in the form of Dora slapping Herr K when he stated his wife meant nothing to him.

Lacan's comments on Dora involve at least two distinct issues. First, Lacan argues that the fundamental question that structures Dora is – 'What is it to be a woman?' Lacan says that Freud's mistake was that he started by asking 'what Dora desires, before asking himself who desires in Dora' (*Book III* 174). It is Herr K with whom Dora identified herself – an imaginary identification as Herr K functions as her ideal ego – and who desires in Dora. Thus, Lacan says, the external point of imaginary identification, as it happens in the mirror stage, is placed in Herr K: 'It is insofar as she is Herr K that all her symptoms adopt their definitive sense' (175).

It is the triangle of Dora, Herr K and Frau K that keeps alive Dora's desire for Frau K – a desire which is otherwise threatened by her father who, Dora believes, desires Frau K over her. The occasional absence of Herr K threatens the collapse of the triangle. It is when Herr K is absent and thus Dora is alone with Frau K that she suffers from aphonia and cough – both being oral symptoms. The threat is all the more intensified when Herr K says that his wife means nothing to him – if Frau K means nothing to Herr K, then the latter cannot be the means (in Dora's imaginary order) to love the former, which further leads to the collapse of the triangle, which is her fear. This is when Dora falsely claims that Herr K made sexual advances towards her, or that her father wants to offer her to Herr K in exchange for Frau K. These somewhat delusional claims, arguably, constitute a second set of symptoms for her.

Through her desire for a woman, her identification with a man, her rivalry with another man and the symptoms which are derived from the collapse of the triangular relations, Dora is in essence confronted with the set of questions that constitute hysteria – 'Am I a man, or am I a woman? What is a woman? What is it to be a woman?'

The second issue Lacan elaborates on, regarding the case of Dora, is that even though Dora shows symptoms which are somewhat psychotic in nature, she is not a psychotic. This is, arguably, one of the most crucial observations made in *Seminar Book III*. Dora makes false, unjustified and somewhat hallucinatory claims against her father and Herr K, whom she sees as acting against her. Such claims could perhaps be considered as small-scale delusions in the sense of Dora manifesting a 'delusion of presumption', or be described as somewhat paranoiac considering a paranoiac is described as 'a touchy, intolerant, and distrustful gentleman [or lady], who is in a state of verbalized conflict with his [or her] surroundings' (*Book III* 92). But such small-scale delusions or paranoia do not, in any way, imply that Dora is a psychotic, since she does not show any disturbances on the level of language in the sense that, for instance, Schreber does. Lacan unequivocally states: 'to have a psychosis, there must be disturbances of language – this at least is the rule of thumb I suggest you adopt provisionally' (92).

Apart from hysteria and obsessional neurosis, phobia is sometimes considered the third form of neurosis in Lacan's teachings. As Bruce Fink emphasises in his seminal work, *A Clinical Introduction to Lacanian Psychoanalysis* (1999), in *Seminar Book VIII* Lacan considers phobia as the 'most radical form of neurosis' (Fink 163). Even then, the status of phobia is not the same as that of the other two neuroses. It is rather, as Evans puts it, 'a gateway which can lead to either of them' (149). The classic case of phobia may be found in the case of Little Hans as elaborated on in Freud's case history titled 'Analysis of Phobia in a Five-Year-Old Boy' (1909). The real name of Little Hans was Herbert Graf (1903–73), the son of a family friend of Freud. When Hans was about five years old, he developed a fear of horses which was so intense that he was reluctant to leave the house in case he encountered them on the street. As Evans notes, Freud divided Hans's experiences into two interconnected phases: the anxiety phase, which had nothing to do with horses, and the fear phase, which was occupied by the idea of horses (148). The first phase derived from Hans's relationship with his mother, while the second phase involved Hans's fear of being punished by his father. It is the second phase which constituted Hans's phobia.

For the phobic subject, the 'no'/'name' of the father is either lacking or, as Fink notes, in a precarious state. The object of phobia, which is ultimately a signifier, is what saves the subject from the anxiety of being engulfed by the desire of the mother and helps him in separating himself from her. The phobic signifier performs the paternal function for the phobic subject and helps him move towards castration/neurosis. As Lacan explains in *Seminar Book IV*, in the case of Little Hans, whose father did not play a strong role in separating him from his mother, the phobic signifier – the horse – functions as the 'no'/'name' of the father (Fink 163). In this regard, phobia is different from hysteria and obsessional neurosis; it is what occurs prior to the other two forms of neurosis.

PERVERSION

Perversion is the third of the clinical structures. In conventional usage, 'perversion' is a derogatory word, but Lacanian psychoanalysts challenge this implication. A pervert is generally considered to be an aberration – one whose sexuality does not aim at normative genital intercourse which enables reproduction of species. However, as Bruce Fink notes, perversion is what constitutes the 'core of human sexuality' when sexual behavior is not aimed at reproduction but at seeking pleasure (166). In fact, sexuality at the subject's infantile state begins with 'polymorphously perverse' dispositions, as Freud states in *Three Essays on the Theory of Sexuality* (1905), and, during this point, sexual instincts exist independent of any chosen objects. The choice of a particular kind of sexual object or so-called 'sexual orientation' is, in this regard, socially motivated and trained.[3] Furthermore, as Fink clarifies, even in the case of neurotics, the sexual tendencies are somewhat perverse in nature. For the obsessive neurotic, sexual partner is reduced to an object – object *a* – and thus, through his sexual desire, the radical otherness of the partner is neutralised. The hysteric, on the other hand, does not reduce the sexual partner into an object of desire but instead tries to desire *through* the partner and desires to be the object that the partner is lacking. In this regard, what is involved in sexuality is not a relation between two 'total' persons or selves but rather the objectification of the partner, which is undeniably fetishistic in nature. Fetishism, or any form of 'perverse fantasy', is also found in sexual tendencies that are conventionally considered 'normal'. If there is any form of sexuality which may be called normal, then perversion definitely forms a part of it. 'Indeed', as Fink notes, 'Lacanian psychoanalysts view the perverse nature of sexuality as a given, as something to be taken for granted – in other words, as "normal"' (166). Perversion, in this sense, is not a stigma.

In Lacan, perversion has a specific definition – it is a clinical structure which is based on the mechanism of 'disavowal' (*Verleugnung*). Thus, even though a subject might engage in perverted behaviour or manifest symptoms of a so-called pervert (sadism, masochism, fetishism, voyeurism, exhibitionism and homosexuality in the main), clinically he might not be considered a pervert. A pervert is one who disavows castration – where the disavowal involves perceiving castration yet refusing to 'accept the reality of this traumatic perception' (Evans 142). What does it mean to perceive castration? A classic case of perceiving castration is that of Little Hans, who, on seeing his six-year-old sister bathing, says: 'Her widdler's still quite small. When she grows up it'll get bigger all right' (qtd. in Fink 167). In such cases, the female genitals are perceived but disavowed. The older male patients sometimes express two attitudes towards a woman's lack of a penis. It is found that 'they disavow the perception, maintaining a belief in . . . the "maternal phallus", but develop symptoms which seem to indicate that this perception has nevertheless been registered at some level' (167). It must be noted that, according to Lacan, the phallus has an imaginary status, as is the case during the first phase of the Oedipus complex in which the imaginary phallus, along with mother and child, constitute the triangle.

In the case of fetishism, which Lacan considers in *Seminar Book IV* to be the 'perversion of perversions', a fetish is a 'symbolic substitute for the mother's missing phallus' (Evans 142). A fetish veils the absence of the maternal phallus. In all cases of perversion, however, the maternal phallus plays a similar role. Lacan thus notes, in 'On a Question Preliminary to Any Possible Treatment of Psychosis':

> The whole problem of the perversions consists in conceiving how the child, in its relationship with its mother – a relationship that is constituted in analysis not by the child's biological dependence, but by its dependence on her love, that is, by its desire for her desire – identifies with the imaginary object of her desire insofar as the mother herself symbolizes it in the phallus. (*Écrits* 462–63)

Also, as Evans notes, perversion is to be understood in relation to drive as well as in relation to how the subject situates himself vis-à-vis drive. In perversion, the subject turns himself into an object – into an instrument for the other's *jouissance*. The pervert thus inverts the structure of fantasy since, in fantasy, the other is turned into an object of enjoyment. A pervert's enjoyment derives from being the object of the other's enjoyment. 'While neurosis is characterised by a question,' Evans reminds us, 'perversion is characterised by the lack of a question; the pervert does not doubt that his acts serve the *jouissance* of the Other' (142). There are two kinds of drive which cause the pervert to turn himself into an object – the scopic drive and the invocatory drive. In scopophilia, the pervert turns himself into the object of the other's gaze (exhibitionism and voyeurism), whereas in sadism/masochism, the pervert turns himself into an object of the other's command/voice. It may be noted that both the sadist and the masochist locate themselves as the object of the invocatory drive. Sadism and masochism are intimately linked. However, unlike Freud, who considered sadism as primary, Lacan considers masochism as primary and sadism as a derivative. In *Seminar Book XI*, he goes to the extent of saying that 'sadism is merely the disavowal of masochism' (qtd. in Evans 171). As Evans explains, 'whereas the masochist prefers to experience the pain of existence in his own body, the sadist rejects this pain and forces the Other to bear it' (171).

Lacan plays with the words perversion and *père-version* and suggests that perversion is *père-version* because it involves an appeal to the father – an appeal for the pronouncement of the law. For the neurotic, the law is what triggers desire; prohibiting the desire for the mother triggers the unconscious desire for her. For the pervert, this prohibition is what has to be brought into existence. Somewhat like phobia, perversion is the consequence of a partial failure or inadequacy of the paternal function. The pervert thus, as Fink puts it, says the following:

> I [the pervert] know full well that my father hasn't forced me to give up my mother and the *jouissance* I take in her presence (real and/or imagined in fantasy), hasn't exacted the 'pound of flesh,' but I'm going to stage such an exaction or forcing with someone who stands in for him; I'll make that person pronounce the law. (170)

In fact, in perversion, two key issues are at stake: law and *jouissance*. 'One of the paradoxical claims Lacan makes about perversion', Fink notes, 'is that while it may sometimes present itself as a no-holds-barred, *jouissance*-seeking activity, its less apparent aim is to bring the law into being: to make the Other as law (or law-giving Other) exist' (180). There is a rupture here between conscious fantasies of perversion (unending *jouissance*) and unconscious anxieties, which, in the case of a masochist, leads to the instating of the limit on *jouissance* by bringing the partner 'to the point of enunciating a law and perhaps pronouncing a sentence' (180). Therefore in perversion, like in any other clinical category, it is the law and language of the father, the 'no' and the 'name' of the father that are at stake.

Finally, another issue that stands out in Lacan's discussion of perversion is that perversion is an exclusively masculine structure. Homosexuality, as a clinical form of perversion, is fundamentally a male category according to Lacan and he writes it as *hommosexualité* with a double 'm' ('man' is *homme* in French). Homosexuality is man's love for man. Lesbianism is a form of heterosexuality to the extent that in it the object of love is a woman or the 'Other sex'. Woman is the Other in many senses, including that she ek-sists the symbolic and thus contributes to the impossibility of sexual rapport. With reference to perversion, men are the 'weaker sex'. Female perversion does not exist and, as Lacan states, 'female masochism is a male fantasy' (qtd. in Fink 173). This is certainly a radical departure from the conventional understanding of sexuality.

NOTES

[1] Also see Lacan's *Seminar Book XXIII*, lesson of 16 March 1976.

[2] For a discussion on the interface between Vico and Joyce with reference to *Finnegans Wake*, see Donald Phillip Verene's *Knowledge of Things Human and Divine: Vico's New Science and Finnegans Wake* (2003).

[3] For a discussion on the concept of polymorphous perversion and its relation to human sexuality, see Tim Dean's 'Lacan and Queer Theory' in *The Cambridge Companion to Lacan*. For the original Freudian text, see 'Three Essays on the Theory of Sexuality' in Volume 7 of *The Standard Edition of the Complete Psychological Works of Sigmund Freud*.

REFERENCES

Cox-Cameron, Olga. 'Lacan's Doctoral Thesis: Turbulent Preface or Founding Legend?' *Psychoanalytische Perspectieven*. Web. 7 Mar 2017. <http://www.psychoanalytischeperspectieven.be/wp-content/uploads/2012/10/Cox-Cameron.pdf>.

Evans, Dylan. *An Introductory Dictionary of Lacanian Psychoanalysis.* London: Routledge, 1996. Print.

Fink, Bruce. *A Clinical Introduction to Lacanian Psychoanalysis: Theory and Technique.* Cambridge: Harvard UP, 1999. Print.

Freud, Sigmund. 'Analysis of a Phobia in a Five-Year-Old Boy.' *The Standard Edition of the Complete Psychological Works of Sigmund Freud, Vol. 10.* Trans. James Strachey, Anna Freud, Alix Strachey and Alan Tyson. London: Vintage Books, 2001. Print.

---. 'Fragment of an Analysis of a Case of Hysteria.' *The Standard Edition of the Complete Psychological Works of Sigmund Freud, Vol. 7.* Trans. James Strachey, Anna Freud, Alix Strachey and Alan Tyson. London: Vintage Books, 2001. Print.

---. 'From the History of an Infantile Neurosis.' *The Standard Edition of the Complete Psychological Works of Sigmund Freud, Vol. 17.* Trans. James Strachey, Anna Freud, Alix Strachey and Alan Tyson. London: Vintage Books, 2001. Print.

---. 'Negation.' *The Standard Edition of the Complete Psychological Works of Sigmund Freud, Vol. 19.* Trans. James Strachey, Anna Freud, Alix Strachey and Alan Tyson. London: Vintage Books, 2001. Print.

---. 'Neurosis and Psychosis.' *The Standard Edition of the Complete Psychological Works of Sigmund Freud, Vol. 19.* Trans. James Strachey, Anna Freud, Alix Strachey and Alan Tyson. London: Vintage Books, 2001. Print.

---. 'Psycho-Analytic Notes on an Autobiographical Account of a Case of Paranoia.' *The Standard Edition of the Complete Psychological Works of Sigmund Freud, Vol. 12.* Trans. James Strachey, Anna Freud, Alix Strachey and Alan Tyson. London: Vintage Books, 2001. Print.

---. 'Some Neurotic Mechanisms in Jealousy, Paranoia and Homosexuality.' *The Standard Edition of the Complete Psychological Works of Sigmund Freud, Vol. 18.* Trans. James Strachey, Anna Freud, Alix Strachey and Alan Tyson. London: Vintage Books, 2001. Print.

---. 'The Loss of Reality in Neurosis and Psychosis.' *The Standard Edition of the Complete Psychological Works of Sigmund Freud, Vol. 19.* Trans. James Strachey, Anna Freud, Alix Strachey and Alan Tyson. London: Vintage Books, 2001. Print.

---. 'Three Essays on the Theory of Sexuality.' *The Standard Edition of the Complete Psychological Works of Sigmund Freud, Vol. 7.* Trans. James

Strachey, Anna Freud, Alix Strachey and Alan Tyson. London: Vintage Books, 2001. Print.

Joyce, James. *A Portrait of the Artist as a Young Man and Dubliners*. New York: Barnes and Noble, 2004. Print.

---. *Finnegans Wake*. London: Penguin Modern Classics, 2000. Print.

---. *Ulysses*. London: Penguin Modern Classics, 2000. Print.

Lacan, Jacques. *Écrits: The First Complete Edition in English*. Trans. Bruce Fink. New York: W. W. Norton & Co., 2006. Print.

---. 'Lituraterre.' *Scribd*. Trans. (unofficial) Jack W. Stone. Web. 6 November 2017. <https://www.scribd.com/document/103886428/Lituraterre-english>.

---. 'The Case of Aimée, or Self-Punitive Paranoia.' *The Clinical Roots of the Schizophrenia Concept: Translations of Seminal European Contributions on Schizophrenia*. Ed. John Cutting and Michael Shepherd. Cambridge: Cambridge UP, 1987. Print.

---. *The Seminar of Jacques Lacan Book III: The Psychoses, 1955–56*. Trans. Russell Grigg. London: W. W. Norton & Co., 1997. Print.

---. 'The Seminar of Jacques Lacan Book XXIII: Le Sinthome, 1975–76.' *Lacan Online*. Trans (unofficial). Luke Thurston. Web. 20 September 2017. <http://www.lacanonline.com/index/wp-content/uploads/2014/11/Seminar-XXIII-The-Sinthome-Jacques-Lacan-Thurston-translation.pdf>.

Rabaté, Jean-Michel. *Jacques Lacan: Psychoanalysis and the Subject of Literature*. New York: Palgrave, 2001. Print.

Verene, Donald Phillip. *Knowledge of Things Human and Divine: Vico's New Science and Finnegans Wake*. New Haven: Yale UP, 2003. Print.

Chapter Four

Literature with Lacan

Poets, as is well known, don't know what they're saying, yet they still manage to say things before anyone else.

Jacques Lacan, *Seminar Book II*

To be taught and to be learned, this technique [the psychoanalytic technique] would require a profound assimilation of the resources of a language . . . specially those that are concretely realized in its poetic texts.

Jacques Lacan, 'The Function and Field of Speech and Language in Psychoanalysis'

It is a remarkable fact that at many points in his teachings, Lacan formulated his psychoanalytic theories with reference to a range of literary authors from ancient times to modern day. The list includes, but is not limited to, the Greek playwrights Sophocles (c. 496–406 BC) and Aristophanes (c. 450–385 BC), Italian poet Dante Alighieri (1265–1321), British playwright and poet William Shakespeare (1564–1616), British author Lewis Carroll (1832–98), Irish authors James Joyce (1882–1941) and Samuel Beckett (1906–89), American writer Edgar Allan Poe (1809–49), French authors Molière (1622–73), Jean Racine (1639–99), Marquis de Sade (1740–1814), Paul Claudel (1868–1955), André Gide (1869–1951), Jean-Paul Sartre (1905–80), Maurice Blanchot (1907–2003), Jean Genet (1910–86) and Marguerite Duras (1914–96), German authors Johann Wolfgang von Goethe (1749–1832) and E. T. A. Hoffmann (1776–1822) and Russian author Anton Chekhov (1860–1904).

Arguably, three literary texts – Sophocles's play *Antigone* (discussed in *Seminar Book VII*), Shakespeare's play *Hamlet* (discussed in *Seminar Book VI*) and Poe's short story 'The Purloined Letter' (discussed in *Seminar Book II*, *Écrits* and *Seminar Book XVIII*) – stand out in Lacan's teachings as they received the most detailed commentaries. In addition to specific readings of literary authors and texts, Lacan delivered a seminar and wrote a corresponding *écrit* on the theme of *lituraterre* to formulate the psychoanalytic notion of literary criticism. 'Lituraterre' (discussed in *Seminar Book XVIII* and included in *Autres écrits*) is a significant albeit dense and cryptic text on Lacan's views on literature.

Some useful interpretations of the above-mentioned texts have already been offered by a number of Lacanian scholars. Two books that may be referred to here are Jean-Michel Rabaté's *Jacques Lacan: Psychoanalysis and the Subject of Literature* (2001) and the excellent collection *The Literary Lacan: From Literature to Lituraterre and Beyond* (2012), edited by Santanu Biswas. These books include exhaustive analyses and there is no need in an introductory book like this one to go into the exposition of Lacan's reading of individual literary texts. Instead, this chapter begins by outlining the basic coordinates of Lacanian literary criticism and then, to demonstrate the same in a new literary context, engages in a Lacanian analysis of a postmodernist text, namely, John Fowles's *The French Lieutenant's Woman*.

SOME COORDINATES OF LACANIAN LITERARY CRITICISM

Two significant issues may be raised and addressed regarding Lacanian literary criticism – what does it aim at and what does it not aim at. Arguably, a Lacanian reading of literary texts aims at isolating the three registers of a literary narrative (the imaginary, the symbolic and the real), the literary figuration of masculine and feminine structures and the fictional demonstration of the three clinical structures (psychosis, neurosis and perversion).

As far as the three registers are concerned, the reader may investigate how, on the imaginary level, the fictional characters try to relate to one another in the domains of romantic love, fantasy, hatred, rivalry and jealousy. These emotions are based on imaginary identification with the other (lowercase 'o'), which can be traced to the mirror stage in the life of a human subject. For instance, in his analysis of Shakespeare's *Hamlet*, Lacan shows how, in the graveyard scene, Hamlet clearly projects Laertes as his imaginary other or 'the mirror image of the perfect other' (Wright 80). Laertes's passionate cry for his dead sister Ophelia triggers in Hamlet a sense of rivalry over matters of love and affection. Thus Hamlet, who had previously abandoned Ophelia, suddenly cries: 'I loved Ophelia; forty thousand brothers/ Could not with all their quantity of love/ Make up my sum. What wilt thou [Laertes] do for her?' (5.1.236–38). Hamlet's sense of rivalry with Laertes is not confined to Ophelia but also extends to the question of revenge vis-à-vis the dead father. As Elizabeth Wright notes, Laertes is 'a man of action who, unlike Hamlet, is prepared to revenge his father' (80). Hamlet's decision to join the fencing match with Laertes is thus an attempt 'to overcome the mirror rival' (80–81).

On the symbolic level, the reader may explore how fictional characters manifest their graphs of desire. It is well known that Lacan formulated man's desire as the Other's desire (uppercase 'O'), that is, desire is not only desire *for* someone (which verges on fantasy) but also desire *of* the big Other whose prototype is the mOther. The latter type of desire, which Lacan predominantly uses to explain the term, involves questions like, 'What does the Other want?' and 'How can I become an object for the Other's desire?' and so on. Hamlet, for instance, is suspended in the desire of the Other. Lacan claims that Hamlet is not a revenge tragedy but a 'tragedy of desire' as his tragedy begins before, not after, he learns of the murder of his father. Hamlet is troubled not so much by the question of revenge as by the question, 'What does my mOther want?' His tragic experience, derived from his mother's hasty remarriage, is perfectly captured in the famous 'Frailty, thy name is woman!' soliloquy (Shakespeare 1.2.129–58). Hamlet's procrastination derives from the riddle related to Gertrude's desire.

On the level of the real, the reader may examine how fictional characters encounter the real in the form of *jouissance*, sexual non-rapport, anxiety, trauma and the nothingness of their symbolic and imaginary subjectivities, and how literary narratives centre on holes and erasures. Encountering the real is the cause of tragedy since it is, in one sense, an encounter with death. Encounter with the real is the essence of tragedy as it is also the essence of psychoanalysis, in that at the end of analysis one encounters the nothingness of one's being. Lacan substantiates the real dimension of literature in his 'Lituraterre', which will be explained in this chapter.

As far as masculine and feminine structures are concerned, a reader may concentrate on how notions of masculinity and femininity are conceived of by the characters and how sexual differences and sexual non-rapport figure in fictional texts. The Lacanian notion of sexuation may be used to engage in a literary study. As far as the three clinical structures are concerned, the reader may attempt to isolate instances of 'unconscious formations' (dream, joke, parapraxes, symptoms) exemplified in the narrative and outline the clinical category the protagonists resemble. However, such an analysis would, by definition, be entirely tentative.

This is where we need to raise the following question: what does a Lacanian criticism not aim at? It does not aim at 'psychoanalysing' the author and characters in the same way in which 'clinical psychoanalysis' is understood. In the clinical chamber, the freely associated words of the analysand serve as a pathway to the unveiling of her unconscious. In the case of literary texts – unlike the oral texts or the analysand's discourse produced within the clinical context – no such pathway to the unconscious of the characters or author is accessible. A fictional character cannot be psychoanalysed as she does not exist outside the narrative in flesh and blood and hence cannot be brought into a clinical chamber. The same holds true for an author who is dead. To reach the unconscious of a fictional protagonist through a literary text is therefore a clinical impossibility. In literature, the psychoanalyst has always found a precise articulation of clinical discoveries. The best example of this is Sophocles's *Oedipus Rex* (c. 429 BC) which, for Freud, articulated what he came to call the Oedipus complex. In fact, in this case, the name of a fictional protagonist becomes the name of a concept which constitutes the bedrock of classical psychoanalysis.

This is precisely why Lacan insisted psychoanalysts should have a wide range of literary knowledge which would better equip them to articulate their concepts. For Lacan, poets always articulate psychoanalytic truths in advance, even though they know not what they say. Literary authors and protagonists, however, can at most exemplify psychoanalytic discoveries, or represent unconscious-formations, but that does not help with diagnosing their clinical structures or the nature of their unconscious.

This point is highlighted by Lacan in his reading of *Hamlet*. According to Lacan, *Hamlet* is a play which offers the structure of the neurotic's desire. The character of Hamlet manifests both hysteric and obsessional symptoms and demonstrates how the neurotic is forced to construct for himself a certain kind of desire. Lacan claims that 'the problem for Hamlet is closer to the desire of the hysteric, because in a way the problem of Hamlet is to rediscover the place of his desire'. A hysteric is marked by a capability of 'creating for himself an unsatisfied desire'. The obsessional's problem, on the other hand, is 'to support himself on an impossible desire' ('Book VI' 18 March 1959). Hamlet thus demonstrates the function of desire in the case of the obsessional neurotic, which is, 'to keep at a distance, to wait for, the desired moment of encounter' (8 April 1959). This is shown when he procrastinates and delays killing Claudius. Even though Hamlet manifests both hysteric and neurotic symptoms, Lacan emphasises that Hamlet is not a clinical case but a poetic creation. Hamlet does not suffer from a neurosis, which can be diagnosed only in the clinic and that too after numerous psychoanalytic sessions, but demonstrates some symptoms of neurosis. As has been discussed in Chapter Three, manifesting neurotic symptoms is different from having a specific neurotic structure. Literary texts thus do contain characters' and even authors' symptoms – and the task of the psychoanalytic critic is to foreground these with the holes and riddles which constitute the narratives – but such symptoms are in no way sufficient to psychoanalyse fictional or dead people. Any Lacanian approach to a literary text must be informed by this clinical limitation.

It may be noted, however, that Lacan does refer to the lives of authors when he analyses literary texts. His analyses of Joyce, Gide and Shakespeare take into account certain facts from their lives. However, such use of biographical detail in the context of reading a literary text does not aim at psychoanalysing the author but at supporting the thesis of how a given literary text demonstrates specific psychoanalytic insights. In the final analysis, this demonstration is not affected by the absence of biographical details.

In this light, what does the title of this chapter, 'Literature with Lacan', imply? In his famous text, 'Kant with Sade' (included in *Écrits*), Lacan used the preposition 'with' because the latter philosopher both completed and rendered true the former philosopher. Although the present context is obviously different, the phrase 'Literature with Lacan' means that Lacanian insights may be profitably used in the critical admiration of literature and in bringing to the fore valuable ideas literary authors may not always know of but articulate. Lacan's conception of love, desire, *jouissance*, masculinity, femininity, neurosis, psychosis and perversion help us make sense of ourselves – be it inside or outside of the clinic. The same conception may be used (and has been used) to understand how fictional characters make sense of themselves or how authors shape the behaviours, motives and conversations of their characters. Indeed, psychoanalytic readings have opened up an entirely new field of literary studies, and Lacanian findings add an altogether new dimension to this field.

LITURATERRE: ENCOUNTERING OR FOREGROUNDING THE REAL IN LITERATURE

Lacan coined the term *lituraterre*. While it could be seen as a combination of the Latin words *litura* (erasure) and *terre* (earth) – Lacan even refers to a complex set of etymological references which 'legitimise' his neologism – he actually coined this term through a spoonerism (on the level of syllables) of *littérature,* the French word for literature. Spoonerism, the *Oxford English Dictionary* (OED) tells us, is 'an error in speech in which the initial sounds or letters of two or more words are accidentally transposed, often to humorous effect, as in *you have hissed the mystery lectures* [instead of saying 'you have missed the history lectures]'. The term, as the OED explains, is named after the English scholar Rev. W. A. Spooner (1844–1930), 'who reputedly made such errors in speaking' (1395). Even though *lituraterre* translates into something similar to 'writing erasure on earth', in a literary context, Lacan specifically refers to the way literature could be considered a site for 'writing erasure' and indicates that the task of psychoanalytic literary critics is to expose how 'literature [or a given literary text] consists of holes and erasures' (Rabaté 33). The holes and erasures in literature refer to what is unreadable, or impossible to be written. The term 'impossible', here, refers to the impossible dimensions of the real. As Evans explains, this impossibility derives from the fact that the real cannot be imagined and cannot be integrated into the symbolic order. 'It is this character of impossibility and of resistance to symbolisation', writes Evans, 'which lends the real its essentially traumatic quality' (163).

To concentrate on the real of literature is to not focus on the representation of reality. Both reality and representation are in the domain of the symbolic. It is the gaps and holes, ellipses and silences, the unknowable and the unspeakable, the traumatic and the void which constitute the sole focus. As Santanu Biswas indicates, the move that Lacan is making in 'Lituraterre' is a move from the idea of literature as 'semblance' that veils the holes/erasures/real to the possibility of a literature that 'might not be a semblance' or that might unveil holes/erasures/real (20). Indeed, this text is part of Lacan's *Seminar Book XVIII,* significantly titled *A Discourse that Might Not Be a Semblance*. Lacan's investigation brings him to the conclusion that literature cannot escape the fate of being a semblance; however, there can be literatures which *sustain* themselves not in terms of semblance but through erasures. A literature that tends not to be a semblance, or tends to be a *lituraterre*, is a literature that moves from 'letter' (semblance) to 'litter' (a piece of trash/ the real). To demonstrate how literature tends to be *lituraterre*, Lacan offers the examples of Poe, Joyce, avant-garde artists and Beckett.

Lacan's take on Poe's 'The Purloined Letter' has been discussed in detail in Chapter Five. For Lacan, what is missing at the heart of Poe's story is the content or message of the letter. No one knows what is written in the letter and Poe deliberately keeps it like that.

And yet, the letter moves from one place to another – from the queen (who is the addressee of the letter) to the minister (who steals it from the queen) to the detective (who steals it from the minister) and finally, so the story implies, back to the queen. This letter, which constitutes the core of the story and which shapes the intersubjective relations among the characters, is marked by a hole or erasure – 'the unreadable content of the letter constitutes an unbridgeable gap in the narrative' (Biswas 182). A letter without a message – a signifier without a signified – is no better than litter or a piece of trash. What matters in the story is the materiality of the letter – its shape, size and location – as opposed to its content. Moreover, this 'littoral' letter exerts a powerful effect on those it is associated with by feminising them – the letter possesses the holder and not vice versa. Indeed, 'Poe was able to demonstrate the effects of the letter at its limit so thoroughly', Biswas explains as he draws on Lacan's ideas, 'because he had effaced its content and thus converted it and the narrative on it into the edges of an unreadable hole, which brings out the letter's littoral condition in the story' (182).

It is in the context of Poe's work that Lacan mentions a crucial detail against psycho-biographical criticism: 'Nonetheless, the ellipsis [the content of the letter] cannot be elucidated by means of some aspect *(trait)* of his [Poe's] psychobiography; rather this would clog it up' ('Lituraterre'). As opposed to psycho-biography, Lacan's attempt is to find out where the letter makes a hole in writing, and he says, 'For me, if I propose to psychoanalysis [sic] the letter as in sufferance, it is because it shows there its failure. And it is by this that I shed light on it: when I thus evoke the *lumières*, it is to demonstrate where it makes a *hole*' ('Lituraterre').

Alongside Poe's 'The Purloined Letter', James Joyce's *Finnegans Wake* is another major example where letter becomes litter. Lacan says there is an '*equivoque* by which Joyce . . . slips from *a letter* to *a litter,* from *a lettre* . . . to a piece of trash' ('Lituraterre'). Joyce, whom we have discussed in the preceding chapter in conjunction with *sinthome* and psychosis, did not have to go to a psychoanalyst even though he was once urged to psychoanalyse himself with Carl Gustav Jung. Lacan claims that Joyce did not need psychoanalysis because through his creative works Joyce reached the end point of psychoanalysis, the point where one recognises oneself as a piece of trash and needs to construct the *sinthome*. How does Joyce slip from letter to litter? Biswas notes that *Finnegans Wake* is a case in point where one experiences 'a comedy of letters/litters' in which the letter slips to the litter. He says:

> While the whole of *Finnegans Wake* . . . is as much 'A comedy of letters!' . . . as it is a comedy of litter, the word litter itself, as well as Joycean derivatives of it, figures throughout the novel, often in connection with writing, literacy, literature or storytelling . . . But, perhaps, Joyce best ratified his slippage from a letter to a litter in [a sentence from the text] . . . : 'writing and with lines of litters slittering up and louds of latters slettering down' (175–76).

Finnegans Wake, it may be noted, is a dream text in which the letters of the English language are displaced and condensed to such an extent that the words they form move beyond recognition. Joyce manipulates the letters of the English language to the point of breaking them into pieces and emptying them of signifieds. It is one of the ways in which the letter, as semblance, turns into litter, as trash. The 'Fin' ('end') in *Finnegans Wake*, Biswas notes, resonates with the notion of 'end of analysis', where the analysand experiences a subjective destitution by encountering the trash of one's being (179–80).

Lacan also talks about avant-garde literature as that which, even though 'made of the littoral', cannot be literature which is not a semblance. But avant-garde literature certainly moves towards *lituraterre*. To quote Lacan, 'There is the question only proposed by the literature called *avant-garde,* which is itself made of the littoral: and thus does not sustain itself by the *semblant,* but for all that proves nothing but the breakage, which only a discourse can produce, with an effect of production' ('Lituraterre').

Avant-garde literature was the literature of 'high modernism'. It involved a lot of experimentation marked by a deliberate discarding of traditional forms of narration. Surrealist art and poetry (foregrounding the unconscious and its formations, especially dream), for instance, dealt a blow against the realist mode of representation. Dadaism, futurism and other artistic movements were similar in spirit. How is such artistic experimentation considered to be 'made of the littoral'? Biswas addresses the issue:

> In terms of its radical departure from traditional forms of narration – by way of unconventional narrative style, wordplay, condensation, neologism, displacement, pun, riddle, allusion, ideogram, misspelling, combination of incongruous words and phrases, use of words from different languages, absence of punctuation, stress on the sounds of words, the fading self, etc. – avant-garde literature comprised texts that were hallucinatory, chaotic and situated at the edge of meaning. By creating holes in meaning and thus eluding sense, it directed the attention of the readers to the very materiality of the letters and their sounds on the one hand, and to the limit of meaning and the impossible void beyond it as the site of *jouissance* on the other. Thus, avant-garde literature comes closest to a form of a discourse that might not be a semblance because, being made of the littoral instead of the literal, it is sustained by the holes in the semblance. (185)

Samuel Beckett's writings, too, serve as an ideal example of Lacan's concept of 'litter'. This is what Lacan says about Beckett:

> It must be said no doubt that I was tired of the wastebasket to which I have channelled my fate. You know that I am not the only one, to be generous, to admit it (*L'avouer*). The admission (*L'avouer*) or, as pronounced of old, *'l'avoir'* (the having) of which Beckett makes a balance to the debt that makes refuse of our being, saves the honour of literature, and relieves me of the privilege I believed owed to my place. ('Lituraterre')

Beckett has saved the honour of literature, Lacan claims, by accommodating the 'refuse of our being' in the literary space. The refuse of our being is the experience the analysand has at the end of psychoanalysis. Like Joyce, Beckett too moves from the letter to the litter by way of foregrounding the litter. Beckett's 1957 play *Endgame* – the title bearing a 'fortuitous resonance' to the end of analysis, as Biswas notes, and the play comprising characters who are 'bottled' in dustbins – as well as his thirty-five second play *Breath* – in which, onstage, there is no character, only scattered rubbish – could be examples of this idea. 'The end of analysis here concerns the subject having a glimpse of the real of his being as waste', Biswas continues, 'as Beckett may have had with or without the assistance of his analysis with [the British psychoanalyst] Wilfred Bion round the beginning of his literary career' (179–180).

Having thus outlined the basic coordinates of Lacanian literary criticism, we may now move on to substantiate the same in terms of a Lacanian reading of a literary narrative not dealt with by Lacan himself.

PHALLIC MYTH, FEMININITY, AND SEXUAL NON-RAPPORT IN *THE FRENCH LIEUTENANT'S WOMAN*

> Who is Sarah? Out of what shadows does she come?
>
> John Fowles, *The French Lieutenant's Woman*

> I meant I am not to be understood even by myself. And I can't tell you why, but I believe my happiness depends on my not understanding.
>
> John Fowles, *The French Lieutenant's Woman*

> There is a *jouissance* . . . 'beyond the phallus'. There is a *jouissance* that is hers, that belongs to that 'she' that doesn't exist and doesn't signify anything. There is a *jouissance* that is hers about which she herself perhaps knows nothing if not that she experiences it – that much she knows. She knows it, of course, when it comes. It does not happen to all of them.
>
> Jacques Lacan, *Seminar Book XX*

Introduction

As a literary writer and thinker, John Fowles was interested in the workings of the unconscious mind and the psychological and psychoanalytical theories pertaining to the same domain. Eileen Warburton, Fowles's biographer, notes that Fowles was fascinated by psychoanalysis and was inspired to analyse his and his wife's minds by interpreting their dreams. His basic techniques of understanding the unconscious were Freudian, though he drew on methodologies developed by Jung, Alfred Adler and Karen Horney as and when necessary. In *John Fowles: A Life in Two Worlds* (1926), Warburton writes:

> Fowles completed an intense period of analysis of his dreams and those of his wife. In his 'method' he made the basic interpretation Freudian – that is, he wrote, 'treat all imagery as illustration of pre-conscious traumas that have to do with (a) withdrawal of the breast-corruption of the pure mother-baby relationship, (b) feelings about parents or the parent substitutes; Oedipus complex and the rest.' Imagery, however, was to be interpreted using Jungian, Adlerian, and Hornerian methodologies. (271)

Fowles's interest in psychoanalysis (Freudian) and analytical psychology (Jungian) is reflected in his literary writings, especially in his novels. A close study reveals that Fowles's texts are very much psychoanalytically informed. His protagonists are subjected to 'psychological tests' conducted by figures supposed to function as psychoanalysts and psychiatrists. His characters speak the vocabulary of psychoanalysis, frequently using in their conversations terms like 'Oedipus complex', 'repetition compulsion', 'case histories', 'sado-masochism', 'hysteria', 'father/mother-substitute', 'gaze', etc. Real or fictional 'case histories' (in the Freudian fashion) constitute or are incorporated in his narratives to the extent that his protagonists undergo some sort of psychological trial or test. That is not to say that Fowles mechanically imitates Freudian case histories, which he found extremely fascinating and which he made use of in his day-to-day life to understand himself and others. With a postmodernist inclination, Fowles maintains an ironic, parodic, even interrogatory distance vis-à-vis the larger discourse of psychoanalysis (predominantly Freudian), as his fictional psychiatrists and psychoanalysts sometimes end up with false interpretations of the protagonists' minds. It has been rightly pointed out that in his novels, Fowles does not merely represent psychical structures, but also 'interprets psychoanalytical meanings' (Kirillova).

Such 'reinterpretations' or 'interrogations', however, do not indicate a rejection of psychoanalysis, especially considering Fowles's preoccupations with understanding the human mind. Throughout his career he maintained a sustained interest in psychoanalysis. For example, later on, when Gilbert Rose penned a Freudian reading of *The French Lieutenant's Woman*,[1] presenting the unconscious significance of the novel to its author, Fowles was highly impressed and inspired to write an essay called 'Hardy and the Hag' (1977), which was a psychoanalytic study of Thomas Hardy's 1897 novel *The Well Beloved*.

Fowles's (re)interpretation of psychoanalysis could also be considered as part of the larger climate of opinions and diversity of followers or schools[2] that Freudian psychoanalysis (both in theory and practice) had generated in Europe. With Lacan's rise in the international psychoanalytic field, most of these schools of Freudian psychoanalysis would eventually recede to the background.

It is highly unlikely that Fowles read Lacan. Fowles was born in 1926 (passed away in 2005) and was younger than Lacan, who was born in 1901 (passed away in 1981), and yet, even though Fowles was psychoanalytically informed, there is a curious absence of any reference to Lacan in his works. In his novels there are direct references to Lacan's contemporaries, like Roland Barthes (1915–80) and Jacques Derrida (1930–2004). In fact, in a text like *The French Lieutenant's Woman,* Fowles is quite deliberately acting as a poststructuralist. Could we then conclude that the absence of Lacan in Fowles's work was due to the relative inaccessibility of Lacan's seminars and *écrits* outside of France? It remains a fact that unlike Derrida and Barthes, whom Fowles fondly and playfully refers to in his novels, Lacan was somehow less known to Fowles, who studied in Oxford and lived in Dorset in the United Kingdom.

It does not matter whether or not Fowles directly used Lacan in his writing; what matters is that both of them had shared interests in Freudian psychoanalysis. Apart from his critical interest in Freudian ideas (as was the case with Lacan, albeit in a more rigorous and clinical way), Fowles, in almost all of his novels, was preoccupied with the workings of the human mind and engaged with the domains of male desire and fantasy, the 'enigma' of femininity and the (im)possibility of a man-woman relationship. These ideas constitute the key concerns Lacan explores (especially later in life) – concerns which evolved into original and immensely significant concepts including feminine sexuality, phallic myth, sexual difference, sexual non-rapport and the limits of love and knowledge, found most notably in his *Seminar Book XX*. From a more critical perspective, the problems which Fowles apparently had with psychiatry (reflected through his attempts to disprove the diagnoses made by his fictional psychiatrists) can be rightly addressed using Lacanian ideas. It appears as though Fowles was eager to present complex psychic situations which could not be easily fathomed. Through his unique engagement with psychoanalysis, Lacan had repeatedly addressed the ungraspable and complex domains of the human psyche (the question of femininity and feminine *jouissance*, for instance) and criticised a class of psychoanalysts and psychiatrists who lacked the necessary rigor in their theoretical and clinical engagements with psychoanalysis. In a sense, Fowles's narratives, especially *The French Lieutenant's Woman*, foreground the riddles, holes and erasures that constitute the 'littoral' condition of the letter as discussed in the early part of this chapter.

Lacanian ideas have significant poststructuralist implications. Indeed, Fowles's major postmodernist preoccupations – his strategies of rewriting, parody and playfulness, his repeated use of unresolved endings, metafictional moments and moments of ontological frame-breaking – could best be understood in poststructuralist terms. Eli Zaretsky has pointed out in his 1966 essay, 'Postmodernism and Psychoanalysis', that Freud's theories, originating as they did in the modernist period, cannot explain all that a postmodern subject might experience. If, as Derrida says, inconclusiveness is one of the hallmarks of postmodernism and indeterminacy marks postmodern subjectivity, then Lacan, Zaretsky concludes, has given us the first postmodernist, poststructuralist conception of psychoanalysis 'that truly broke with modernist assumptions concerning subjectivity and sexual difference' (163). Hence, he adds, a meaningful history of postmodernism should assign relatively more importance to Lacan (168). Zaretsky's point might appear to be rather simplistic here, especially in his understanding of Freud as a 'modernist' and the kind of unproblematic relation between Derrida and Lacan that his approach seems to indicate. He has, however, as it were, hit the nail on the head and echoed a point that Slavoj Žižek makes in his studies on postmodernism. Žižek, while talking about the later films of Alfred Hitchcock, has stated that a poststructuralist reading of a postmodern text and another reading of the same text, not informed by poststructuralist ideas, would be fundamentally different from one another – the earlier one alone disentangling the true significance of the postmodern narrative (1–2).

Truth of the Feminine and Fictionality of the Masculine

One of the ways to introduce the concept of truth/fiction would be to say a few words about the Japanese film *Rashomon* (1950), which won the Golden Lion Award (1951) and established Akira Kurosawa as an international film-maker. Famously, in this film, a murder incident and a related rape incident are presented in four different and somewhat contradictory versions narrated from four different subject positions, each of which is initially, equally convincing. Through this film, Kurosawa gives us a number of critical insights on the question of truth. The original incident (murder or rape), or the primal scene, is always already lost – this is what constitutes the hole or erasure of the film-text. But the loss is unbearable which is why a re-presentation of the primal scene becomes imperative. It is only with the subjective re-presentation (with all the unconscious nuances of the word 'subjective') of the traumatic moment that the truth of that moment can be constructed. In other words, truth cannot be accessed in its own abode in an unmediated way. Truth exists only through its narration, that is, through the mediation of discourse/visuals. What is more important is that the discursive representation of truth is precisely what *creates* the truth, which would otherwise be non-existent. Truth is devoid of any singularity and authenticity; it would exist as 'truths', in the plural, in multiple versions and variations derived from the different positions of the subjects. Here, Kurosawa seems to have hit upon a major Lacanian insight (as proposed by Lacan in his 1957 essay 'Seminar on the "Purloined Letter"') – truth is structured like fiction, or truth reveals a 'fictional ordering' (*Écrits* 11) where truth is in close proximity to the real as well as the symbolic. Even if fiction is considered to be deception or lie (or based on either as is the case with Fowles's narrative, which will be further discussed in this chapter), such falsity may be said to be located within the very text of truth. In terms of fiction being broadly understood as the domain of language or the symbolic, truth can only be half-said or half-articulated, for there is always something in truth which escapes symbolisation, or remains unsayable. It is this domain of the unsayable in truth that makes truth similar to the real, or that which escapes signifierisation (Evans 242). The unsayable would be close to the unreadable and impossible to write, as discussed in connection with Lacan's essay 'Lituraterre'.

In a Lacanian sense, the proliferation of fiction or discourses in human life is directly linked to an attempt to avoid the void; to avoid an encounter with the real or with a traumatic truth. A literary example here could include *Arabian Nights* (1704): a sequence of interconnected stories which, as planned by Scheherazade, the would-be storyteller-queen, have their roots in traumatic events such as the betrayal of the first Queen, her murder by her Sultan-husband and his consequent desperation to avenge the betrayal by marrying and murdering one virgin after another. The proliferation of stories, meant to approximate 1001 stories, is an attempt to defer another traumatic moment – the death of Scheherazade at the hands of her Sultan-husband and the succession of marriages and murders that would follow. Here, murder/death would be the domain of the real or traumatic domain of beyond-the-language, while the constantly increasing stories would constitute the fictional/symbolic universe which helps one in avoiding/hiding the real. For Lacan, the domain of language is predominantly the domain of the symbolic, which is precisely what creates and categorises reality. The entry of the human subject into the domain of the symbolic, or vice versa, is necessarily related to the exclusion of the real from reality. However, the domain of reality/symbolic is not just an exclusion of the real/truth; the symbolic is also that which bears a truth – the truth about its origins in the real. The real does not 'exist' in the symbolic as such, but it 'ek-sists' (exists outside but insists on) the symbolic and, like the umbilical cord's relation to the body, always functions as a remainder/reminder, setting the symbolic in motion. The symbolic, or the domain of discourse and representation, has its origins in the real/the unrepresentable/truth and carries within itself the remainder or traces of the real.

The proliferation of signifiers to avoid the void can be illustrated by one of my favourite metaphors – the metaphor of the onion –

which I learnt from my teacher, Professor Santanu Biswas, who first introduced me to Lacan. The onion has multiple layers which, when peeled away, one after another, reveal that at its centre there is a void. The layers could be compared to the discursive layers of the symbolic reality which disguise a lack by containing it. It is understandable why Lacan has stated that every discourse is a semblance;[3] every discourse offers a semblance of truth while, in reality, in the place of truth there is only a lack. In his analysis of courtly love in *Seminar Book VII*, Lacan has pointed out that the discourse of courtly love in medieval times was not a mimetic exercise – it didn't represent what was there in reality; rather, it represented what was *not* there (139–54). Courtly love, for Lacan, was based on a lack of sexual advances or, on the part of the knight, maintaining a proper physical distance from the lady. The discourse of love and romance represented an inevitable truth – that no such ideal love-relation could take place in actuality, that the relationships between lord/knight and lady had an underlying tension that would lead to the eventual decline of feudalism and a 'waning of the middle ages' (a phrase used by Johann Huizinga).[4] Courtly romance could be considered a kind of wish-fulfilment on the part of the upholders of feudalism – a wish that was far from being fulfilled in the domain of social reality. Hence the need for literary discourse.

It may be noted that the French word for truth, *vérité,* is a feminine noun. By and large, Lacan brings out the link between truth and femininity. It can be argued that femininity, in the purest sense, is essentially a domain outside phallocentric language. Masculinity, for Lacan, is a fiction which is structured in law, logic and language, whereas femininity is the domain of truth (which is fundamentally the lack of truth, the holes in the symbolic), the domain beyond language and representation, the domain that challenges the concepts of law and logic. The myth of masculinity, or the phallic myth, derives from the notion of the phallus. Lacan explains that the phallus does not just refer to the biological organ (we have already talked about the imaginary, the symbolic and real phallus with reference to the Oedipus complex) but is also predominantly a symbolic entity or a set of traditionally inherited concepts like virility, power and superiority, supposed to symbolise or construct the identity of the masculine subject. Phallus is an overcoat that the male subject is made to put on by society in order to achieve 'manhood'. In a sense, one could say that one is not born a man but becomes a man (a play on Simone de Beauvoir's famous 'One is not born, but rather becomes, a woman'), that is, one must internalise existing notions of masculinity in order to construct one's subjectivity.

Taking forward Lacan's idea, one can state that a woman's existence (understood not as a biological but a psychoanalytical category) qua woman, or as 'purely feminine', is the Other to language, and that woman cannot exist entirely qua woman since that would make her entirely incomprehensible and unrepresentable to others as well as to herself. For Lacan, woman is not entirely cut by language and since she is not cut by language, since she verges on the real, she is a potential threat to the fiction called masculinity and patriarchy. Patriarchy can exist and sustain itself as long as it can avoid encountering the purely feminine. Women, as subjects, are trained from the beginning of their lives to uphold and authenticate the patriarchal institution at the cost of keeping aside, or sacrificing, the purely feminine or that which is fatal to the phallic. One could say that women function as the gatekeepers of patriarchy.[5] Gatekeepers exist at the margins of an institution but are instrumental in protecting the institution.

There are two ways in which women authenticate the phallic myth: by apparently sacrificing 'pure femininity' and by fitting into the domain of language and understanding. These are what could be called, based on Garry Leonard's excellent exposition of these concepts in *Reading Dubliners Again* (1993), 'woman as masquerade' and 'woman as symptom' (8–10). As 'masquerade', a woman upholds and authenticates the phallic myth – the fiction about the virility, heroism, superiority and power of the masculine subject. In other words, a woman masquerades or masks, or does not trigger disturbing questions regarding a masculine subject's sense of being superior to women or, for example, his right to exert power over women. As 'masquerade', woman protects man from experiencing existential crisis. Woman, in the Lacanian sense, is also the symptom of man. Here, symptom would refer to woman as a site for the disguised fulfilment of man's repressed sexual desire. Sexual desire is repressed in the classical Freudian sense because the first sexual impulse was directed towards the mother (Freud 262) and had to be repressed due to paternal prohibition. For the masculine subject, woman is not an original object of desire but rather a *substitute* for the first object of desire – the mother. If symptom is understood as a return of the repressed in a disguised form, then for man, woman qua man's substitute object of desire stages the return of man's repressed sexual desire. Because the original object is always already lost, woman is less an object than an *object cause* of man's desire and fantasy. Woman as a substitute object cannot fulfil man's desire but can bring back his repressed desires with the caveat that a fulfilment of desire is impossible. Desire, thus caused, may not be fulfilled, or may not aim at fulfilment, but does contribute to the articulation and recognition of the masculine subject as a desiring subject. It may also be noted that man's desire, as Lacan demonstrates in his analysis of Hamlet's desire in *Seminar Book VI*, is the other's desire. In the case of Hamlet, it is the desire of the mother and not desire for the mother which constitutes the question of 'to be or not to be' (Shakespeare 3.1.56) for the masculine subject. Lacan's take on man's desire, as opposed to Freud's take, is that man does not desire the other as such but rather desires to emulate the desire of the other. Man is troubled by the question, 'what does the other lack and desire?' and thinks of ways to fulfil the lack in the other. In a sense, the notion of woman as symptom would mean that woman is the site where the desire for her, as well as the desire to be the object of her desire, aims at recognition, if not fulfilment.

Both as 'masquerade' and as 'symptom', a woman contributes to a rather ironical sense of self-importance and security in the masculine subject. As 'masquerade', woman contributes to the masculine subject's false sense of superiority and power, and as 'symptom', woman contributes to the sustenance of the masculine subject as a desiring subject. Furthermore, both as 'masquerade' and as 'symptom', a woman is understandable and explainable since she thereby fits into the man's coordinates of desire and fantasy and is, hence, graspable in language. However, woman qua woman is an Other to language and in this regard remains a perpetual threat to the entire symbolic domain and phallic myth. As will be discussed in Fowles's female protagonist in *The French Lieutenant's Woman*, the encounter with this Other side of woman can lead to an absolute destitution of the masculine subject. It is obvious that these three aspects of femininity correspond to the three Lacanian registers – the imaginary (woman as object of fantasy or as man's symptom), the symbolic (woman as 'masquerade') and the real (woman ek-sisting the phallic domain).

Because masculinity is a fiction, for a woman to be related to man is to participate in the authentication of this fiction, and sexual 'relationships' are by implication based on a kind of emptiness and falsehood. It is in this context that Lacan states that there cannot be any 'sexual rapport' between man and woman. We have already discussed the notion of sexual non-rapport in Chapter Two. A few things may be added here. The hyphen in the expression 'man-woman' (as in 'man-woman relationship') is crucial. The hyphen is like the bar between signifier and signified in Ferdinand de Saussure's formulation of the linguistic sign:

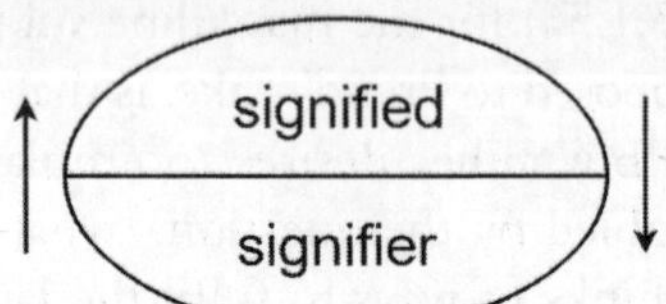

Figure 9: Linguistic sign, Saussure's modified drawing (Saussere 114)

Lacan draws attention to the bar in Saussure's diagram. Lacan says that because of the bar the signifier and signified are eternally alienated from one another, hence the arrows signifying an interaction between signifier and signified in Saussure's drawing make no sense (Lacan criticises Saussure on other fronts as well, an issue which has been discussed in Chapter Two). In this regard, the hyphen keeps 'man' and 'woman' forever apart. The hyphen and the bar could also be considered as phallus, where phallus stands for fiction of masculinity and for woman's participation in the same as 'masquerade' and 'symptom'. To quote Garry Leonard:

> For Lacan, the sexual relation consists of two interrelated gender myths: the myth of psychic unity and coherence that is the masculine subject and the corresponding myth of the feminine subject as the site of the otherness and absence that guarantees the supposedly self-evident unity of man. The irony of this is that by believing in the Phallus, and in the law and order that it represents, a man is symbolically castrated because his penis is, subsequently, just an uneasy rem(a)inder of his insatiable desire that must, henceforth, be completed and authenticated by something outside of himself. (9)

Phallic Myth and Femininity in *The French Lieutenant's Woman*

John Fowles's novel *The French Lieutenant's Woman* is set in nineteenth-century Victorian England and tells the story of a village girl, Sarah Woodruff, an outcast (a 'fallen woman' since she *supposedly* had a liaison with a certain French lieutenant) who apparently falls in love with the male protagonist, Charles Smithson. Charles leaves his fiancée Ernestina for Sarah, yet Sarah eventually betrays him to make her way into the heart of London and the famous household of the Rossettis. Charles later on discovers that Sarah is a virgin and has fooled everybody by circulating the story that she was the French lieutenant's 'woman', and we are left to ponder – why did Sarah do this? After they have intercourse, Charles leaves Sarah and promises to return shortly. But Sarah disappears. Charles desperately looks for her for years and we are left to reflect on the question – why did she disappear? While Fowles successfully constructs one of the strongest and most complex female characters in literary history through Sarah, he adds an unprecedented twist to the narrative by assigning three different endings to the story. The first ending has Charles and Ernestina enter an unhappy marriage and, apart from being mentioned in passing, Sarah plays no role in their lives. This ending is dismissed by the narrator as a daydream. The second ending sees Charles and Sarah have intercourse and Charles realising Sarah is a virgin. He decides to end his engagement to Ernestina and promises to marry Sarah, but due to his circumstances he falls into disgrace. He leaves for America while Sarah flees to London without informing him. She appears to have manipulated his feelings, but when they are eventually reunited she reveals, to Charles and the reader's astonishment, their child. There is a sort of union at last: Sarah's 'head against his breast shakes with a mute vehemence' (Fowles 462). What does this imply? Reconciliation? What will they do? Get married? Would Sarah take him as an extension of her happiness? Any such resolution is kept uncertain. The third ending sees events take place as they do in the second ending, only this time their reunion is acrimonious and the parentage of the child, Lalage, is left unclear. Although the narrator has his reasons for dismissing the earlier endings as inappropriate, the third ending is just as inconclusive as the previous two.

The multiple endings and the enigma that is Sarah Woodruff (similar to the heroine in Luis Buñuel's 1977 film *That Obscure Object of Desire*) have, for their obvious significance, repeatedly received critical attention. While the literary theorist Linda Hutcheon, among others, has attempted to analyse the formal structure of the novel, special attention has been paid to Sarah and Charles's psychic universe by Robert Huffaker, Bruce Woodcock, Gilbert Rose, Olga Kirillova, and others.[6] Theories developed by Jung and Freud are central to the majority of writings of this kind, except for one article written by Olga Kirillova which is from a Lacanian viewpoint. Additionally, all these scholars, in different ways, indicate the kind of impact Sarah's character has on Charles. Huffaker, for example, tries to understand Sarah in conjunction with Jung's insights through analytical psychology of the female mind. He contends that Sarah, by maintaining a passive attitude, aids Charles in his self-realisation and, in that way, holds him. Lauren Barral presents a somewhat similar insight by keeping a sustained focus on Charles, as 'within the enigmatic narrative, the protagonist Charles Smithson first initiates a quest for Sarah's mystery. Progressively, the quest for Sarah turns into a quest for his own self-knowledge' (Barral 2). Woodcock makes the point that Charles is forced into a realisation of self and autonomy through his ironical or contradictory idealisation of Sarah and his attempts to appropriate her. Bonnie Zare, in her powerful reading of Sarah Woodruff in 'Reclaiming Masculinist Texts for Feminist Readers' (1997), talks about the richness of Sarah's character which motivates feminist readings. She refers to the author's ambiguous take on the changing roles of women in Victorian England and concludes that 'the text is finally ambiguous enough to allow Sarah to transcend the bounds of the words which try to circumscribe her' (Zare 191). While such a conclusion is indeed of great importance to the present analysis, Zare does not consider significant Lacanian theories in the understanding of femininity. Rose's article is probably the first proper attempt to read Fowles psychoanalytically, in conjunction with Freud, with an emphasis on the theme of loss in the creative process. Kirillova's article, in Lacanian terms, considers the French lieutenant a phallic signifier for Sarah and the relations between the characters as one of transference. Some of these articles provide new perspectives, no doubt, but also have their limitations. According to both Huffaker and Woodcock, Sarah apparently aids in the formation of Charles's self, but their discussions seem to present Sarah as merely a part of Charles's consciousness and hence not being read as having a strong sense of individuality. Rose's Freudian reading, in spite of the fact that it appealed to a lot to readers including Fowles himself, at times does not seem entirely convincing because of its psychobiographical inferences – given the kinds of limitations a piece of psychobiographical criticism might have (problems with psychoanalysing an author through one of his published books). Kirillova's clinically inspired reading (focusing solely on the concept of 'transference') is undeniably a novel Lacanian engagement with Fowles, but in no way does it exhaustively make use of Lacanian theory in the literary universe of the text.

Critically differing from all of these existing readings and specifically focusing on Lacanian ideas, my claim is that it would be insufficient to say that the novel, with its multiple endings, is an experiment with the narrative form. There is something more in it – an impasse which resists any straightforward resolution. Focusing on Sarah Woodruff, I claim that she is this impasse and that the content of her character produces multiple and contradictory effects on and possibilities for both the narrative as well as the male protagonist. Fowles's biographical details suggest that the author was actually indecisive when it came to concluding the story, given the kind of characters he had constructed. Warburton writes that the ending of the novel, as initially composed by Fowles, was as follows (it included a twist even in the initial draft):

> After a twenty-month search Charles finds Sarah living in Clapham, presumably married. Denying she ever loved him, she sends him away. Leaving with bruised pride, Charles cynically sends flowers of farewell and learns from the seller that Mrs. Smithson [Sarah] lives alone, supporting her baby son by modelling at the Royal Academy of Art. Joyfully, Charles rushes to a tender reconciliation to the promise of marriage and another child. (295)

Fowles's wife, Elizabeth Fowles, rejected this ending by calling it 'too pat'. Elizabeth is quoted as saying:

> Sarah was the one person who should come through strong as part of the twentieth century conditions of complicated male/ female [sic] intellect . . . should stand as the tragic figure in some way. [As an] . . . inconclusive *modern* human being . . . Therefore I do not think you can end with the ending you have. (qtd. in Warburton 295)

Warburton adds: 'In July 1968 Fowles wrote both a stronger version of the conventional happy ending and a new "tragic" ending in which the couple part and Sarah continues mysteriously, as "your inconclusive *modern* human being"' (295).

The expression 'inconclusive modern human being' (with all the rich connotations of the word 'modern', which includes the word 'postmodern' in the sense that it is an extension of, or a response to, the modern) is key to my understanding of Sarah as a psychologically rich and complex female character who baffles anybody (male protagonist, other characters, narrator and reader) who attempts to draw simple or straightforward conclusions about her. My attempt here would be to show that for some substantial psychoanalytic reasons, Sarah embodies what Lacan would have called an instance of 'dédoublement', whereby she attracts the attention of others only to frustrate their understanding of her, participates in the construction of phallic myth only to 'unconceal' the nothingness of it and becomes the agent of both fiction and truth at the same time.[7] My argument is that Sarah's incomprehensibility derives from her embodying the truth or the real of femininity in the Lacanian sense, which puts the symbolic/discursive/phallic/fictional universe at a loss, alongside her functioning as 'masquerade' and 'symptom' or as creator and upholder of the phallic myth and desire.

Sarah as 'Masquerade' and 'Symptom'

In the narrative, Sarah creates and upholds the fiction of selfhood and the phallic myth in many ways. The idea of the 'French lieutenant's woman' is based on a lie. She invents and circulates a false story about her liaison/sexual intercourse with a French lieutenant, whom, as the story goes, she nursed after he was rescued from a shipwreck. Sarah disguises herself as a fallen woman, as socially outcast. It is this falsehood and disguise that actually creates her identity or selfhood. She seems to imply that her 'I' is a 'lie'. Of course, in this case, Sarah deliberately resorts to a lie to project herself as an outcast. By way of this fiction, she can fool the Victorian mindset, turn conventions upside down and assert her agency.

Sarah's participation in the creation of the fiction of masculinity happens on a more subtle, unconscious level. To my mind, the key to the narrative is her enigmatic gaze which is described in the very first chapter. This chapter, beginning with an epigraph from Thomas Hardy's poem 'The Riddle' (thus enhancing the sense of enigma surrounding Sarah as well as resonating with the riddles that Lacanian criticism asks us to concentrate on), describes Charles and Ernestina at length before concluding with a description of Sarah standing by the sea:

> But where the telescopist would have been at sea himself was with the other figure on that somber, curving mole. It stood right at the seawardmost end, apparently leaning against an old cannon barrel upended as a bollard. Its clothes were black. The wind moved them, but the figure stood motionless, staring, staring out to sea, more like a living memorial to the drowned, a figure from myth, than any proper fragment of the petty provincial day. (Fowles 5)

In the film adaptation (1981) directed by Karel Reisz, this moment is tellingly captured. Sarah, whom Charles does not yet know, is found dressed in black, standing by the seaside of Lyme Regis and staring at the sea. As she stands there, amidst a violent storm and rains, she is noticed by Charles, who arrived at that place with his fiancée Ernestina. Like a chivalric hero, he approaches her to rescue her from the impending disaster of the rains and the storm. For a few seconds she looks at him – a stranger to her – in a cold and indifferent way, after which she once again turns back towards the sea. Charles is thus, in a way, forced to leave her alone.

Sarah's enigmatic gaze is what attracts Charles and sets in motion his desire. The crucial quest for Charles lies in answering the questions – 'Who is Sarah?', 'Out of what shadows does she come?' (Fowles 94). In a sense the entire symbolic order of the narrative is built around this gaze, which functions both as an *objet petit a* as well as the unsignifiable trace of the real. At one point in the narrative, Dr Grogan tells Charles, 'don't blame yourself for falling for that girl. I think I know why that French sailor ran away. He knew she had eyes a man could drown in' (226). The apt expression, 'eyes a man could drown in', refers to the dual possibilities of Sarah's gaze – eyes that attract and then destroy the masculine subject. Indeed, Charles's devastation is somewhat similar to the subjective destitution experienced at the end of psychoanalysis.

Lacan says that the other, as a whole, does not cause desire; something in the other, for example, the voice or the look, causes desire. It is the blank look that Sarah gives Charles – a look which, for Charles, turns into a gaze full of mystery and in need of exploration – that sets in motion his desire and fantasy. At length, Sarah adds fuel to Charles's desire and fiction about himself by convincingly stating that he is the only person in the world who can take care of her, that he is a kind of omniscient, omnipotent and potentially heroic figure. Charles gradually starts to believe in this fiction and sexually fantasises about Sarah, leaving his fiancée for her and, after she disappears, deciding to spend his whole life searching for Sarah.

Sarah, as 'masquerade' in relation to the phallic myth, seems to deliberately affirm the mastery, heroism, virility and protective power of the male subject. For example, by paying attention to Charles, she enhances his confidence: 'As he talked, and was listened to with a grave interest, his disapproval evaporated' (Fowles 139). Again, when Sarah says, 'I have no one to turn to . . . I am weak . . . I have sinned' (140–41), she implies that Charles is the only person she can turn to, the only person who can save and protect her. She makes Charles believe that while he is strong, she is weak. This authentication of Charles as a superior being is remarkably intensified by the following conversation:

> [Charles] I am most sorry for you. But I must confess I don't understand why you should seek to . . . make me your confidant . . .
>
> [Sarah] Because you have travelled. Because you are educated. Because you are a gentleman. Because . . .
>
> [Charles] It is beyond my powers – the powers of far wiser men than myself – to help you here [in the countryside where Sarah is living almost as an outcast].
>
> [Sarah] I do not – I will not believe that. (Fowles 142–43)

Sarah, during such conversations, enhances Charles's superiority as a masculine subject. How does Charles react to this? He is 'obscurely flattered' (141). He gains an inflated image of himself which fits into the masculine position he desires. The sea tests (sea urchins) or shells she gives – 'they are all I have, to give' (165) – to Charles is also symbolic of her total surrender to this masculine subject. This is also the case when she completes Charles's unfinished sentences, thus bringing completion to his selfhood:

> [Sarah] I have no one to turn to.
>
> [Charles] I hoped I had made it clear that Mrs. Tranter –
>
> [Sarah] Has the kindest heart. But I do not need kindness.
>
> [Charles] If I can speak on your behalf to Mrs. Tranter, I shall be most happy . . . but it would be most improper of me to . . .
>
> [Sarah] Interest yourself further in my circumstances. (Fowles 140)

To the extent that Sarah acts as 'masquerade' vis-à-vis Charles, Charles seems to play the father with Sarah and we are told he has 'a desire to protect' her (248). On his first encounter with her, Charles was 'overcome by an equally strange feeling – not sexual, but fraternal, perhaps *paternal*' (71; italics mine). A similar description is found in the lines, 'for a moment she was like a child, both reluctant and yet willing to be cozened – or homilized – out of tears' (184). Charles, here, exerts a paternal authority over Sarah which also includes taming her of her 'wildness', and this gives him a sense of superiority. He may well replace Sarah's father. Her father sending her to boarding school is similar to Charles sending her to Exeter (for mental treatment). In both cases, the upholding of the masculine myth is involved. In both cases, Sarah obediently listens to the demand of the masculine subject and thus authorises the masculine position. Like other masculine subjects in the novel, Charles too takes pride in being charitable towards her, in offering to send her to a respectable asylum and in proudly bearing the expenses. Sarah's acceptance of these offers authorises his superiority.

Apart from performing as 'masquerade' in the various ways discussed, Sarah is also a 'symptom' of Charles's masculine position. As the signifier of Charles's repressed sexual desire, Sarah signifies the source of his pleasure. When Sarah tells Charles about her affair with the French lieutenant, Charles's fantasy is tellingly at work: 'He saw the scene she had not detailed: her giving herself. He was at one and the same time Varguennes [the French lieutenant] enjoying her and the man who sprang forward and struck him down' (Fowles 177). Charles striking down Varguennes is the myth of Charles's heroism authorised by Sarah's 'masquerade' that is ironically derivative of a fiction – the lie that she had a liaison with the French lieutenant. Sarah, here, becomes the 'symptom', that is, the means for fulfillment of Charles's fantasy and sexual desire. Sarah thus functions as 'masquerade' while authorising Charles's phallic myth, and as 'symptom' as she arouses desire in him.

Sarah and the Real of Femininity

While Sarah initially upholds the phallic myth, she gradually, sometimes simultaneously, becomes instrumental in its destitution. If Sarah's gaze at the outset of the narrative sets Charles's desire in motion, it also reveals to Charles his emptiness as a subject and gradually leads to his destruction. After his first meeting with her, we are told that Charles has so far experienced emptiness in his life and Sarah 'made him aware of a deprivation. His future had always seemed to him of vast potential; and now suddenly it was a fixed voyage to a known place' (Fowles 130). As he falls desperately in love with Sarah, who eventually stops reciprocating his love, he states, 'But you [Sarah] must say that [you never loved me]! You must say, "I was totally evil, I never saw in him other than an instrument I could use, a destruction I could encompass"' (452). He adds, 'This is my reward. To succour you . . . and now to know I was no more than the dupe of your imaginings' (359).

In fact, the novel ends with Charles confronting the harsh truth about the vanity of masculinity as exposed by his apparent separation from Sarah: 'And at the gate, the future made present, he found he did not know where to go . . . it meant thirty-four years of struggling upwards – *all in vain, in vain, in vain, all height lost*' (468–69). Metaphorically, Charles's realisation of the nothingness of his high-sounding masculinity is represented by the corpse in the final description: 'along that other deserted embankment Charles now begins to pace, a man behind the invisible gun carriage on which rests his own corpse'. Charles has 'at last . . . begun, though he would still bitterly deny it . . . to realize that life . . . is to be, however inadequately, *emptily*, hopelessly . . . endured' (470; emphasis mine). This emptiness is the truth of the phallic myth. This emptiness, Charles realises, is what characterises his selfhood. As is obvious, the destitution of Charles's masculine position is a result of Sarah's refusal to function as 'masquerade' and as 'symptom'.

While Sarah initially shows her dependence on the masculine subject by projecting herself as a weak being in need of assistance, she later tells Charles, 'It is as I told you before. I am far stronger than any man may easily imagine' (Fowles 359). Sarah reiterates her feminine position: 'I do not want to share my life. I wish to be what I am, not what a husband, however kind, however indulgent, must expect me to become in marriage' (453). She is a different woman here, not what Charles or the reader imagined her to be (a woman in need of protection and security from a male subject like Charles). Here, she shows the other side of her character which tries to do away with the masculine position. She attempts to make it clear that she had actually loved Charles as she says, 'There is one thing in which

I have not deceived you. I loved you . . . I think from the moment I saw you. In that, you were never deceived'. But she hastily adds, 'What duped you was my loneliness. A resentment, an envy, I don't know. I *don't know*. Do not ask me to explain what I have done. I cannot explain it. It is *not to be explained*' (358; italics mine). I claim that Sarah, here, is being very honest about her state of mind. She is certainly trying to express herself, but language fails her. It is in the gaps of the letters and in the ellipses that the feminine, as the real, exists. These gaps and ellipses are what constitute the holes around which the entire narrative develops. Sarah, at this point, becomes the unexplainable 'other' to language. This otherness makes her an enigma, even to herself. Sarah functions here not as 'masquerade' or as 'symptom', but rather as the real, as the feminine reveals itself through her in an unsettling way.

This aspect of Sarah's femininity figures in another point in the narrative in a remarkable way, as we discover Sarah's relation to her father (this point has unfortunately not received much critical attention). The narrator of *The French Lieutenant's Woman* tells us that Sarah has an uncanny ability to 'see through' people, to 'classify other people's worth' (53). Her father's vanity and worthlessness is devastatingly brought to light by Sarah. Her father is a vicar who believes in his ancestry, especially of once belonging to the gentry, even though his current social status is not very respectable. He boasts about it, in spite of his diminished social circumstances. In other words, his past was a source of pride and confidence. Due to this pride, he sent Sarah, his only child (and also the only woman in his life since his wife was dead), for education at a boarding school for those of a higher social status. Although she went to the boarding school, thus partially authenticating her father's false sense of social superiority, in the main Sarah did not view her father's boastfulness sympathetically. After she came back from the boarding school, she 'sat across the elm table from him and watched him when he boasted, watching with a quiet reserve that goaded him, goaded him like a piece of useless machinery (for he was born a Devon man and money means all to Devon men), goaded him finally into madness' (55). To prove his masculinity, to prove his worthiness to his daughter, he then bought a farm of his own. 'But it was cheap and bad . . . For several years he struggled to keep up both the mortgage and a ridiculous facade of gentility' (55). Metaphorically, her father's struggles are desperate attempts to veil the harsh truth about his weakness as a male subject – a weakness he is afraid to confront. The 'mortgage' and 'gentility' correspond to the two contradictory parts of his selfhood, and the unity of his selfhood depends on 'keeping up both' – it is a unity which is actually a falsity. However, he did not gain any authorisation or support from a female subject as Sarah vehemently resisted it, and so he went mad, quite literally, and was sent to the Dorchester Asylum where, a year later, he died.

As is obvious, both in the case of her father and Charles, Sarah's look – her 'seeing through', her 'gaze' which pervades the narrative (she 'saw through' the vanities of her suitors and made all possibilities of man-woman relationship impossible) – has a disconcerting characteristic about it which is so devastating for a man that it can potentially strip him of the façade of masculinity, thereby leaving him with a bare minimum which can easily result in a pathological disorder.

It would be a mistake to state that Sarah, as an individual, deliberately engages in acts of authentication and the dissolution of masculinity. Whatever Sarah does is strongly informed by the position she occupies – the feminine subject position which is not entirely included in the symbolic order or the order of language and which resists understanding, even to the woman herself. Sarah indicates this 'beyond' of understanding and articulation by referring to the fact that she cannot help her contradictory attitudes – that she does not know why she does certain things and that she cannot help doing those things. For example, as noted earlier, she says, 'Do not ask me to explain what I have done. I cannot explain it. It is not to be explained'. At another point, as noted in the epigraph of this section, she states, 'I am not to be understood even by myself. And I can't tell you why, but I believe *my happiness* depends on my not understanding' (455; italics mine). The key words here are 'happiness' and 'not understanding'. It may be said, at this point, that Sarah is not expressing her vanity, as Charles would like to think, but rather she is demonstrating an important psychoanalytical finding, that is, the Lacanian notion of Other *jouissance*. The Other *jouissance* is what can be experienced but not understood, known, or articulated, since articulation involves the intervention of language, which is predominantly phallic.

How Lacan understands the relation between *jouissance* and knowledge is important. Knowledge, according to Lacan, is motivated by some failure or insufficiency of pleasure – in a word, dissatisfaction. Displeasure relates to knowledge, pleasure relates to a lack of knowledge. In the Lacanian RSI schema, pleasure, or more specifically *jouissance*, verges more on the real (the unrepresentable) and knowledge verges more on the symbolic (the linguistic). Sarah seems to make a striking point here by linking 'enjoyment' with 'I do not know why', or linking the feminine *jouissance* with the real.

Conclusion

At the heart of the narrative of *The French Lieutenant's Woman* is the real of femininity which manifests itself through Sarah Woodruff and which direly needs to be avoided, represented and supplemented. As Sarah is known as the French lieutenant's woman, she can be categorised and thereby understood as a 'fallen woman'. As Sarah performs as 'masquerade' and as 'symptom', upholds the myth of masculinity (for Charles, her father and the reader) and remains the object of male desire and fantasy (in the eyes of Charles and the reader), she can be represented. However, such an easy and smooth understanding of Sarah is repeatedly disrupted throughout the narrative; disruptions which lead to subjective destitution (for her father and Charles) and discursive indeterminacy (involving the multiple endings of the narrative). There are moments in the narrative which show a significant interface between the real and the symbolic – moments when the entire domain of language and discourse is challenged and is almost on the verge of dissolution. Why does Sarah circulate a false story about her liaison with a French lieutenant? Why does Sarah ego-massage her father and, more elaborately, Charles, thereby creating and upholding a falsity only to eventually destroy the same? Why does she, at different points in the three endings, tell a different kind of lie about her present status? Questions of this kind refer to the impasse that the real of femininity puts forward for the phallic domain of the symbolic. The fictional domain of the narrative and the fiction of selfhood are, time and again, punctuated by the intrusion of the real. The symbolic has to rush in to come to terms with the unbearable truth of the real. In a sense, it is the real which triggers the symbolic, or it is the real of Sarah's femininity which demands symbolic representation. Fowles's narrative becomes a prime instance of what happens to a discourse that is constantly punctured by truth (embodied via the *dédoublement* of Sarah Woodruff) that has an existence and resists representation through phallocentric discourse. It also exemplifies the different effects exerted on a masculine structure by the imaginary, symbolic and real registers of femininity.

NOTES

[1] For more information, see Gilbert J. Rose's *Trauma and Mastery in Life and Art* (1987).
[2] Theorists include Carl Gustav Jung, Alfred Adler, Karen Horney, Melanie Klein and Anna Freud, among others. Schools include Ego Psychology, Object Relations School and Analytical Psychology.
[3] Lacan delivered a series of lectures constituting his Seminar of 1971 (*Seminar Book XVIII*) which he significantly titled 'A Discourse that Might Not Be a Semblance'.
[4] For more information, see Johan Huizinga's *The Waning of the Middle Ages* (1987), translated by F. Hopman.
[5] I am once again indebted to Professor Santanu Biswas for discussing the notion of women as gatekeepers of patriarchy.
[6] I have consulted the following secondary resources: Bruce Woodcock's *Male Mythologies: John Fowles and Masculinity* (1984), Robert Huffaker's *John Fowles* (1980), Olga Kirillova's "If the French Lieutenant Never Existed, He Should Have Been Invented" and Gilbert Rose's *Trauma and Mastery in Life and Art*.
[7] Lacan talks about a splitting (*dédoublement*) vis-à-vis the female subject. For more information, see Geneviève Morel's 'Feminine Conditions of *Jouissance*' in *Reading Seminar XX*.

REFERENCES

Barral, Lauren. 'Mystery, Knowledge, and Freedom in *The French Lieutenant's Woman*.' *HAL Archives-Ouvertes*. Web. 6 November 2017. <https://dumas.ccsd.cnrs.fr/dumas-00710543/document>.

Biswas, Santanu, ed. *The Literary Lacan: From Literature to Lituraterre and Beyond*. London: Seagull Books, 2012. Print.

Concise Oxford English Dictionary. Eds. Catherine Soanes and Augustus Stevenson. New Delhi: OUP, 2007. Print.

Evans, Dylan. *An Introductory Dictionary of Lacanian Psychoanalysis*. London: Routledge, 1996. Print.

Fowles, John. *The French Lieutenant's Woman*. London: Vintage Books, 2004. Print.

Freud, Sigmund. 'The Interpretation of Dreams Part I.' *The Standard Edition of the Complete Psychological Works of Sigmund Freud, Vol. 4*. Trans. James Strachey, Anna Freud, Alix Strachey and Alan Tyson. London: Vintage Books, 2001. Print.

Huffaker, Robert. *John Fowles*. Boston: Twayne Publishers, 1980. Print.

Huizinga, Johan. *The Waning of the Middle Ages*. Trans. F. Hopman. London: Penguin Books, 1987. Print.

Kirillova, Olga. 'If the French Lieutenant Never Existed, He Should Have Been Invented.' *Lacan Dot Com*. Web. 6 November 2017. <http://www.lacan.com/olgak.htm>.

Lacan, Jacques. *Écrits: The First Complete Edition in English*. Trans. Bruce Fink. New York: W. W. Norton & Co., 2006. Print.

---. 'Lituraterre.' *Scribd*. Trans (unofficial). Jack W. Stone. Web. 6 November 2017. <https://www.scribd.com/document/103886428/Lituraterre-english>.

--- .*The Seminar of Jacques Lacan Book II: The Ego in Freud's Theory and in the Technique of Psychoanalysis, 1954–55*. Trans. Sylvana Tomaselli. London: W. W. Norton & Co., 1991. Print.

---. 'The Seminar of Jacques Lacan Book VI: Desire and Its Interpretation, 1958–59.' *Lacan in Ireland*. Trans (unofficial). Cormac Gallagher. Web. 20 September 2017. <http://www.lacaninireland.com/web/wp-content/uploads/2010/06/Book-06-Desire-and-its-interpretation.pdf>.

---. *The Seminar of Jacques Lacan Book VII: Ethics of Psychoanalysis, 1959–60*. Trans. Dennis Porter. London: Routledge, 1997. Print.

---. *The Seminar of Jacques Lacan Book XX (Encore): On Feminine Sexuality, Limits of Love and Knowledge, 1972–73*. Trans. Bruce Fink. London: W. W. Norton & Co., 1998. Print.

Leonard, Garry. 'Spilling the Whisky on the Corpus.' *Reading Dubliners Again: A Lacanian Perspective*. New York: Syracuse UP, 1993. Print.

Rabaté, Jean-Michel. *Jacques Lacan: Psychoanalysis and the Subject of Literature*. New York: Palgrave, 2001. Print.

Rose, Gilbert J. *Trauma and Mastery in Life and Art*. New Haven: Yale UP, 1987. Print.

Saussure, Ferdinand de. *Course in General Linguistics*. Trans. Wade Baskin. New York: Columbia UP, 2011. Print.

Shakespeare, William. *Hamlet, Prince of Denmark*. Ed. Philip Edwards. New Delhi: Cambridge UP, 2012. Print.

Warburton, Eileen. *John Fowles: A Life in Two Worlds*. London: Viking, 2004. Print.

Woodcock, Bruce. *Male Mythologies: John Fowles and Masculinity*. New Jersey: Barnes and Noble, 1984. Print.

Wright, Elizabeth. *Speaking Desires Can Be Dangerous: The Poetics of the Unconscious*. Cambridge: Polity Press, 1999. Print.

Zare, Bonnie. 'Reclaiming Masculinist Texts for Feminist Readers: Sarah Woodruff's "The French Lieutenant's Woman".' *Modern Language Studies*, vol. 27, no. 3/4, 1997, pp. 175–95. *JSTOR*. Web. 6 November 2017. <http://www.jstor.org/stable/3195400>.

Zaretsky, Eli. 'Psychoanalysis and Postmodernism.' *American Literary History*, vol. 8, no. 1, 1996, pp. 154–69. *JSTOR*. Web. 6 November 2017. <http://www.jstor.org/stable/490236>.

Žižek, Slavoj. *Everything You Always Wanted to Know About Lacan (But Were Afraid to Ask Hitchcock)*. London: Verso, 1992. Print.

Chapter Five

Lacan in the Field of Culture

> I have another question, which has been troubling me for years, which is – What do Americans want? – I have the answer! A partial answer. They want Slavoj Žižek! They want the Lacan of Slavoj Žižek. They like it better than the Lacan of the Freudian Field, for the time being perhaps. The question is, do they want very definite concepts? Or do they want some room to wrangle? Some negotiating space? And that is the case with the concepts of psychoanalysis.
>
> Jacques-Alain Miller, 'Ordinary Psychosis Revisited'

Lacanian psychoanalysis is fundamentally a clinical practice. Whenever Lacan refers to issues outside of the clinical field – for example, philosophical and literary texts – he does so to 'elucidate a precise clinical problem' (Žižek, *How to Read Lacan* 5). The field of culture – cultural theories, cultural representations – has a place in Lacan in that it demonstrates clinical discoveries. In this sense, while the clinical constitutes the bedrock of Lacan's teachings, the cultural seems to have a sort of secondary status. Elucidation of Lacan in terms of cultural forms, or elucidation of culture in terms of Lacanian concepts, runs the risk of losing the essential clinical aspect of his teachings which are located in the context of clinical analysis of analysands. In fact, there is an ongoing cold war between clinical Lacanians and Lacanian cultural theorists. This is particularly evident in the way Slavoj Žižek's works have been received. Žižek has, quite consistently, used Lacan in the study of contemporary culture, politics and society. To provide just one aspect of his wide-ranging works, in the two film-presentations, namely, *Pervert's Guide to Cinema* (2006) and *Pervert's Guide to Ideology* (2012), and in his 1992 edited collection *Everything You Always Wanted to Know About Lacan (But were Afraid to Ask Hitchcock)*, Žižek shows how film-texts demonstrate and make clear Lacanian insights. Žižek proclaims that the clinical is everywhere in the field of culture and the demonstrability of Lacan's ideas in a non-clinical field further authenticates Lacan's teachings. This is how Žižek justifies the 'exclusion of clinical concerns' in his Lacanian cultural analysis:

> Lacan was first of all a clinician, and clinical concerns permeate everything he wrote and did. Even when he reads Plato, Aquinas, Hegel, Kierkegaard, it is always to elucidate a precise clinical problem. The very ubiquity of these concerns is what allows us to exclude them: precisely because the clinical is everywhere, one can short-circuit the process and concentrate instead on its effects, on the way it colors everything that appears non-clinical – this is the true test of its central place. (*How to Read Lacan* 5)

Žižek's works are extremely popular and have generated stimulating insights into the way we make sense of ourselves and our surroundings. At the same time, they have created controversies. Miller's response to the 'Lacan of Slavoj Žižek', as quoted in the epigraph, is a case in point. In fact, the American study of Lacan has mainly been along cultural lines, whereas the French (including Miller, Millerians and clinical Lacanians across the globe) have, in a sort of orthodox manner, preserved the legacy of the 'clinical' Lacan. Indeed, as Marie-Helene Brousse and Maire Jaanus confirm, 'Both in France and the United States, psychoanalysis in the Lacanian orientation has developed in two directions – psychoanalysis applied to mental suffering and psychoanalysis applied to culture' (vii). Rather than resolving the issue in terms of making psychoanalysis either clinical or cultural, the journal *Clinic/Culture* – the first issue of which was edited by Miller and Maire Jaanus and was subtitled *Applied Lacanian Psychoanalysis* – was founded to debate the apparent opposition between culture (social, collective) and clinic (concerned with the individual analysand). Furthermore, this journal attempted to move beyond the impasse created by this binary opposition by showing that in Lacan's teachings such an opposition, in one sense, is 'untenable', and that both fields could be addressed from within Lacan:

> [Clinic and culture posit] a paralyzing opposition between the individual and the social. Two cornerstones of Jacques Lacan's thought – 'The unconscious is structured like a language' and 'The social bond is a discourse' – allow a movement beyond this impasse. Lacan's reduction of the psychical apparatus to language, speech, and discourse renders this opposition untenable and enables culture and clinic, with their differing emphases, to focus on what is common to them both, the real of the symptom. (Brousse vii)

This passage carries with it a number of implications. First, Lacan talked about both the individual and the social, the clinical and the cultural. If his notion of the unconscious as 'structured like a language' is a clinical finding, then his 'four discourses' (master's discourse, university discourse, hysteric's discourse and analyst's discourse) are insightful commentaries on the 'social bond' between people. Second, the very notion of the psychical apparatus is constructed by and operative in the elements which are fundamentally cultural – language, speech and discourse. Third, what is common to both culture and clinic – as far as Lacan's teachings are concerned – is 'the real of the symptom'. In a sense, both the clinician and the cultural theorist focus on the real in relation to which discourses, representations and symptoms are built. In 'Lituraterre', as has already been noted, Lacan asks us to focus on the impossible-to-be-written or the 'holes and erasures' – the real – in a literary text (Rabaté 33). The real, in the clinical context, is the 'trash' or nothingness that the analysand experiences herself to be at the end of psychoanalysis. Like the individual, the social too is constituted by veiling the real. 'Symptoms' in both cases are a means to avoid the void.

Lacan should probably not be confined to the clinical context. On the contrary, the significance of Lacan in the field of culture is immense. The purpose of this chapter is to demonstrate how Lacan has been read, received and advantageously used in the domain of culture, especially in culture studies and critical theory. To accomplish this task, four issues are elaborated on – Lacan and film studies, Lacan and gender studies, Lacan and postcolonial studies and Lacan and deconstruction.

LACAN AND FILM STUDIES: ŽIŽEK'S READING OF HITCHCOCK

Slavoj Žižek's *Everything You Always Wanted to Know about Lacan (But Were Afraid to Ask Hitchcock)* is a milestone in film criticism, though not the first attempt at psychoanalytic film criticism. In his book, Žižek, among other Lacanian critics who contributed to the volume, uses Lacan to bring to the fore the psychoanalytic significance of Alfred Hitchcock's movies. The title of the collection, which attests to the sense of humour that pervades Žižek's works, is actually a parody of a 1972 Woody Allen film titled *Everything You Always Wanted to Know About Sex* (*But Were Afraid to Ask)*. The book is a collection of Lacanian readings of select movies by Hitchcock, offered by the likes of Fredric Jameson, Mladen Dolar, Michel Chion and others. Žižek, the editor of the collection, has written the introduction, a chapter on Hitchcock's sinthoms (Žižek spells *sinthome* as *sinthom*) and a concluding section on *Psycho*. The expression 'Everything . . . about Lacan' is used by Žižek to mean a number of key concepts which are demonstrated through, and which bring out, the truths of Hitchcock's films. These concepts include the subject and the big Other, the three orders (RSI), *sinthome*, the three clinical structures, intersubjectivity and truth, gaze, voice, desire, drive, *jouissance* and object *a*.

Žižek, using Fredric Jameson's system of classification, divides the history of cinema into three phases – realism (1930–40), modernism (1950–60) and postmodernism (1960 onwards). According to his reading, the realist film is marked by closure, conclusiveness, easy comprehensibility and a feeling of homeliness for the audience; everybody can enjoy the narrative, irrespective of their critical ability. Modernist and postmodernist narratives, on the other hand, demand the 'artifice of interpretation' to be understood and enjoyed. The modernist narrative is deliberately made incomprehensible. It is only when one is equipped with the interpretative tools that one 'recognises' the truth behind the disquieting 'mess' of the film, and this recognition leads to pleasure. Modernist films are characterised by the director playing the role of the auteur. It was the French magazine *Cahiers du Cinema*, and the writings of François Truffaut which were published in it, that promoted the auteur theory in the mid-1950s. The defining feature of auteur cinema is the notion that the director is the most significant person in the making of the film. Indeed, auteur cinema, as Satyajit Ray described Akira Kurosawa's *Rashomon* as indicative of, gives 'sustained and dazzling proof of a director's command over every aspect of film-making' (Ray 180). The director, in these kinds of films, is the auteur since he uses the camera in the same way a literary author uses the pen (hence the notion of *caméra-stylo*), and the auteur film, sometimes but not always the so-called 'art film', thus bears the 'signature' of the director. The postmodernist film-narrative, in comparison, is marked by a mix of high culture and low culture, leaving the viewer at risk of believing the film is easy to understand and appreciate. Even though, on the surface, postmodern films have a distinct mass appeal, viewers gain a different perspective on the film if they use the 'artifice of interpretation' (poststructuralist theories, for instance), a perspective which is completely estranged from their initial experience. They discover they had 'totally missed the point'. To quote Žižek:

> If, then, the pleasure of the modernist interpretation consists in the effect of recognition which 'gentrifies' the disquieting uncanniness of its object ('Aha, now I see the point of this apparent mess!'), the aim of the postmodernist treatment is to estrange its very initial homeliness: 'You think what you see is a simple melodrama even your senile granny would have no difficulties in following? Yet without taking into account . . . /the difference between symptom and *sinthom*; the structure of the Borromean knot; the fact that Woman is one of the Names-of-the-Father; etc., etc./ you've totally missed the point!' (*Everything You Always Wanted to Know About Lacan* 2)

According to Žižek, in the history of cinema, Hitchcock verges on the borders of all three '-isms'. Hitchcock's movies include ideological narrative closure, a typical Oedipal trajectory and the classic Hollywood narrative. Hitchcock was also a great auteur and, among other things, his cameo appearances in his own films and his subversion of classical Hollywood narrative codes constitute his 'signature'. But then, Hitchcock also epitomises the interpretive pleasure of estranging the most banal and, as 'a theoretical phenomenon' given the substantial and diverse body of academic responses to his works, is a postmodern event (*Everything You Always Wanted to Know About Lacan* 2). According to Žižek, however, chronologically his career is divided into three central phases. Films by Hitchcock the realist include all that came before *The Lady Vanishes* (1938). These films comprise themes like 'the Oedipal trajectory of the couple's initiatory journey', test of love and reunion (3). Films by Hitchcock the modernist range from *Rebecca* (1940) to *Under Capricorn* (1949) and include the theme of the female heroine traumatised by 'an ambiguous paternal figure' (4). And films by Hitchcock the postmodernist range from *Strangers on a Train* (1951) to *Birds* (1963) and encompass the themes of voyeurism and allegory and, most significantly, exhibit the perspective of the male hero whose access to 'normal' sexual relations is blocked by the maternal super-ego (5).

In addition, Žižek identifies the three 'Hitchcockian objects' that predominantly define the three phases in the filmmaker's career. Hitchcock the realist makes use of the so-called 'McGuffin' object. This object is described as 'nothing at all' or an 'empty place'. What this object in itself contains is not the issue. This object is important in that it sets in motion the story or motivates the characters to act. Such an object 'is totally indifferent and, by structural necessity, absent; its signification is purely auto-reflexive, it consists in the fact that it has some signification . . . for the principal characters of the story' (*Everything You Always Wanted to Know About Lacan* 6). This object is 'pure semblance' and it exposes the real dimension or the gap in the symbolic order of the film-text. Žižek defines this object as object *a*. The uranium bottle in *Notorious* (1946) is an example of such an object. The work by Hitchcock the modernist involves another category of object that Žižek characterises as 'decidedly *not* indifferent, *not* pure absence'. This object operates as a 'material presence of a fragment of reality' and is defined as 'an object of exchange circulating among subjects, serving as a kind of guarantee, pawn, on their symbolic relationship'. An example would be the cigarette lighter exchanged between the two 'strangers' in *Strangers on a Train*. Žižek suggests this second category of object enables the 'crystallization of the symbolic' as well as the symbolisation of the imaginary (8). The third category of object, used by Hitchcock the postmodernist, is described by Žižek as functioning as an 'imaginary objectification of the real'. 'This object', he writes, 'has a massive, oppressive material presence; it is not an indifferent void like the McGuffin, but at the same time it does not circulate between the subjects, it is not an object of exchange, it is just a mute embodiment of an impossible *jouissance*' (7). Examples of the third kind of object include the birds in *The Birds* (1963) and Mount Rushmore in *North by Northwest* (1959).

The three phases of the filmmaker's career are interconnected on the level of what Žižek calls 'Hitchcock's *sinthoms*'. Hitchcock, as an auteur, displays a continuum of visuals, motifs and repeated details like 'the woman who knows too much', 'the person who is suspended from another's hands', 'the glass full of white milk' and so on (*Everything You Always Wanted to Know About Lacan* 125). These motifs and details constitute *sinthoms*, which are to be understood as the constellation of signifiers that works as 'the inscription into the texture of a specific visual enjoyment' (126). The *sinthoms* do not involve a common meaning; rather, they pose limits to any systematised interpretation of a specific film-text. For Žižek, they are indicative of Hitchcock's compulsion to repeat. They enable us to establish links connecting Hitchcock's films which, on the level of their 'official content', seem to have nothing whatsoever in common (126).

The third part of Žižek's contribution to Hitchcock studies is titled 'In His Bold Gaze My Ruin Is Writ Large' and comprises his analysis of the classic film *Psycho*. To provide some of the key details of the plot: the first part of *Psycho* is the story of Marion Crane, who steals a huge amount of money from her employer and leaves home. She stops for the night in a motel owned by Norman Bates. She learns that Norman has a mentally-ill mother who does not want him to have a life outside of her. That night, while taking a shower, Marion is stabbed to death by a woman. The second part of the movie is an investigation into the murder. During the course of this investigation the detective, Arbogast, who enters Norman's house to talk to Norman's mother, is also murdered. It is finally revealed that Norman has a case of personality disorder and has been living two lives – his own, which is almost non-existent, and the life of his dead mother whom he killed ten years ago along with her lover. Norman's uncontrollable guilt made it impossible for him to accept that his mother was dead and he consequently preserved her corpse in the house and treated her as if she were still alive. He was also occasionally possessed by her. The killing of Marion (by Norman disguised in his mother's clothes) was a victory for Norman the mother over Norman the son in that, through this killing, the latter's object of desire was annihilated. At the end of the film, when Norman speaks in his mother voice and looks with eyes open but inert, it is revealed that the (deceased) mother has permanently taken possession of the son. In the final scene, Norman's face dissolves into the skull of his mother.

Žižek's analysis of the film comprises a set of points. Some of these are as follows. First, Žižek claims that Hitchcock's films contain two distinct subject positions – that of the director and that of the viewer. All the narrative figures and all the characters in his films assume any one of these two positions. This is also the way in which a relation between Hitchcock and his viewers is developed – a relation that Žižek, drawing upon the ideas of William Rothman, describes as 'benevolent-sadist' (*Everything You Always Wanted to Know About Lacan* 218). Hitchcock is notorious for manipulating, shocking and even exposing the hidden desires of his audience.

Second, Žižek explains the differences between the representation of Marion and Norman. Marion is a desiring subject; she is in a relationship and she is also someone who falls for money – a symptom of the capitalistic world (money being the object cause of desire). In clinical terms, Marion shows clear signs that, for her, the Oedipus complex has worked (and she hence can move into relationships with other men) and that she is like the majority of neurotics. The audience can identify themselves with Marion.

But this is not the case with Norman. The Oedipus complex has not been successfully completed and he hence cannot move into relationships with other women but remains fatally trapped in the mother-child dyad. He is caught in and even devoured by the maternal other. He has foreclosed the Name-of-the-Father. Marion has undergone the normal course of neurotic repression, has lost the maternal object and is thus caught up in the graph of desire which is based on this loss. For Norman, no such loss has taken place which is why he is caught up not in desire but in a primordial drive – all his libidinal energy is invested in encircling and preserving the maternal object. Norman behaves like a psychotic; his belief that his mother is still alive is a delusion. The audience cannot identify with Norman. They are baffled, shocked and intimidated by him.

Third, Žižek carefully considers the significance of the two murder scenes. Marion's murder illustrates the intrusion of the real. The camera is on a beautiful woman taking a bath in the motel following a conversation with Norman, perhaps implying an upcoming sexual liaison between the two. All of a sudden, a shadowy female figure breaks into the bath and stabs Marion. The murder of Arbogast, on the other hand, is a more endurable shock considering it comes after the first murder and is expected since the detective, curious to know more about Norman's mother, takes it upon himself to explore the old family house. It may be noted that in both cases the camera is on the victims, whom the audience identifies themselves with, and the sudden attacks are almost attacks on the audience themselves. Their shock is intensified by the fact that the camera does not clearly show the murderer. It is almost as if Hitchcock himself is murdering the viewer by way of a malicious camera movement.

Fourth, Žižek notes that the two murder locales are significantly different. The motel is a modern locale while the old family house is a traditional locale. On account of the tension between the two locales – between past and present – *Psycho*, for Žižek, is still a modernist film. In a postmodern *Psycho,* according to Žižek, 'the motel itself would be rebuilt as an imitation of old family houses' (*Everything You Always Wanted to Know About Lacan* 232).

Fifth, Žižek claims that the film, on a number of levels, produces subversive effects (in terms of subverting classical Hollywood narratives and a normative understanding of the human subject). For instance, the shower scene could serve as the logical end to the film, or at least, to Marion's story. Norman's story could be presented as a self-contained whole. The entire subversive effect of *Psycho*, according to Žižek, hinges on putting together the two heterogeneous, inconsistent pieces. Žižek points out that the structure of *Psycho* mockingly reverses Aristophanes's myth of androgyny. In Plato's *Symposium*, while talking about love, Aristophanes claims that at the dawn of civilisation there were three gender identities – females, males and androgynes. Each person had four hands, four legs, two heads and two sets of genitals. While each male had two sets of male genitals and each female had two sets of female genitals, those who were androgynous had one set of male genitals and one set of female genitals. These three types of people were huge and powerful and their actions angered the gods, resulting in Zeus deciding to cut each of them into halves. Consequently, each human being has two legs, two hands, one head, one set of genitals and is fated to look for their other half. Aristophanes explains the sexual desire of men for other men is derived from an originally male person being cut into two, the sexual desire of women for other women is derived from an originally female person being cut into two and the sexual desire of men for women, or vice versa, is derived from an originally androgynous person being cut into two. But in Norman Bates exists a woman and a man, mockingly reversing Aristophanes's thesis on androgynous humans. Aristophanes believed that the masculine and feminine halves of an androgynous person were consistent and harmonious, but Norman serves as an example which challenges the Greek myth as his one half is bent on dislodging the other. Žižek's emphasis, however, is more on narrative structure; how Marion's story and Norman's story – the neurotic's story and the psychotic's story, the woman's story and the man's story – are put together in *Psycho*, and how this structural heterogeneity is a challenge to the larger implications of Aristophanes's thesis as well as to the conventional mode of storytelling.

Sixth, Žižek describes Norman the mother, who completely takes over Norman the son, as an uncanny figure linked to the real. She is an absolute otherness and strangeness that unsettles and threatens the viewers. She is also the 'pure creature of the super-ego' – full of prohibitions against Norman the son – though 'totally powerless in itself' (*Everything You Always Wanted to Know about Lacan* 234). Drawing on points made by Michel Chion, a contributor to his collection, Žižek says that *Psycho* is ultimately the story of a voice in that it is the mother's voice which is in search of a bearer or a body whom it can possess. This voice resists identification and produces absolute Otherness for the audience and the characters.

Alongside voice, there is the aspect of gaze. Drawing on Lacan's theories, Žižek differentiates between glance and gaze. Gaze is not the glance exchanged between two people; it is how the person glanced at reads the glance from the position of his or her desire. In Žižek's words, 'The gaze is not the Other's glance as such, but the way this glance concerns me, the way the subject sees him/herself affected by it as to his/her desire' (214). Or, to put it another way, gaze is not related to the one who glances, but to the one who is glanced at. At the end of the film the glance that is thrown at the camera and thus to the audience by Norman is described by Žižek as empty and 'soulless' (257). It is a gaze generated by the monsters and the living dead. For Žižek, it is the ultimate hollow that constitutes the 'secret' of *Psycho*. It is this gaze that marks the manner in which Norman has irrevocably lost his identity in his mask and how, by killing Marion, he annihilated his desiring self.

It is in connection with this that Žižek describes Hitchcock as a director of the subjective camera. His masterstroke is the presentation of a gaze of the object-thing (the dead mother, the skull) that leads to the subjective destitution of Norman as well as of the viewers. In the end, all subjective identifications are cleared away and the subject is pinned to the object. The 'ultimate socio-ideological lesson of *Psycho*', for Žižek, 'is the collapse of the very field of intersubjectivity as medium of Truth in late capitalism, its disintegration into the two poles of expert knowledge and psychotic "private" truth' (262). In a sense, the pole of expert knowledge belongs to the domain of the symbolic and the site of identification, whereas the pole of psychotic private truth belongs to the domain of the real and the site that resists identification.

LACAN AND GENDER STUDIES: THE 'PHALLUS' AND THE MOVE 'BEYOND THE PHALLUS'

In the introduction to her 1990 book, *Jacques Lacan: A Feminist Introduction*, Elizabeth Grosz writes: 'while providing arguably the most sophisticated and convincing account of subjectivity, psychoanalysis itself is nevertheless phallocentric in its perspectives, methods, and assumptions' (3). Historically, there have been a number of conflicts between Lacanians and feminists (including Lacan's own students). Two instances are provided here. First, the expulsion of Luce Irigaray from Lacan's EFP after she published her 1974 thesis, *Speculum de l'Autre femme* (Speculum of the Other Woman), in which she accused Lacanian psychoanalysis as phallocentric. Second, Lacan prohibiting Michèle Montrelay, herself a Lacanian, from conducting her seminar in the EFP on the subject of male sexual fulfilment and femininity in men (as a response to Lacan's Seminar on feminine sexuality). This was after Lacanians accused her of being more a feminist than a psychoanalyst.

Even though Lacan's teachings have been criticised as 'phallocentric', it is a fact that, later in his career, he moved 'beyond the phallus'. The notion of feminine *jouissance* and ek-sistence of woman qua woman are concepts which bear testimony to this move. His thesis on feminine sexuality as developed in *Seminar Book XX* remains an invaluable clinical finding. In fact, many feminists have since made use of Lacan's psychoanalytic insight into feminine alterity, so much so that an entire critical trend of 'psychoanalytic feminism' has come into being. Rather than blaming Lacan as, ultimately, a phallocrat, the approach these feminists have taken is to utilise psychoanalytic ideas to sharpen feminist discourse. Moreover, Lacan's evolving ideas regarding feminine sexuality were also impacted by contemporary feminist movements in France, including the writings of Simone de Beauvoir. Rather than homogenising the entire field of psychoanalysis as phallocentric, a more judicious approach would perhaps be to see how feminism and psychoanalysis mutually inform each other. This idea has been succinctly articulated by British feminist Juliet Mitchell in her 1974 book *Psychoanalysis and Feminism*, even though she refers to Freud in her work and not Lacan: '[a] rejection of psychoanalysis and of Freud's works is fatal for feminism. However it may have been used, psychoanalysis is not a recommendation *for* a patriarchal society, but an analysis *of* one. If we are interested in understanding and challenging the oppression of women, we cannot afford to neglect it' (qtd. in Luepnitz 221).

Indeed, a psychoanalyst like Lacan is not prescribing a patriarchal order but largely exposing how patriarchy works. What is up for debate is how far, both on a personal and theoretical level, Lacan remained a phallocrat. However, Lacan's clinical exposition of how our universe is phallocentric would perhaps be useful for women's movements. In her 1982 essay, 'Jacques Lacan: Feminism and the Problem of Gender Identity', the Lacanian analyst Ellie Ragland-Sullivan does not consider Lacan a phallocrat as she claims, 'His description of the structures underlying the patriarchal order is certainly not an ideological support for maintaining that order' (11). Over the course of her article, she pointedly dismisses Luce Irigaray. The opening paragraph is unequivocally radical; Ragland-Sullivan states that Lacan considered Freud's formulation of the Oedipus complex to be incorrect and in its place offered his own theory of the paternal metaphor using the concepts of phallus, castration, desire and *jouissance*. According to her, Lacan thus largely differed from Freud as he introduced the element of the Name-of-the-Father into the mother-child dyad, thereby moving away from the mythological and biological implications of the Oedipus complex. The move is described by her as a shift from 'the Freudian sexual triangle to . . . [the realm of] symbolic effect', whereby Lacan 'leaves the scene of the incest taboo to dramatists and anthropologists'. This is why a feminist critic must be cautious while criticising Lacan. 'Sexual identity is not based on biological gender, or any other innate factor', as far as Lacan is concerned, 'but is learned through the dynamics of identification and language' (Ragland-Sullivan 11).

Ragland-Sullivan's opening paragraph – in fact, her entire essay – deconstructs the notion that Lacan was implicitly promoting male supremacy by making 'phallus' the central term in his psychoanalytic discourse. She contends that Lacan's interest is not biological or anthropological but structural, that is, 'the structural drama of patriarchy' inscribed in the structures of language and law. The formation of 'sexual identity', she asserts, is linked with the mirror stage: 'Identity is built up as a composite of images and effects – i.e., mental representations – taken in from the outside world from the start of life, which are developed in relation to the Desire for recognition and the later social requirements for submission to an arbitrary Law' (Ragland-Sullivan 7).

There are in fact two stages in the formation of this identity – the mirror stage (imaginary identification) and castration (symbolic identification). While each individual encounters these stages uniquely, the stages themselves play an instrumental role in the formation of every subject. Irigaray, however, misreads these two stages as outlined by Lacan and criticises him: in *Speculum of the Other Woman* (*Speculum de l'Autre femme*), Irigaray 'accuses psychoanalysis of a "masculine bias", of being arrested in the phallic phase, and equating female sexuality with motherhood' (Ragland-Sullivan 10). In her 1977 book *This Sex Which is Not One* (*Ce Sexe qui n'en est pas un*), Irigaray 'portrays Lacan as a profiteering cynic who gains pleasure, power and love from being a Master'. Furthermore, she considers the mirror stage as 'a phallic fixing of a child's sexual destiny' and thus as 'implicitly male' (10).

According to Ragland-Sullivan, Irigaray is mistaken on a number of points. First, the mirror stage, unlike what Irigaray thinks, is neither literal nor biological. The mirror stage is rather a metaphor 'for a mimetic process which occurs in intersocial relations with or without a mirror' (11). Second, Raglan-Sullivan explains, the imaginary identification which involves identifying with a centre (mother or specular image) outside of oneself is the crucial moment when 'human perception of difference starts out based on a lie' (11). The mirror stage is thus not marked by phallocentrism but by a fiction that structures and victimises the subject. Third, unlike what Irigaray thinks, the phallic signifier is not the penis but the first signifier of the symbolic order exposed to the child. Ragland-Sullivan elaborates on this by describing the signifier as the cause of disintegration of the subject's imaginary sense of unity with the mother and of a unified selfhood (following the sense of fragmentation at the mirror stage). Civilisation's success is derived from making the child learn to compromise, submit and repress the mOther by means of introjecting the Name-of-the-Father as the law.

In this context, Ragland-Sullivan extends Lacan's thesis by conceptualising what she calls women's 'double Castration'. At the moment of symbolic/phallic identification, there takes place a primary castration when 'both males and females experience loss, and gain an unconscious and a social personality' (Ragland-Sullivan 16). The loss is fundamentally a repression of the imaginary identification, or a sense of oneness, with the mother. The discourse that the subject is exposed to, in the aftermath of primary castration, is fundamentally a patriarchal discourse that castrates the woman a second time by displacing the 'mother within' onto the figure of the woman. The woman is thus perceived as 'someone to fear, deny, ignore, fight, conquer, or conversely to worship and enshrine'. This symbolic drama of 'double Castration', which paradoxically extols and denigrates women, is further justified by means of 'finding their validity in theology, biology, genetics, science, politics, economics, mythology, and so on' (16).

Ragland-Sullivan's clarifications regarding Lacanian notions of the phallus and castration and her use of the same for understanding how patriarchy subordinates women are, of course, not the only ways in which Lacan has been or can be used in feminist theory. With reference to the later teachings of Lacan, the notions of masculinity and femininity have not only been understood in imaginary and symbolic terms but increasingly in terms of the real. As has been elaborated on in Chapter Two, masculinity and femininity are not biological terms but rather psychological structures which can cut across biological barriers. In Lacan's emphasis on *jouissance* and its relation to sexual difference we see how he distinguishes between the phallic and the feminine/supplementary *jouissance*. Phallic *jouissance* is fundamentally a sexual enjoyment which is found as incomplete; phallic *jouissance* is what generates satisfaction through dissatisfaction. Feminine *jouissance*, on the other hand, is extra-linguistic/extra-phallic – something that can be experienced but not articulated. Whereas the masculine subject has access to phallic *jouissance*, the feminine subject can access both phallic and supplementary *jouissance*.

Gender differences are thus formulated by Lacan not in terms of biological differences but in terms of the subject's relation to language. It is based on this logic that the notion of 'male hysteria' is effectively accommodated within Lacanian psychoanalysis, whereas in conventional understanding which draws its support from the etymology of the word – the word 'hysteria' derives from the Greek root 'hysteron', meaning 'womb' – hysteria is considered a female disease (Evans 79). The same logic is also what extends Lacanian theories beyond a narrow heterosexual worldview. To reiterate a point already made in Chapter Two, the notion of sexual difference, formulated on the basis of masculine and feminine 'structures', does not promote heteronormativity since such a difference is equally applicable to 'homosexual' partners. 'In female homosexuality', Bruce Fink highlights, 'both partners could come under feminine structure, masculine structure, or one of each; the same goes for male homosexuality' (41). Lacan's ideas have consequently opened up new directions for gender and sexuality studies with, for instance, research being done to utilise Lacan in the field of queer theory.

LACAN AND POSTCOLONIAL STUDIES: ON THE RSI OF COLONIALIST DISCOURSE

As is well-known, the ideas of the so-called 'poststructuralist' thinkers like Michel Foucault, Jacques Derrida and Jacques Lacan (I say 'so-called' as these thinkers objected to the term 'poststructuralism') influenced major postcolonial theorists like Homi Bhabha, Edward Said, Gayatri Spivak, Frantz Fanon and Abdul JanMohamed, among a host of others. As far as Lacan's ideas are concerned, works like Bhabha's *The Location of Culture* (1994), or Fanon's *Black Skin, White Masks* (1952), or JanMohamed's 'The Economy of Manichean Ideology' (1985) have quite obviously benefited from Lacanian psychoanalysis in the formulation of postcolonial issues. Quite appropriately, *The Post-Colonial Studies*

Reader (1995) and *Key Concepts in Post-Colonial Studies* (1998) – two of the most-cited volumes which help with the mapping and preliminary understanding of postcolonial studies – bear testimony to how Lacan's ideas have influenced the postcolonial conception of 'the Other/other', 'Othering', 'Subject/subjectivity', 'Manicheanism' and other such issues. By 'Lacan's ideas', however, one does not mean Lacan's teachings as a whole. It is rather a curious fact that only a few of Lacan's texts were cited by these theorists. These texts are Lacan's 1938 essay on the family complex, Alan Sheridan's controversial English translation of select articles from *Écrits*, the original French *Écrits*, Lacan's *Seminar Book XI* titled *The Four Fundamental Concepts of Psychoanalysis* and Lacan's 1953 'Rome Discourse' titled 'The Function and Field of Speech and Language in Psychoanalysis', which was translated and annotated by Anthony Wilden and published in the form of a 1968 book titled *The Language of the Self: The Function of Language in Psychoanalysis*. The almost exclusive attention to these texts, however, is perhaps conditioned by the fact that Lacan's other seminars and *écrits* were inaccessible – and have, for the most part, remained inaccessible – to the English-speaking world. In this section I attempt to briefly present some of the ways in which Lacan's ideas have shaped the thinking of postcolonial theorists.

A major way in which Lacan has been used in postcolonialism is through his distinction between the imaginary other and the symbolic Other. Lacan's distinction between 'other' with a lowercase 'o' and 'Other' with an uppercase 'o' has been used to formulate the distinction and relation between the colonised other and the colonising Other. According to Lacan, the imaginary other is the specular image the child encounters at the mirror stage or the stage of the intrusion complex when he encounters his siblings. It may be noted that to turn the sibling other into an imaginary other is to objectify a person and reduce that person to the viewer's own terms and not explore the infinite otherness of the other. The encounter with the imaginary other takes place at a time when the child himself is 'an uncoordinated mass of limbs and feelings' (Ashcroft et al. 155), in opposition to the imaginary other who is considered both similar to and yet more autonomous than the child. Due to this opposition, the imaginary other is a source of anxiety, identification and mastery. Indeed, it is this other whom the child attempts to master and with reference to whom the ego of the subject is formed. In postcolonialism, the colonised others constitute the imaginary other as imperial discourse marginalises them on the basis of their differences from the colonisers. They also 'become the focus of anticipated mastery by the imperial "ego"' (155). As such, the colonial discourse is ambivalent; the colonised has to be mastered because she is, on one level, a source of anxiety for the coloniser. The colonised is different, but the different must be subjugated or rendered inferior. The otherness of the colonised – for instance, the unique value or truth value of the native culture – is not explored; the colonised is reduced to the way the coloniser defines himself and affirms his superiority.

The symbolic Other, on the contrary, is not the visual image but the big Other which stands for a number of issues including the 'names' and 'no' of the father and the absolute and abstract addressee for the subject (language, mOther, the unconscious and so on – in opposition to the specular other). The subject is caught up in the symbolic Other and is produced by it. For Lacan, the task of the signifier, which constitutes the symbolic, is to represent the subject for another signifier – which is why the subject, as such, is produced in and by language. The child's entry into language, his becoming a 'speaking subject', is what leads to the formation of him as a subject (as different from the formation of the ego at the mirror stage). The symbolic Other is thus linked to what Lacan calls the 'paternal metaphor' – the event of castration or the substitution of the desire of the mother by the Name-of-the-Father. The prohibition is partly the prohibition of incest, on which the edifice of civilisation stands, and, as such, is triggered by the symbolic. The loss of oneness with the mother or the sacrifice of the desire of the mother defines or redefines the subject's desire; in other words, desire gets fundamentally linked to an impossible, always already lost, object. Law and desire are thus born simultaneously – since it is law (of prohibition and repression) that leads to the loss of the primordial object and thereby to desire.

In a number of ways, the symbolic Other is at work in the process of colonisation. First, it works in the form of 'imperial centre, imperial discourse, or the empire itself' (Ashcroft et al. 155), which constitute the imperial big Other. Second, the imperial Other dictates the terms which generate a sense of dependence and inferiority for the colonised and define the latter's identity accordingly. Third, the imperial Other functions as the absolute 'ideological framework' with reference to which the colonised is made to make sense of the world (156). Fourth, the sense of selfhood and subjectivity is perpetually 'located in the gaze of the imperial Other'. The colonising power is projected as having a 'maternal and nurturing function', as words like 'mother England' or 'Home' indicate (156). While talking about 'surveillance' as a powerful strategy of imperial dominance, Ashcroft et al. suggest that the gaze of the imperial Other – that which keeps an eye on the colonised from an elevated position – *objectifies* the colonised 'within the identifying system of power relations' and *confirms* the 'subalternity and powerlessness' of the colonised (207). Fifth, the colonised is 'inducted' into the imperial language – and by extension, is caught up in the entire symbolic network of the coloniser – whereby he is made to see and internalise that the coloniser stands for power and supremacy (156).

In this regard, there are two processes of 'O/othering' in colonial discourse. First, the imaginary othering – turning the colonised into an image of the different, the rival, the inferior – which makes the coloniser anxious to master, marginalise and degrade the other and institutes his 'imperial ego'. Second, the symbolic Othering – turning the coloniser's discourse into the absolute supreme 'imperial Other' – in relation to which the colonised is made to refashion his identity and undermine his native roots. These processes are interconnected as the construction of the imperial Other is also the process which simultaneously constructs the colonised other (Ashcroft et al. 156). However, it may be mentioned that even though the two kinds of O/othering are sometimes used in an overlapping manner by postcolonial theorists (though not by all; Spivak adheres to the technical difference between the two terms), what remains absolutely central to their arguments is how the very construction of self is completely dependent upon the O/other (156).

Abdul R. JanMohamed, in his essay 'The Economy of Manichean Allegory: The Function of Racial Difference in Colonialist Literature', thought-provokingly extends the imaginary and symbolic dimensions of the colonial discourse. The notion of 'Manicheanism' is central to this essay. Ashcroft et al. explain the term as deriving from the so-called 'Manichaean heresy'. This heresy, propounded in the third century AD, dismissed the dual nature of Jesus or the idea that Jesus was both Man (flesh, matter) and God (spirit). Christ was considered only as spirit, and the idea of matter, defined as evil, was dissociated from Him. Such an idea made Satan 'coeternal with God' and proposed that 'the two realms of spirit and matter were always and eternally separate and could never be linked' (Ashcroft et al. 119). The postcolonial usage of the term 'Manichean' involves the question of 'an extreme form of binary structure' that shapes the coloniser-colonised relationship (119).

JanMohamed's essay, which develops the idea of Manicheanism, begins with a critique of Homi Bhabha's 1983 essay, 'The Other Question'. JanMohamed claims that Bhabha's work is based on two unproblematic, unwarranted and unacceptable assumptions – the idea that the 'colonial subject' (both the coloniser and the colonised) manifests a 'unity' and that the colonial discourse is marked by 'ambivalence'. According to JanMohamed, the problem is aggravated by Bhabha's rejection of the theses put forth by Edward Said ('colonial power and discourse is possessed entirely by the colonizer') and Frantz Fanon ('definition of the conqueror/native relation as a "Manichean" struggle') (59–60).

Indeed, JanMohamed elaborately shows that the Manichean ideology – the supremacist ideology that transforms racial difference into moral and metaphysical difference – is what predominantly informs colonialist literature.

Within colonial discourse, the colonial authority, unlike what Bhabha thinks, is not confused or undecided about the meanings of things, or of their relation with the colonised (JanMohamed 60). Even if there is any 'evident ambivalence' in colonial discourse, that ambivalence is a deliberate strategy and inevitably indicates 'imperialist duplicity' which basically hides the Manichean ideology. In the final analysis, even those colonial narratives written by 'enlightened and critical colonial writers' end up positing oppositions on the lines of race and metaphysics, albeit subtly or unwittingly (61).

JanMohamed distinguishes between the two phases of colonialism by labelling one the dominant phase and the other the hegemonic phase. In the dominant phase, European colonisers directly coerce the natives on bureaucratic and military levels and the natives only passively give consent to this coercion (JanMohamed 61). Contrastingly, in the hegemonic phase the colonised accepts the coloniser's 'values, attitudes, morality, institutions, and, more important, mode of production' (62). He further distinguishes between the covert and overt aspects of colonialism, which respectively correspond to the materialistic and discursive practices. The covert form of colonialism involves a ruthless exploitation of a colony's natural resources. The overt form of colonialism, on the other hand, disguises this materialistic exploitation by creating a discourse of civilising the 'savage' or introducing him to 'all the benefits of Western culture' (62). The overt aim, JanMohamed contends, is embedded as an assumption in colonialist literature which ends up justifying 'imperial occupation and exploitation'. He asserts that if such literary discourse can show that the native is irrevocably barbaric or at least 'deeply ingrained' then the civilising mission of the coloniser, which is another name for exploitation of native resources, can be continued uninterruptedly (62). Indeed, a rigorous sub-conscious logic is at work which defines the interrelationship between the covert and overt aims of colonialism, both of which exploit the colonised. As JanMohamed puts it: 'Just as imperialists "administer" the resources of the conquered country, so colonialist discourse "commodifies" the native subject into a stereotyped object and uses him as a "resource" for colonialist fiction' (64). There is thus a 'symbiotic relationship' found between imperialism's discursive and materialist dimensions. Whereas the imperialist author constructs the 'linguistic presence' of the native by objectifying and commodifying the native and his stories, the imperialist administrator exploits the native on the physical and materialist level. Both these forms of commodification are equally heinous and inform each other.

Even though the Manichean ideology lies at its heart, colonialist literature, as a form of colonial discourse, cannot be homogenised. This is where JanMohamed, borrowing Lacan's terms, claims there exists a major division in colonialist literary texts between 'imaginary' texts and 'symbolic' texts. The encounter with the colonised Other (he uses the Other with an uppercase 'O', not strictly adhering to Lacan's distinction), as enacted in these literary texts, takes either an imaginary or a symbolic turn.

The imaginary text is the 'essentially specular literature' which, 'instead of seeing the native as a bridge towards syncretic possibility, . . . uses him as a mirror that reflects the colonialist's self-image' (JanMohamed 65). Such a colonialist text aims at representing encounters with the racial other but implicitly promotes European cultures as superior (65). JanMohamed makes distinct the following features of such imaginary texts. These texts objectify the colonised other and the approach to the alterity of the colonised is marked by aggression and rivalry. The native, made to function 'as an image of the imperialist self', ends up exposing the self-alienation of the coloniser. The authors of such imaginary texts promote and 'fetishize' a Manichean opposition whereby the 'native' is unequivocally projected as evil (65).

The symbolic texts, on the contrary, manifest 'the inevitable necessity of using the native as a mediator of European desires' (JanMohamed 66) – as opposed to reducing the native to an 'image' that justifies the coloniser's supremacy. The writers of such texts, JanMohamed explains, are firmly grounded in the 'egalitarian imperatives of Western societies'. They not only explore the differences between Europeans and the natives but also examine the supposed superiority of the assumptions, values, and habits of the colonisers (66). He divides works by such writers into two categories. The first category includes texts which are a combination of the imaginary and the symbolic – their emotive portions are imaginary and cognitive portions are symbolic. E. M. Forster's *A Passage to India* (1924) and Rudyard Kipling's *Kim* (1901) are two such texts which are 'conceived in the "symbolic" realm of intersubjectivity, heterogeneity and particularity but are seduced by the specularity of the "imaginary" Otherness' (66). The first type of symbolic text aims at fusing Manichean oppositions but, nevertheless, is incapable of transcending the imaginary order which promotes imperial supremacy. This is why these texts demonstrate the power of a Manichean binary in the colonial context more so than those texts which are covertly 'imaginary' (66). The second type of symbolic text engages in a rigorous examination of the imaginary mechanism of colonialist mentality and thus frees itself from the Manichean allegory. The novels of Joseph Conrad and Nadine Gordimer belong to this category. The writer of such a text recognises the impossibility of any kind of syncretism due to the fact that they themselves are trapped within the strict relations of power that constitute colonial society (66). However, be it to avoid the specular universe of colonialism or to critique 'fetishized' racial barriers, the authors of both types of symbolic texts have to pay a price. What is the price these writers might have to pay to 'avoid the narcissistic world of the colonialist' (81)? An impossible price – the negation of one's being. The ability to achieve a completely objective exploration of the Other implies the negation of one's own cultural assumptions which constitute one's very being. Even though JanMohamed does not mention it, it is perhaps on the level of the second type of symbolic fiction that an encounter with the real takes place. The realisation of the coloniser's being as trash, as litter, does perhaps have the potential to turn the colonialist's literature into a form of *lituraterre*. The novels of Conrad and Gordimer, in this sense, may be said to tend towards *lituraterre*.

LACAN AND DECONSTRUCTION: THE DEBATE OVER POE'S 'THE PURLOINED LETTER'

A major critical theorist who challenged Lacan was Jacques Derrida. Derrida's criticism of Lacan is best exemplified in his response to Lacan's reading of Poe's critically acclaimed story, 'The Purloined Letter'. An overview of the debate would help us make sense of the difference between Lacanian literary criticism and a Derridean deconstructionist critique of literature.

Simply put, deconstructionist literary criticism involves the idea that the meaning of a literary text is undecided, indeterminate and inconclusive. Any reading of a literary text runs the risk of proposing singular and absolute interpretation. This is especially the case with those conventional readings which rely on authorial intention – in the form of a biographical detail about the author, for instance, or considering the author as the 'origin' of the work – as the authoritative explanation of a literary work. In 'Signature Event Context' (1972), Derrida states that literary writing has an 'iterative' character and is 'orphaned and separated at birth from the assistance of its father' (8). This not only implies that a singular and absolute authorial intention cannot be deciphered but also that a literary text remains open to infinite kinds of interpretation. Furthermore, in a Derridean sense, one should be skeptical about literary representation of binary oppositions (villain vs. hero, for instance) because a literary text not only posits such binaries but might also subtly reverse or blur them. Yes, one ought to look at how certain terms, characters or ideologies are privileged or centralised at the cost of others being marginalised. But one also needs to highlight those parts of the text which problematise such privileging or which create an impasse to any conclusive interpretation. Deconstructionist critique also involves an exposition of how literary criticism risks being implicated in the fallacy of essentialism – positing a definitive meaning, for instance – if it remains unaware of how texts resist conclusive interpretation. In fact, a major part of Derrida's own writings involve interpretation of already existing interpretations. As he states in the epigraph to 'Structure, Sign and Play in the Discourse of Human Sciences' (1967): 'We need to interpret interpretations more than to interpret things' (351). The interpretation of a literary text might reveal more about the politics of interpretation than about the text itself. By implication, a deconstructionist reading needs to be aware of its own limitations as well.

Poe's story is the third of his Dupin trilogy; the two other stories being 'The Murders of Rue Morgue' (1841) and 'The Mystery of Marie Rogêt' (1843). The central character of the trilogy is a detective named C. Auguste Dupin, and these stories are considered to have paved the way for the genre of detective fiction. Poe was translated into French by one of his admirers, Charles Baudelaire, in the 1850s and 60s. This period marked Poe's entry into the French intellectual circle. It was followed by a number of French (psychoanalytic) interventions in Poe studies in the twentieth century, including Marie Bonaparte's Freudian analysis of Poe's life and works entitled *Edgar Poe: Etude psychanalytique* (1933), Lacan's reading of 'The Purloined Letter' (*Seminar II, Écrits, Seminar XVIII*) and Derrida's response to Lacan in his article 'The Purveyor of Truth' (*La facteur de la vérité*, 1975).[1] Poe's story occupied such a significant position in critical theory that in 1988 an entire collection of critical approaches to 'The Purloined Letter', titled *Purloined Poe: Lacan, Derrida and Psychoanalytic Reading*, was published by Johns Hopkins University Press.

Before comparing Lacan and Derrida's readings, a brief outline of the story is presented here. Barbara Johnson, in her oft-cited article 'The Frame of Reference: Poe, Lacan, Derrida' (1977), paraphrases the story in the following words:

> 'The Purloined Letter' is a first-person narration of two scenes in which dialogues occur among the narrator, his friend C. Auguste Dupin, and, initially, the Prefect of the Parisian police. The two scenes are separated by an indication of the passage of a month's time. In each of the two dialogues, reported to us verbatim by the narrator, one of the other two characters tells the story of a robbery: in the first scene, it is the Prefect of Police who repeats the Queen's eyewitness account of the Minister's theft of a letter addressed to her; in the second scene, it is Dupin who narrates his own theft of the same letter from the Minister, who had meanwhile readdressed it to himself. In a paragraph placed between these two 'crime' stories, the narrator himself narrates a wordless scene in which the letter changes hands again before his eyes, passing from Dupin – not without the latter's having addressed not the letter but a check to himself – to the Prefect (who will pocket the remainder of the reward) and thence, presumably, back to the Queen. (215)

The most striking aspect of the story is that, as Poe writes, even though the Prefect of Police apparently 'read aloud a minute account of the internal, and especially of the external, appearance of the missing document' (qtd. in Johnson 216), the narrator does not tell us what this 'account' actually involves. The letter is central to the story and shapes the intersubjective relationships between characters, but its message is never revealed.

Lacan claims that the two scenes at the heart of the story are structurally similar; the first scene is what he calls the primal scene and the second scene a repetition of the first scene. Each of the scenes involves three characters. The first scene takes place in the boudoir, with the Queen trying to hide a letter from the King when the Minister enters the room. The Minister notices the letter on the table and, over the course of his conversation with the King and Queen, replaces it with a similar letter he was carrying. The Queen notices what he has done but is unable to say anything for reasons unstated. The second scene takes place in the Minister's hotel room. The Prefect has been appointed the task to find the letter, which the Minister is using as blackmail. Unable to find the letter despite repeatedly searching the hotel room, the Prefect contacts Dupin. Dupin visits the Minister. During his visit he does not do what the Prefect did, which was to search the room from top to bottom, but instead deduces that the letter is where it should not be, that is, not hidden but in open sight. Scanning the room, he discovers the Minister has left the letter crumpled in an ugly, pasteboard card-rack hanging in the middle of the mantlepiece. He bids farewell to the Minister, deliberately leaving behind his snuff box. The next day he returns on the pretext of taking back his snug box. Having appointed someone to cause a scene on the street, Dupin seizes the opportunity when the Minister is distracted and looking out the window to replace the original letter with a replica. We are told that Dupin made it a point to write a few words in the replica so that the Minister would know, once he re-examined its contents, that he had been duped. This is Dupin's revenge for a past wrong committed against him by the Minister.

In his 'Seminar on "The Purloined Letter"', Lacan argues that each of the scenes is marked by 'three moments, ordering three glances, sustained by three subjects, incarnated in each case by different people' (*Écrits* 10). In each of the scenes, the first glance is that which 'sees nothing' (10). The King does not see the Queen's distress or the theft of the letter. In the second scene, the Prefect is completely ignorant of the location of the letter. The second glance is 'a glance which sees that the first [glance by the first person] sees nothing and deceives itself into thereby believing to be covered what it hides' (10). The Queen in the first scene and the Minister in the second scene are defined by this glance. In the first scene, the Queen takes pride in the fact that the King is ignorant of the letter, but she is fooled by the Minister. In the second scene, the Minister takes pride in the fact that the Prefect can never find the letter, but he is fooled by Dupin. The third glance is a glance that 'sees that the first two glances leave what must be hidden uncovered to whomever would seize it' (10). The Minister in the first scene and Dupin in the second scene are characterised by this glance: the Minister seizes the opportunity to steal the letter, which lies out in the open on the royal table, and Dupin steals the letter from the hotel room, where it is paradoxically hidden by being left out in the open.

The letter is purloined not only because it is stolen but also because it has a trajectory as it moves from one hand/receiver/destination to another. The letter is instrumental in shaping the intersubjective relationships between the characters. Moreover, the individuality of the characters is not important in the triangles they are part of; the important thing is the place they occupy in the triangles constructed around the letter, which ultimately shapes the characters' actions, thoughts and behaviours. Lacan describes these three positions as analogous to 'the politics of the ostrich'. The technique of shielding itself from danger is divided among three ostriches thus: 'the second believing himself invisible because the first has his head stuck in the ground, and all the while letting the third calmly pluck his rear' (10). Lacan claims that the letter, in Poe's story, produces an ostrich policy among the characters.

Lacan goes on to interpret the letter as an 'allegory of signifier' (Johnson 217). Signifiers are what constitute the symbolic network of language which, in turn, leads to the formation of the human subject. The symbolic also connects the subjects in their intersubjective relationships. The subject is, for Lacan, an effect of the signifier. The letter in the story functions by exerting effects on the characters even though no one is bothered about the contents of the letter. It is the trajectory of the letter, resembling the itinerary of the signifier, that orients the subjects. Johnson draws on Lacan's points to argue that the position of the letter within the group decides the actions of each person. Here, the character of the individual subjects is not important; nor are the contents of the letter. The letter does not constitute a unit of meaning, that is, a signified. It functions by producing an effect on the subjects exactly the way the subject in Lacan is considered to be the effect of the signifier (217).

Relying on Johnson's exhaustive analysis, I have provided below some of the key points in Derrida's criticism of Lacan's reading.

First, Derrida accuses Lacan of (a) considering 'The Purloined Letter' as an independent story and therefore not incorporating an analysis of how this story is linked with the Dupin trilogy as a whole and (b) reducing the story to a single meaning – the allegory of the signifier. Johnson notes that according to Derrida, 'To cut out part of a text's frame of reference as though it did not exist, and to reduce a complex textual functioning to a single meaning are serious blots indeed in the annals of literary criticism' (Johnson 218). However, Derrida's own reading of Lacan is no better than what he claims to be Lacan's reading of Poe, as he himself commits the same crime he accuses Lacan of committing. Derrida does not, for instance, explore the fact that Lacan's reading of Poe is just a small part of his Seminar (*Seminar Book II*), and it is with reference to his Seminars as a whole that the text on Poe should be read. Additionally, Derrida considers Lacan's text as containing a single unequivocal message.

Second, Derrida accuses Lacan of setting aside the very elements that constitute a sort of 'literariness' of literature (a notion which is, obviously, debatable). Derrida claims that Lacan, in his triangular schemes, does not provide a place for the narrator of the story. It is by eliminating the narrator that Lacan constitutes the triangular relationships in what he calls the two scenes of the story. According to Derrida, as Johnson notes, 'The elimination of the narrator is a blatant and highly revealing result of the way "psychoanalysis" does violence to literature in order to find its own schemes' (Johnson 222). Derrida believes that by bringing in the fourth reference, the narrator, Poe's story challenges the triangles that a psychoanalytic reading tries to develop. Derrida thus claims that there are quadrangles or 'even' numbers and not triangles or 'odd' numbers that constitute the structure of the story. Moreover, he argues that Lacan solely considers sets of three characters instead of sets of two. For example, the narrator and Dupin constitute a dual pair. Johnson, however, refutes Derrida's claims by pointing out that the narrator and Dupin cannot be considered a dual pair since their original meeting happened due to their rivalry over a rare and remarkable book they were both seeking. This book acts as the third reference point, thereby constituting not a dual but a triangular relationship.

Moreover, Derrida omits the fact that, in connection with the seminar on Poe, Lacan developed 'Schema L' (named because of its resemblance to the uppercase Greek *lambda*), which is not a triangle but a quadrangle comprising four elements – the Other (A), the subject (S), ego (a), and the imaginary other (a'). The schema, as Evans explains in his *An Introductory Dictionary of Lacanian Psychoanalysis*, demonstrates the opposition between the symbolic and the imaginary, or how the symbolic relation between the subject and the Other is blocked by the imaginary relation between the ego and the other (172). The quadrangular implications of Schema L must be used to understand Lacan's reading of Poe. It may also be noted that the number 'three', as in the three orders (RSI), is also somewhat undermined by Lacan himself through his four-ring Borromean knot (the fourth ring being the *sinthome*).

Third, there is a lack in the message of the letter. Derrida claims that Lacan uses this lack to exemplify the truth of castration; by putting meaning where there is a lack of it, Lacan has committed a mistake. The irony here is that Lacan never uses the word 'castration' in his seminar on Poe. Johnson hence retorts, 'Lacan himself, however, never uses the word *castration* in the text of the original Seminar. That it is suggested is indisputable, but Derrida, by filling in what Lacan left blank, is repeating precisely the gesture of blank-filling for which he criticises Lacan' (217–18).

Fourth, Derrida argues that in Lacan's reading of the story the letter is equal to the phallus. Although Lacan does not use the words 'phallus' and 'castration', only suggests them, it is nevertheless necessary to explain the implications of their association with the letter. Arguably, there are four such implications suggested by Lacan which we must note.

(a) The letter is a substitute for the phallus which the Queen does not have; this is what the idea that the letter *belongs* to the Queen implies. In a sense, the letter thus exposes and compensates for the castration of the Queen. Because of its association with the (maternal) phallus, castration and woman (the Queen), the letter feminises or castrates those who hold it over the course of the story.

(b) The association of the letter with the maternal phallus (phallus that fills in the lack that figuratively defines the mother, for the child) is substantiated by the analogy between 'the shape of the fireplace from the centre of whose mantelpiece the letter is found hanging' and the 'point on a woman's anatomy from which the phallus is missing' (Johnson 225).

(c) For Lacan, the letter's significance in Poe's story derives from its materiality and not from its message. This materiality is defined by the fact that the letter is indivisible – the letter, torn or crumbled, will still have the same significance. Derrida claims that such a notion is necessary for Lacan's conception of the phallus; the integrity of the phallus, which is an essential aspect of psychoanalysis, is hereby upheld through the notion of the letter's indivisibility.

(d) For Lacan, the trajectory of the purloined letter shows that 'a letter always arrives at its destination' (*Écrits* 30). Derrida completely opposes this claim by stating that such an idea implies the possibility of an unequivocal meaning and makes the letter (signifier) equivalent to its destination (signified). If the return of the letter qua the phallus to the Queen implies the inevitable reaching of the letter to its destination, then such an idea, according to Derrida, serves psychoanalysis well. This is what constitutes the phallogocentrism of psychoanalysis, and in Derrida's reading this phallogocentrism ends up mercilessly repressing 'the uncontrollable multiplicity of ambiguities,

> the disseminating play of *writing*, which irreducibly transgresses any unequivocal meaning' (Johnson 226).

How tenable is Derrida's criticism of Lacan? The phallogocentrism that is claimed to be Lacan's flaw – both by a number of feminists and by Derrida – has already been challenged in this chapter in the section 'Lacan and Gender Studies'. On the other hand, Derrida's objection to Lacan's statement that the letter always reaches its destination has been refuted by both Johnson and Žižek. It would be wrong to assume that, in this statement, Lacan is foreclosing Derridean theses on undecidability, indeterminacy and inconclusiveness that characterise the relation between the signifier and the signified. This is because Lacan's concerns are different from such Derridean concerns. One of the most elaborate interpretations of Lacan's statement has been offered by Žižek.

In his book *Enjoy Your Symptom: Jacques Lacan in Hollywood and Out* (1992), Žižek begins his discussion with a section titled 'Why Does a Letter Always Arrive at Its Destination?' He claims that Derrida's objection to Lacan's statement does not constitute 'a refined theoretical sensitivity' but rather is 'a primordial response of common sense' (9). Lacan's idea that the letter always reaches its destination should not be dismissed in terms of commonsensical objections like the letter getting lost or failing to reach its correct recipient. Lacan's concerns are far more technical. On a preliminary level, Žižek gives the example of 'the limit case of a letter *without* addressee, of what is called in German *Flaschenpost,* a message in a bottle thrown into the sea from an island after shipwreck' (10). The moment the message in a bottle is thrown into the water, it reaches its destination, where destination does not stand for an empirical other but for the big Other. More precisely, the letter reaches its destination the very moment it is 'put in circulation' or the moment the sender 'externalises' the message. To put the letter in circulation is to deliver it to the big Other; 'the moment the Other takes cognizance of the letter . . . [it] disburdens the sender of responsibility for it' (10).

Žižek, however, goes deeper into the problem and demonstrates that Lacan's statement is justified on three levels – the imaginary or on the level of 'imaginary (mis)recognition', the symbolic, or on the level of 'symbolic circuit', and the real, or on the level of 'real encounter'.

Žižek claims that, on the imaginary level, the letter always reaches its destination 'since its destination is wherever it arrives' (*Enjoy Your Symptom* 10). The destination of the letter, in this sense, is not predetermined but rather depends on contingent factors. Žižek explains the contingency of the destination of the letter in terms of the following joke: 'Daddy was born in Manchester, Mummy in Bristol and I in London: strange that the three of us should have met!' (10). The meeting of these three people is marked by contingency. The letter, once it leaves the sender, always reaches somewhere – the right or the wrong destination – depending on contingent factors. From another perspective, the 'call of the ideological big Other' (12), like Nation, Democracy, Party, God and so on, is a letter which reaches its destination in those who (mis)recognise (*méconnaissance*, related to the imaginary) themselves as the addressee of that call. Žižek says that he who recognises himself as the addressee of such a call is an addressee not because he was fixed as the addressee in advance, but because he *becomes* its addressee the moment he recognises himself in the call. '*This* is the reason why a letter always reaches its addressee,' Žižek writes, 'because one becomes its addressee when one is reached' (12). He refutes Derrida's claims by arguing that when one says the letter might miss its destination, one presupposes the addressee. Such a presupposition exhibits 'the traditional teleological trajectory with a preordained goal' (12). Explaining such an attitude in terms of the above-mentioned joke, the Derridean argument – regarding the letter missing its destination or going astray – 'discloses a typical obsessional apprehension of what would happen if my father and mother had *not* come across each other – all would have gone wrong, I would not exist' (12).

On the symbolic level, the letter always reaches its destination due to the basic premise that 'there is no metalanguage', which Žižek explains in terms of the following propositions from Lacan: 'the sender always receives from the receiver his own message in reverse form', 'the repressed always returns', 'the frame itself is always being framed by part of its content' and 'we cannot escape the symbolic debt, it always has to be settled' (*Enjoy Your Symptom* 12).

With reference to Poe's story, for instance, Dupin's vengeful message to the Minister in the replica is a return, to the Minister, of the message (of being betrayed, being fooled) he sent to the Queen. On another level, 'the letter arrives at its destination when the subject is finally forced to assume the true consequences of his activity' (*Enjoy Your Symptom* 13). The ending of Sophocles's *Oedipus Rex* serves as a relevant literary example of this where Oedipus is forced to accept the verdict of ostracisation and banishment that he himself had passed at the beginning of the play upon the undiscovered criminal who had killed King Laius. Žižek notes: 'Lacan defines "hero" as the subject who . . . fully assumes the consequences of his act, that is to say, who does not step aside when the arrow that he shot makes its full circle and flies back at him – unlike the rest of us who endeavour to realize our desire without paying the price for it' (13–14).

Additionally, the letter always reaches its destination because the repressed always returns to the subject. The formations of the unconscious would, for instance, be examples of the letter reaching its destination. If one follows Derrida and concludes that a letter might miss its destination, then one is, by implication, stating that the repressed might not return. It is also to be noted that the repressed and the return of the repressed are the same thing, that is, there is no repressed before the return of the repressed. In this sense, the letter (or the repressed) comes into existence the moment it reaches its destination (or returns).

On yet another level, the letter inevitably reaches its destination, in the sense that one (destination) can never escape one's fate (letter) that is constituted in the symbolic network of language. The very notion of subject is based on how she is constructed, or excluded, from the domain of the symbolic (law, logic, language, history and so on) – the subject's very existence is dependent upon her position in the symbolic. Every subject has to repay her debt to the symbolic order. The symbolic not only turns the individual into a subject, but also *returns* to ask for the repayment of its debt from the subject.

On the level of the real, a letter always reaches its destination since we will all inevitably die. Death is the real – the encounter which cannot be avoided. Žižek notes, 'the only letter that nobody can evade, that sooner or later reaches us, i.e., the letter which has each of us as its infallible addressee, is death. We can say that we live only in so far as a certain letter (the letter containing our death warrant) still wanders around, looking for us' (*Enjoy Your Symptom* 21). He also states that the imaginary, symbolic and real dimensions of the letter reaching its destination are not mutually exclusive: 'at the end of the imaginary as well as the symbolic itinerary [of the letter], we encounter the real' (21). With reference to Oedipus, especially in the context of what happens in Sophocles's *Oedipus at Colonus* (401 BC), Žižek draws attention to Oedipus's statement, 'Am I made man in the hour when I cease to be?' (qtd. in *Enjoy Your Symptom* 21). At Colonus, after the fatal incidents at Thebes, Oedipus is 'reduced to a kind of soap bubble burst asunder' and he finds himself as a thing of nothing. This is the moment when Oedipus's symbolic destiny has been fulfilled, but this is also the point when he gets a glimpse of 'a scrap of the real, the leftover of a formless slime without any support in the symbolic order' (21).

However, as Žižek clarifies, the Lacanian real is not only related to death but also to life itself. The tension between life and death, as between Eros and Thanatos, is not something that takes place in the domain of the symbolic; it is fundamentally related to the pre-symbolic (before the subject enters language) and extra-symbolic (that which ek-sists language) dimensions of the real. The very notion of life, Žižek explains, is alien to the symbolic. Not only that, the core element of life – enjoyment and surplus *jouissance* – turns out to be a source of traumatic shock for the symbolic order. In this regard, the letter always reaches its destination because *jouissance* always sticks to the subject – 'you can never get rid of the stain of enjoyment' and 'the very gesture of renouncing enjoyment produces inevitably a surplus enjoyment that Lacan writes down as the "object small a"' (*Enjoy Your Symptom* 22). Every act involving the sacrifice of enjoyment is linked to a surplus enjoyment produced by that very act. Human beings are inevitably caught up in the 'dialectic of enjoyment and surplus enjoyment' (22).

Thus, Žižek's explanation of Lacan's statement 'the letter always arrives at its destination' – a statement that Derrida vehemently opposes – indicates that Derrida has misread Lacan. Furthermore, as Johnson's reading of the Lacan-Derrida debate demonstrates, Derrida himself committed the same mistakes he accused Lacan of committing. It may be stated that, overall, the Lacanian reading of Poe makes some crucial points regarding 'letter', 'subject', 'lack' and literature, which the deconstructionist critique fails to mention.

NOTES

[1] For more information, see Derrida's 'Purveyor of Truth' in *The Purloined Poe: Lacan, Derrida, and Psychoanalytic Reading*.

REFERENCES

Ashcroft, Bill, et al. *Post-Colonial Studies: The Key Concepts*. London: Routledge, 2007. Print.

Brousse, Marie-Helene, and Maire Jaanus. 'Editors' Introduction.' *Culture/Clinic* 1. U of Minnesota P, 2013. Print.

Derrida, Jacques. 'Signature Event Context.' *Limited Inc*. Trans. Samuel Weber and Jeffrey Mehlman. Evanston: Northwestern UP, 1988. Print.

---. 'Structure, Sign and Play in the Discourse of Human Sciences.' *Writing and Difference*. Trans. Alan Bass. London: Routledge Classics, 2001. Print.

Evans, Dylan. *An Introductory Dictionary of Lacanian Psychoanalysis*. London: Routledge, 1996. Print.

Fink, Bruce. *The Lacanian Subject: Between Language and Jouissance*. New Jersey: Princeton UP, 1995. Print.

Grosz, Elizabeth. *Jacques Lacan: A Feminist Introduction*. London: Routledge, 1990. Print.

JanMohamed, Abdul R. 'The Economy of Manichean Allegory: The Function of Racial Difference in Colonialist Literature.' *Critical Inquiry* 12, no. 1 (Autumn 1985): 59–87. *JSTOR*. Web. 3 May 2017. <http://www.jstor.org/stable/1343462>.

Johnson, Barbara. 'The Frame of Reference: Poe, Lacan, Derrida.' *The Purloined Poe: Lacan, Derrida, and Psychoanalytic Reading*. Eds. John P. Muller and William J. Richardson. London: Johns Hopkins UP, 1988. Print.

Lacan, Jacques. *Écrits: The First Complete Edition in English*. Trans. Bruce Fink. New York: W. W. Norton & Co., 2006. Print.

Luepnitz, Deborah. 'Beyond the Phallus: Lacan and Feminism.' *The Cambridge Companion to Lacan*. Ed. Jean-Michel Rabaté. Cambridge: CUP, 2003.

Miller, Jacques-Alain. 'Ordinary Psychosis Revisited.' *Dissertation. xlix.info.* Trans. Adrian Rice. Web. 13 Mar 2017. <http://www.dissertation.xlibx.info/d1-psychology/728794-1-i-want-first-congratulate-marie-h-l-ne-brousse-for-organising-t.php>.

Rabaté, Jean-Michel. *Jacques Lacan: Psychoanalysis and the Subject of Literature*. New York: Palgrave, 2001. Print.

Ragland-Sullivan, Ellie. 'Jacques Lacan: Feminism and the Problem of Gender Identity.' *SubStance* 11, no. 3 (1982): 6–20. *JSTOR*. Web. 03 May 2017. <http://www.jstor.org/stable/3684310>.

Ray, Satyajit. *Our Films Their Films*. Hyderabad: Orient Blackswan Pvt. Ltd., 2013. Print.

Žižek, Slavoj. *Enjoy Your Symptom: Jacques Lacan in Hollywood and Out*. New York: Routledge, 1992. Print.

---. *Everything You Always Wanted to Know About Lacan (But Were Afraid to Ask Hitchcock)*. London: Verso, 1992. Print.

---. *How to Read Lacan*. New York: W. W. Norton and Co., 2007. Print.

Conclusion

He who interrogates me also knows how to read me.
Jacques Lacan, *Television*

In *Television*, Miller questioned Lacan regarding his style of writing and the impenetrability of his texts. Alluding to the French poet Boileau, Miller asked how Lacan would like to respond to the statement, 'What is well conceived can be clearly stated'. Lacan's reply is now famous: 'Ten years is enough for everything I write to become clear to everyone' (45). As I reach the end of this book, I can sense how Lacan's remark is deceptively simple. What does he imply by 'ten years'? Does he suggest that we engage with his works (which were produced over a period longer than fifty years) twenty-four hours a day for ten years? What does he mean by the words 'enough', 'everything' and 'everyone'? Are these not rather problematic expressions? Does a Lacanian clinician have a clear understanding of *every* aspect of Lacan? Can a reader of Lacan, not clinically oriented, make sense of *everything* Lacan wrote? Does an English speaker, without any knowledge of French, fall under Lacan's *everyone*?

Given the scope of the book, I did not concentrate on many aspects of Lacanian psychoanalysis. For instance, clinical psychoanalysis, in the Lacanian orientation, is now practiced in many countries of the world. A history of the spread, scope and success of Lacanianism in the field of mental health would definitely have been worth investigating. The issue of Lacan's own clinical practice and how a Lacanian clinic functions could be included in the same research. The invention of new concepts like Miller's idea of 'ordinary psychosis', which Miller describes as a 'Lacanian clinical category' though not a term introduced by Lacan himself, could also be discussed in the same vein ('Ordinary Psychosis Revisited'). There are many topics I have touched upon which could certainly have been further developed. Some of these include the history of Lacan's conflict with the IPA, his use of mathematical ideas, his critique of philosophy and his approach to the question of religion. I also did not discuss in detail the various controversies that surrounded him. Nor did I elaborate on Lacan's personal and intellectual relations and conflicts with other great minds like Louis Althusser, Claude Lévi-Strauss, Michel Foucault, Jean-Paul Sartre, Simone de Beauvoir, Luce Irigaray, and Julia Kristeva.

The larger purpose of this book is not to engage in the impossible task of discussing everything related to Lacan but to trigger questions and curiosity in the minds of the readers. The motto is taken literally from Lacan himself: 'He who interrogates me also knows how to read me' (1). If readers of this book feel motivated to explore the Lacanian universe, then that in itself would be counted as a success.

REFERENCES

Lacan, Jacques. *Television: A Challenge to the Psychoanalytic Establishment.* Trans. Denis Hollier, Rosalind Krauss, Annette Michelson, Jeffrey Mehlman and Bruce Fink. London: W. W. Norton and Co., 1990. Print.

Miller, Jacques-Alain. 'Ordinary Psychosis Revisited.' *Dissertation. xlix.info.* Trans. Adrian Rice. Web. 13 Mar 2017. <http://www.dissertation.xlibx.info/d1-psychology/728794-1-i-want-first-congratulate-marie-h-l-ne-brousse-for-organising-t.php>.

Glossary

Anxiety: Lacan defines anxiety as the lack of a lack and thus places it in opposition to the idea of desire. If desire is triggered by the lack of an object, anxiety is experienced when the lack itself is lacking. Put differently, whereas desire is caused by object *a*, indicative of the primordially lost object, anxiety is caused when something fills the place of object *a* or when the lack related to object *a* is lacking. Ruling out anxiety as an emotion, Lacan defines it as the only affect that, unlike emotions, does not deceive us. Anxiety does not deceive us in the sense that being related to the real order it has the potential to expose the illusions of the subject's imaginary and symbolic identifications. 'Acting out', an impulsive action meant to draw the attention of others due to their failure to listen to the subject's words, and 'passage to the act', an impulsive attempt at self-destruction, are described as the last recourse against anxiety. Lacan's *Seminar Book X* (1961–62) is devoted to the discussion of anxiety.

Borromean Knot: See page 36.

Castration Complex: Lacan mentions two experiences of castration – castration of the mother and castration of the child. During the early phase of the Oedipus complex, the mother is considered by the child as castrated or as lacking something which Lacan calls the 'imaginary phallus'. That is the first castration. The second castration takes place when the subject realises he cannot be the object of his mother's desire because he himself is, in some respects, 'lacking'. Castration of the subject involves a renunciation of desire of the mother and *jouissance*. The outcome of castration is symbolic identification, that is, identification with the 'name' and 'no' of the father or with logic, language, and law. By implication, castration involves the formation of the ego-ideal and super-ego.

Cogito: The concept of *cogito* – from René Descartes's dictum '*cogito ergo sum*', translated as 'I think therefore I am' – offers a particular notion of selfhood characterised by certainty, autonomy, indivisibility, consciousness and knowability. One primary criticism of Cartesian *cogito* which Lacan offers is that the 'I' in Descartes's 'I think' is not the same as the 'I' in 'I am' since there is an unrecognised split on a number of levels: between the thinking 'I' and being 'I', between the unconscious and consciousness, between the subject as something and subject as nothing. It is this division which turns the individual into a 'barred subject' or one who is barred from knowing his unconscious thoughts or from realising the truth of his being as 'trash'. Lacan refers to the Cartesian dictum to articulate the psychoanalytic conception of the subject. For instance, he rewrites the dictum to read '*cogito ergo es*' or 'I think therefore you are, or I think therefore Id is', where '*es*' is Latin for 'you are' and German for 'Id'.

Desire: According to Lacan, desire refers to both desire for an object and desire to be an object of the Other's desire. For Lacan, during the Oedipus complex the child not only desires the mother but desires to be the sole object of the mother's desire. By positing the phallus as the 'imaginary' object that he thinks the mother lacks, he desires embodying the phallus. In this sense, desire does not relate to an object but rather to the lack or loss of an object. Additionally, to mould one's desire in accordance with the desire of the other is key to Lacan's conclusion that man's desire is the other's desire. Furthermore, the object of desire is defined by Lacan as 'metonymical' because it is always 'part object', or substitute object, as the original object (mother) is primordially lost. This metonymical object does not fulfil desire but causes it – in fact, it is the *source* of man's desire. Lacan hence talks about 'object cause' (object *a*) instead of object *per se*. He explains the notion of desire as something that seeks recognition and not fulfilment. Lacan also relates desire to his understanding of 'ethics of psychoanalysis'. For him, from the perspective of psychoanalysis, the experience of guilt is derived from attempting to recover or articulate or follow one's own desire instead of the desire of the other. Accessing one's desire is what constitutes the only good – in the ethical sense. However, one always has to pay a price for accessing and pursuing one's desire. Lacan's discussion of desire is not confined to the desire of the analysand. He also talks about the desire of the analyst which must be annihilated. The analyst must surrender all notions of authority and domination since he has to reduce himself to an object – the object *a*, that is, the 'object cause' of the analysand's desire. By playing such a role, the analyst helps the analysand recognise truths about his unconscious.

Drive: Drive is a key concept in Lacan's understanding of human sexuality. For Lacan, human sexuality is different from animal sexuality precisely because the so-called 'instinct' that defines the latter has to be curbed and moulded for the former to be in accordance with the norms of civilisation. Lacan replaces 'instinct' with 'drive' while developing the concept of human sexuality. Drives are divided into four categories corresponding to four objects: breast is the object of oral drive, faeces the object of anal drive, gaze the object of scopic drive and voice the object of invocatory drive. Drive, however, is not just related to sexuality; Lacan links it to death in terms of 'death drive'. On one level, the death drive is a push towards suffering, destruction and death which characterise every organism (this can be seen via the push to return to an original inanimate state of existence). Lacan also relates death drive to *jouissance* in that *jouissance* involves a suffering which offers satisfaction. In a sense, every drive involves *jouissance* and thus is a form of death drive.

Écrits: Lacan's psychoanalytic works are generically divided into two categories – his weekly lectures or seminars on psychoanalysis and his writings on psychoanalytic themes. The seminars have been grouped into twenty-seven books. His writings are largely derived from his seminars as most of them were written *for* the seminars, or were elaborate rewritings of issues discussed *in* the seminars. To differentiate his writings from his seminars, and to highlight their specific nature (clinical context, writing as different from speech and so on), Lacan called them *écrits*. '*Écrits*' literally translates as 'writings', but the word is kept untranslated in English for its unique connotations. Around thirty-five *écrits*, produced by Lacan up to the mid-1960s, were put together and published in 1966 in a single volume called *Écrits*. Some articles from this volume were translated by Alan Sheridan and published in 1977 while a complete and corrected translation by Bruce Fink was published in 2006. In 2001, another collection of Lacan's writings was published with the title *Autres écrits*. *Autres*, in French, means 'other'. This collection contains forty-four articles spread across eight sections. Although some of the texts included in this collection have been translated, *Autres écrits* as a whole has not yet been translated into English.

ECF (École de la Cause Freudienne): Lacan founded the School of the Freudian Cause in October 1980 in the aftermath of his dissolution of the EFP.

EFP (École Freudienne de Paris): The Freudian School of Paris was founded by Lacan in 1964 after his resignation from the SFP. He remained its president till 1980, when he himself dissolved the school.

End of Analysis: For Lacan, the end of undergoing psychoanalysis is when the analysand recognises the truth about his unconscious desire and realises the real of his being as 'trash'. Lacan defines the end of a successful psychoanalysis in terms of identification with the *sinthome*.

Fantasy: In a Lacanian sense, fantasy is a veil which saves the subject from encountering the real. Unlike the Klein group of psychoanalysts, Lacan refuses to reduce fantasy to the imaginary even though the very notion of fantasy is analogous to images on a cinema screen and hence to the notion of the imaginary (or identification with images). Lacan conceptualises the structure of fantasy vis-à-vis the symbolic register, which is the domain of law, logic, and language. He also develops the idea of 'logic of fantasy', explained in terms of the relation of the barred subject to the object *a*.

Identification: Identification is a process through which the idea of selfhood is constructed. Lacan talks about three kinds of identification. First, imaginary identification or identification with the mirror image or the image of the semblable other which leads to the construction of the ideal-ego. This process is also called 'projection'. Second, symbolic identification or the identification with the Name-of-the-Father (signifier for law, language, logic) which causes the construction of the ego-ideal. This process is also called 'introjection'. An encounter with the real may lead to temporary disillusionment with these identifications or to subjective destitution. Third, the subject's identification with *sinthome*, which takes place at the end of a successful psychoanalysis. *Sinthome* is understood as the fourth ring in the Borromean knot which ties together the real, symbolic and imaginary registers.

Imaginary: see page 12.

IPA (International Psychoanalytical Association): The IPA was established at the Psychoanalytical Congress held in Nuremberg in March 1910. Zurich was made the official centre of the IPA and Carl Gustav Jung was elected its first president.

Jouissance: A French term kept untranslated for its uniqueness, *jouissance* can be understood as orgasmic bliss and involves the paradoxical notion of pleasant pain or painful pleasure. *Jouissance* is placed in opposition to the notion of pleasure. *Jouissance*, related to the body, is an enjoyment that is limitless. Civilisation functions in such a way as to prevent limitless pleasure. This is why society sets various 'pleasure principles', that is, laws which regulate and channel sexual pleasure (through marriage, morality, abstinence, etc.). While the idea of pleasure involves enjoyment in accordance with pleasure principles, the idea of *jouissance* involves enjoyment that transgresses such principles. To be socialised is to learn to sacrifice or control one's *jouissance*. In his later teachings, Lacan distinguishes between phallic and feminine *jouissance*. Phallic *jouissance* is fundamentally a sexual enjoyment which is found as incomplete. Phallic *jouissance* is what generates satisfaction through dissatisfaction. Feminine *jouissance*, on the other hand, is what is extra-linguistic or extra-phallic, something that can be experienced but not articulated. The masculine subject has access to phallic *jouissance*, whereas the feminine subject can access both phallic and supplementary *jouissance*.

Lalangue: The term '*lalangue*' is Lacan's coinage and is understood in terms of its relation with language. *Lalangue* is different from language in a number of ways. First, language is composed of signifiers and belongs to the domain of the symbolic, whereas *lalangue* belongs to the domain of the real. Second, language is primarily a means of communicating meaning, while *lalangue* relates to affect – *lalangue* is what endows the subject with affects like anxiety. Third, *lalangue*, according to Lacan, is a kind of substrate ('the primary chaotic substrate') or underlying substance out of which language itself is constructed. Language is also the function of *lalangue*. Fourth, order, grammar and logic place language in the symbolic register, but *lalangue* is chaotic (almost like babble) and lacks such rules. In his later teachings, Lacan changed his famous dictum 'the unconscious is structured like a language' to 'the unconscious is structured like *lalangue*'.

Lituraterre: The term *lituraterre* is Lacan's coinage and is a combination of the Latin words *litura* (erasure) and *terre* (earth). Literally, the term might imply erasure on earth. In literary criticism it refers to how narratives contain erasures in the form of gaps and holes, ellipses and silences, obscurities and neologisms, the unknowable and the unspeakable, the traumatic and the void – all of which make the tasks of reading and writing almost impossible. *Lituraterre* is that kind of literature which does not veil these gaps but rather foregrounds them. Whereas literature, as conventionally written or understood, is considered to be a representation of reality (which is symbolically constructed), *lituraterre* is that unconventional avant-garde kind of literature which engages in foregrounding or encountering the real. *Lituraterre* thus paves the way for a new theory of literature.

Matheme: The term 'matheme' is Lacan's coinage and is a combination of the words 'mathematics' and 'mytheme'. Mytheme, a term taken from the works of Claude Lévi-Strauss, stands for the minimal unit of any mythological system. Mytheme is analogous to phoneme, which is the unit of sound of a specified language. Lévi-Strauss's structural analysis of myths was inspired by Ferdinand de Saussure's theorisation of language as a system of signs. Lacan's theorisation of psychoanalysis was influenced by the structuralist ideas formulated by both Saussure and Lévi-Strauss. Lacan used mathemes to formalise psychoanalytic concepts and prevent imaginary or subjective misunderstandings.

Metaphor and Metonymy See page 78.

Mirror Stage: The mirror stage is a crucial stage in the development of a child's subjectivity. It occurs between the ages of six and eighteen months. Unlike animal offspring, a human child, despite a lack of motor coordination at this age, is capable of recognising its own image as well as that of its surroundings in a mirror, and also engages in 'illuminative mimicry'. The specular image of the body appears coordinated as opposed to the uncoordinated body. This contrast generates a sense of rivalry, tension and aggressivity in the subject towards its own image. This tension is resolved through identification with the specular image and this identification leads to the constitution of the ego. Such a form of identification is also an example of *méconnaissance* or 'imaginary' self-knowledge, related to an illusory sense of unified selfhood and self-mastery. Recognition of the specular image thus leads to an essential misrecognition of the selfhood as unified. Identification with the specular image additionally causes alienation since the 'I' is literally located outside of the subject.

Name-of-the-Father: The original French version of this term reads '*nom du père*'. Lacan plays on the words *nom* ('name') and *non* ('no') – which in French have the same pronunciation – to indicate that Name-of-the-Father stands for both 'name' or language and 'no' or law, norms and prohibition. The successful completion of the Oedipus complex is marked by castration, which is defined by Lacan as a substitution of desire of the mother by Name-of-the-Father. This substitution, otherwise called paternal metaphor, is also described as phallic signification or phallicisation. Put differently, Name-of-the-Father is understood primarily as the first signifier that the child has access to, as the primary signifier which names and positions the subject in the symbolic order, and as the signifier of law, logic, and language that constitute social reality.

Neurosis: Neurosis is one of the three clinical structures in Lacanian nosography (the other two being psychosis and perversion). Neurosis is defined by the repression (*Verdrängung*) of the paternal function. Alongside this, the neurotic is one who bars the desire of the mother and avoids or sacrifices *jouissance*. Neurosis is of three kinds – hysteria, obsessional neurosis and phobia.

Object a (objet petit a): The lowercase 'a' in object *a* stands for the imaginary other (*autre*). Object *a* is related to Lacan's conception of desire and, in one sense, stands for the imaginary other as the object of desire. This object, however, does not fulfil desire but helps in its recognition. This is due to a number of reasons. First, object *a* is a substitute object as the original object of desire (mother) is primordially lost. Second, object *a* is only a 'part' in the sense that one does not desire the other as a whole but desires *something* in the other (the voice of the partner, for instance). Third, this is not really an object but rather an 'object cause' – object *a* is responsible for causing or triggering desire in the subject. Object *a* has other implications as well. For instance, Lacan considers it as the real that remains as a residue once the symbolic is introduced to the subject's psychical universe.

Other: See page 23.

Paternal function: The term father (*père*) has various connotations according to Lacan. For instance, in his formulation of the three 'moments' of the Oedipus complex in *Seminar Book V*, Lacan introduces the concepts of 'imaginary father' and 'real father'. While the first moment of the Oedipus complex comprises the child, mother and 'imaginary phallus' (or that 'something' which the child imagines the mother is lacking), the second moment replaces the imaginary phallus with an imaginary father (the imago of the father figure who is considered as controlling the mother's desire). The third moment replaces the imaginary father with a real father (the biological, potent, terrifying father). It may be noted that in Lacan's conception of the paternal function, the father is considered predominantly as a 'symbolic father' – one who embodies law, language and logic. Successful completion of the Oedipus complex breaks the mother-child dyad and results in the child getting caught up in the symbolic network of the 'name' and the 'no' of the father. In this sense, paternal function is composed of the sacrifice of the desire of the mother, controlling of *jouissance* and the internalisation of the Name-of-the-Father which together lead to the socialisation of the subject.

Perversion: Perversion is one of the three clinical structures in Lacanian nosography (the other two being neurosis and psychosis). It is defined by the disavowal (*Verleugnung*) of the paternal function. Alongside this, a pervert is one who makes it a point to bar the desire of the mother, set a limit to *jouissance*, and brings into being or asserts the Name-of-the-Father – the internalisation of which is disavowed in the aftermath of the Oedipus complex. Perversion is mainly of three kinds – sadism, masochism and fetishism.

Phallus: See page 23.

Psychosis: Psychosis is one of the three clinical structures in Lacanian nosography (the other two being neurosis and perversion). Psychosis is defined by the 'foreclosure' (a term introduced by Lacan to translate Freud's term *Verwerfung*) of the paternal function. To not internalise the Name-of-the-Father is to not bar or repress the desire of the mother, which is to say, in the case of the psychotic, the mother-child dyad is not successfully broken since the Name-of-the-Father does not shape their psychical universe. There is no symbolic identification for a psychotic, and this is precisely why there is no question of sacrificing *jouissance*. Psychosis is predominantly of two kinds – paranoia and schizophrenia.

Real: See page 12.

Seminars: The bulk of Lacan's psychoanalytic teaching is in the form of oral discourses delivered on a weekly basis to an audience mostly comprising psychoanalysts and analysts-in-training. His weekly deliberations were called seminars (or sometimes 'lessons' or 'sessions' due to their analytic significance). Seminars based on an annual theme constituted the book of seminars for that particular year. In 1951, Lacan started organising weekly private seminars with small groups of analysts in his Parisian residence. From 1953, however, the seminars went public and Sainte-Anne Hospital was used as the first venue. His so-called 'public' seminars were delivered over twenty-seven years and there are thus twenty-seven books of seminars. Even though Lacan took up a different theme each year, the seminars are, in one way or the other, interconnected.

Sexuation: Sexuation is the 'logic' of masculinity and femininity. Men and women, in Lacan's formulation, are not defined in terms of chromosomes or biological characteristics but predominantly in terms of *jouissance*. A man is someone who is capable of experiencing either phallic *jouissance* or feminine *jouissance* but not both. A woman is someone who is capable of experiencing both kinds of *jouissance*. The idea of sexuation renders impossible the sexual relationship between men and women as the real of femininity has the potential to disrupt the symbolic and imaginary myths of masculinity.

SFP (Société Française de Psychanalyse): The French Society of Psychoanalysis was established by Lacan and his colleagues in the aftermath of his resignation from the SPP in 1953. Lacan resigned from the SFP in 1963 following the IPA's demand that for the SFP to get official accreditation, Lacan, the practitioner of 'variable-length sessions', had to be deprived of the right to train new analysts.

Sinthome: According to Lacan, *sinthome* is an archaic way of spelling the word 'symptom'. Psychoanalysis not only involves the removal of pathological symptoms but also necessitates identification with or construction of a new kind of symptom. This new kind of symptom, called *sinthome* by Lacan, is explained as the fourth knot in the Borromean knot of the real, symbolic and imaginary registers of psychical experience. While the rings of RSI remain separate, a successful analysis leads to their being knotted together with the help of a *sinthome* which, theoretically speaking, brings psychical stability to the subject.

SPP (Société Psychanalytique de Paris): The Psychoanalytic Society of Paris was established in 1926. Lacan became its candidate member in 1934, a full member in 1938 and a member of the teaching committee in 1948. He resigned from the Society in 1953 following disagreements with some of the other members over his stance against the medicalising of psychoanalysis as a branch of neurobiology and his practice of variable-length sessions.

Subject: Lacan uses the term 'subject' to not only critique conventional notions of the individual, self, being and consciousness, but also to advance a radical idea of human subjectivity. Drawing on Freud's ideas, the subject in Lacan is understood as: (a) a divided subject – divided between the unconscious and consciousness, between being and thinking, between the idea of oneself as something and the idea of oneself as nothing; (b) subject of the unconscious – or how the agency of the unconscious determines human thought and action; (c) subjectivity defined in terms of the logic of sexuation – the masculine and feminine subjects; and (d) subjectivity defined in terms of clinical structures – neurosis, perversion and psychosis.

Symbolic: See page 12.

Variable-length sessions: A crucial and controversial clinical technique introduced by Lacan was the variable-length session. The idea behind this innovation was that the length of an analytic session cannot be predetermined but follows the logic of the analysand's discourse and the analyst's appropriate punctuation of the same. Analytic sessions need not be bound by a 'routine framework', the fixity of which might interrupt rather than facilitate the analysand's recognition of the truths of her unconscious desire. In order for these sessions to be effective, Lacan freed them of their temporal restraints and focused solely on the analysand's discursive thread. For Lacan, the ending of an analytic session is to be determined by the analyst, whose efficiency is defined by his ability to punctuate the analysand's speech (free association) and intervene at the right moment. By introducing variable-length sessions, Lacan provoked the ire of the IPA (which had standardised the length of such sessions at forty-five minutes). The consequence of this was that Lacan was eliminated from the list of training analysts on the IPA.

Texts for Further Reading

Biswas, Santanu, ed. *The Literary Lacan: From Literature to Lituraterre and Beyond*. London: Seagull Books, 2012. Print.

Clark, Michael. *Jacques Lacan: An Annotated Bibliography Vol. I.* London: Routledge, 2014. Kindle File.

Evans, Dylan. *An Introductory Dictionary of Lacanian Psychoanalysis.* London: Routledge, 1996. Print.

Fink, Bruce. *A Clinical Introduction to Lacanian Psychoanalysis: Theory and Technique.* Cambridge: Harvard UP, 1999. Print.

---. *Lacan on Love: An Exploration of Lacan's Seminar VIII, Transference.* Cambridge: Polity Press, 2016. Print.

---. *The Lacanian Subject: Between Language and Jouissance*. New Jersey: Princeton UP, 1995. Print.

Freud, Sigmund. 'Analysis of a Phobia in a Five-Year-Old Boy.' *The Standard Edition of the Complete Psychological Works of Sigmund Freud, Vol. 10*. Trans. James Strachey, Anna Freud, Alix Strachey and Alan Tyson. London: Vintage Books, 2001. Print.

---. 'Fragment of an Analysis of a Case of Hysteria.' *The Standard Edition of the Complete Psychological Works of Sigmund Freud, Vol. 7.* Trans. James Strachey, Anna Freud, Alix Strachey and Alan Tyson. London: Vintage Books, 2001. Print.

---. 'From the History of an Infantile Neurosis.' *The Standard Edition of the Complete Psychological Works of Sigmund Freud, Vol. 17*. Trans. James Strachey, Anna Freud, Alix Strachey and Alan Tyson. London: Vintage Books, 2001. Print.

---. 'Neurosis and Psychosis.' *The Standard Edition of the Complete Psychological Works of Sigmund Freud, Vol. 19*. Trans. James Strachey, Anna Freud, Alix Strachey and Alan Tyson. London: Vintage Books, 2001. Print.

---. 'Psycho-Analytic Notes on an Autobiographical Account of a Case of Paranoia.' *The Standard Edition of the Complete Psychological Works of Sigmund Freud, Vol. 12*. Trans. James Strachey, Anna Freud, Alix Strachey and Alan Tyson. London: Vintage Books, 2001. Print.

---. 'Some Neurotic Mechanisms in Jealousy, Paranoia and Homosexuality.' *The Standard Edition of the Complete Psychological Works of Sigmund Freud, Vol. 18*. Trans. James Strachey, Anna Freud, Alix Strachey and Alan Tyson. London: Vintage Books, 2001. Print.

---. 'The Interpretation of Dreams Part I.' *The Standard Edition of the Complete Psychological Works of Sigmund Freud, Vol. 4*. Trans. James Strachey, Anna Freud, Alix Strachey and Alan Tyson. London: Vintage Books, 2001. Print.

---. 'Three Essays on the Theory of Sexuality.' *The Standard Edition of the Complete Psychological Works of Sigmund Freud, Vol. 7*. Trans. James Strachey, Anna Freud, Alix Strachey and Alan Tyson. London: Vintage Books, 2001. Print.

Gallop, Jane. *Reading Lacan*. Ithaca: Cornell UP, 1985. Print.

JanMohamed, Abdul R. 'The Economy of Manichean Allegory: The Function of Racial Difference in Colonialist Literature.' *Critical Inquiry* 12, no. 1 (Autumn 1985): 59–87. *JSTOR*. Web. 3 May 2017. <http://www.jstor.org/stable/1343462>.

Johnson, Barbara. 'The Frame of Reference: Poe, Lacan, Derrida.' *The Purloined Poe: Lacan, Derrida, and Psychoanalytic Reading*. Eds. John P. Muller and William J. Richardson. London: Johns Hopkins UP, 1988. Print.

Lacan, Jacques. *Écrits: The First Complete Edition in English*. Trans. Bruce Fink. New York: W. W. Norton & Co., 2006. Print.

---. 'Lituraterre.' *Scribd*. Trans. (unofficial) Jack W. Stone. Web. 6 November 2017. <https://www.scribd.com/document/103886428/Lituraterre-english>.

---. *Television: A Challenge to the Psychoanalytic Establishment*. Trans. Denis Hollier, Rosalind Krauss, Annette Michelson, Jeffrey Mehlman and Bruce Fink. London: W. W. Norton & Co., 1990. Print.

---. *The Seminar of Jacques Lacan Book II: The Ego in Freud's Theory and in the Technique of Psychoanalysis, 1954–55*. Trans. Sylvana Tomaselli. London: W. W. Norton & Co., 1991. Print.

---. *The Seminar of Jacques Lacan Book III: The Psychoses, 1955–56*. Trans. Russell Grigg. London: Norton, 1997. Print.

---. 'The Seminar of Jacques Lacan Book V: The Formations of the Unconscious, 1957–58.' *Lacan in Ireland*. Trans (unofficial). Cormac Gallagher. Web. 20 September 2017. <http://www.lacaninireland.com/web/wp-content/uploads/2010/06/Book-05-the-formations-of-the-unconscious.pdf>.

---. 'The Seminar of Jacques Lacan Book VI: Desire and Its Interpretation, 1958–59.' *Lacan in Ireland*. Trans (unofficial). Cormac Gallagher. Web. 20 September 2017. <http://www.lacaninireland.com/web/wp-content/uploads/2010/06/Book-06-Desire-and-its-interpretation.pdf>.

---. *The Seminar of Jacques Lacan Book VII: Ethics of Psychoanalysis, 1959–60*. Trans. Dennis Porter. London: W. W. Norton & Co., 1997. Print.

---. *The Seminar of Jacques Lacan Book X: Anxiety, 1962–63*. Trans. A. R. Price. Cambridge: Polity Press, 2014. Print.

---. *The Seminar of Jacques Lacan Book XI: The Four Fundamental Concepts of Psychoanalysis, 1964*. Trans. Alan Sheridan. New York: W. W. Norton & Co., 1998. Print.

---. *The Seminar of Jacques Lacan Book XVII: The Other Side of Psychoanalysis, 1969-70*. Trans. Russell Grigg. New York and London: W. W. Norton & Co., 2007.

---. *The Seminar of Jacques Lacan Book XX (Encore): On Feminine Sexuality, Limits of Love and Knowledge, 1972–73*. Trans. Bruce Fink. London: W. W. Norton & Co., 1998. Print.

Leonard, Garry. *Reading Dubliners Again: A Lacanian Perspective*. New York: Syracuse UP, 1993. Print.

Miller, Jacques-Alain. 'Lacan's Later Teaching.' *Lacanian Ink*. Trans. Barbara P. Fulks. Web. 5 September 2017. http://www.lacan.com/frameXXI2.htm

Muller, John P., and William J. Richardson. *Lacan and Language: A Reader's Guide to* Écrits. New York: International UP, 1982. Print.

Nobus, Dany, ed. *Key Concepts of Lacanian Psychoanalysis*. New York: Other Press, 1998. Print.

Rabaté, Jean-Michel. *Jacques Lacan: Psychoanalysis and the Subject of Literature*. New York: Palgrave, 2001. Print.

Ragland-Sullivan, Ellie. 'Jacques Lacan: Feminism and the Problem of Gender Identity.' *SubStance* 11, no. 3 (1982): 6–20. *JSTOR*. Web. 03 May 2017. <http://www.jstor.org/stable/3684310>.

Roudinesco, Elisabeth. *Jacques Lacan*. Trans. Barbara Bray. New York: Columbia UP, 1997. Print.

Saussure, Ferdinand de. *Course in General Linguistics.* Trans. Wade Baskin. New York: Columbia UP, 2011. Print.

The Pervert's Guide to Cinema. Dir. Sophie Fiennes. Perf. Slavoj Žižek. P Guide Ltd., 2006. DVD.

The Pervert's Guide to Ideology. Dir. Sophie Fiennes. Perf. Slavoj Žižek. Zeitgeist Films, 2012. DVD.

Voruz, Véronique, and Bogdan Woolf, eds. *The Later Lacan: An Introduction*. Albany: SUNY Press, 2007. Print.

Žižek, Slavoj. *Everything You Always Wanted to Know About Lacan (But Were Afraid to Ask Hitchcock)*. London: Verso, 1992. Print.

Index

act, 27–28, 31–32, 70, 100, 126, 158, 171, 198–99, 204
acting out, 27, 31–32, 204
Aimée, 4, 8, 95–102, 105
alienation, 28, 31, 57–60, 187, 210
anxiety, 11, 23, 27, 40, 58, 83–84, 99, 103, 124, 134, 183, 204, 208
Aristophanes, 131, 175
Ashcroft, Bill, 182, 184–85, 200
auteur, 170–172
avant-garde literature, 137, 139–140, 209

Beauvoir, Simone de, 36, 148, 177
Beckett, Samuel, 131, 137, 140–41
bejahung, 104, 117–18
Bhabha, Homi, 181, 185
Biswas, Santanu, 33, 91, 132, 137–40, 147, 163–64, 214
Borromean knot, 36–37, 39–40, 42, 90, 111–12, 115–117, 170, 194, 207, 212
Brousse, Marie-Helene, 167–68, 200

castration, castration complex, 9, 20, 23, 31, 55, 58, 60, 62–63, 81, 90, 103–10, 117–18, 124–26, 178–80, 183, 194–95, 204, 210
Chomsky, Noam, 29
Clark, Michael, 7, 10, 14, 44, 47–48, 58, 60, 91, 214
cogito, 13, 16, 26, 29, 31, 54, 80, 205
Conrad, Joseph, 188

death drive, 25, 206
Derrida, Jacques, 143–44, 181, 188–200
desire, desire of the mother, graph of desire, 12, 19–27, 30–31, 34, 40, 60–65, 69, 76, 79, 81–82, 86, 89, 94, 101, 104, 109–10, 120–27, 133, 135, 136, 143, 149, 155–58, 162, 169, 173–76, 179, 183, 187, 198, 204–07, 210–13
disavowal (*verleugnung*), 18, 94, 125, 127, 211
Dora, 122–23
drive, 28, 30, 81–82, 107, 126–27, 169, 174, 206

ECF, 7, 44, 207
EFP, 7, 10, 43, 177, 207
ego, ego-ideal, ideal-ego, super-ego, ego-psychology, 3, 11–12, 15–18, 22–24, 26, 55–60, 63–68, 77, 80, 82–83, 102, 122, 162–63, 171, 176, 183–84, 194, 204, 209
end of analysis, 12, 32, 37, 40, 89, 134, 139–40, 207
enunciation, 80–81
Evans, Dylan, 8, 13–14, 16, 19–20, 24–25, 27, 29, 31–35, 39–42, 48, 55–59, 63–65, 76, 77–79, 81, 84, 89, 91, 124–27, 129, 137, 146, 164, 181, 194, 200, 214

Fanon, Franz, 181, 185
fantasy, 23, 31, 34, 60, 107–08, 120, 125–28, 133, 143, 149–50, 156, 158, 162, 207
father, 12, 18, 20, 23, 26, 35, 39–40, 56, 60–65, 79, 96, 108, 110, 112–15, 122–24, 127–28, 133, 142, 157–58, 160–62, 170, 189, 197, 204, 210–11
femininity, 24, 38, 55, 83, 86, 134, 136, 141–63, 177, 180, 212
film studies, 169–77
Fink, Bruce, 34–35, 45, 48–49, 51, 80–81, 83–87, 91–92, 94, 124–30, 164–65, 181, 200–01, 203, 206, 214–16
foreclosure (*verwerfung*), 18, 40, 65, 90, 93, 104–05, 114–19, 211
Foucault, Michel, 31, 181, 203
Fowles, John, 141–144, 150–65
Freud, Sigmund, 1, 3, 8–10, 13–21, 24, 27–28, 31, 43, 45–47, 54, 56, 61, 66–68, 70–74, 82–83, 88, 90, 94–96, 101–12, 117–30, 134, 141–44, 149, 152–53, 163–64, 178, 190, 211, 213–15
(works of)
'Analysis of a Phobia in a Five-Year-Old Boy', 129, 214
Beyond the Pleasure Principle, 8, 17
Civilization and Its Discontents, 24

'Fragment of an Analysis of a Case of Hysteria', 122, 129, 214
'From the History of an Infantile Neurosis', 103, 129, 214
Group Psychology and the Analysis of the Ego, 27
Inhibitions, Symptoms and Anxieties, 28
'Negation', 117, 129
'Neurosis and Psychosis', 19, 120, 129, 214
'Psycho-Analytic Notes on an Autobiographical Account of a Case of Paranoia', 129, 215
'Some Neurotic Mechanisms in Jealousy, Paranoia and Homosexuality', 8, 102, 129, 215
'The Ego and the Id', 102
The Interpretation of Dreams, 17, 66, 119, 164, 215
'The Loss of Reality in Neurosis and Psychosis', 19, 120, 129
The Psychopathology of Everyday Life, 66–67
'Three Essays on the Theory of Sexuality', 125, 128–29, 215
Wits/Jokes and their Relation to the Unconscious, 66–67

Gallagher, Cormac, 14, 35–36, 39, 49–52
Gallop, Jane, 2, 5, 44–45, 49, 215
gaze, 28, 30–31, 86, 127, 142, 155–56, 158, 161, 169, 176, 184, 206
Grigg, Russell, 6, 47, 49–50, 90, 92, 130, 216

hallucination, 8, 18, 90, 96, 103–06, 119
Hardy, Thomas, 143, 155
Hegel, G. W. F., 16, 28, 167
Hitchcock, Alfred, 64, 94, 144, 166, 169–76
homosexual, homosexuality, 34, 87, 102, 107, 125, 128, 181
Huffaker, Robert, 152–53, 163–64
hysteria, 19, 35, 93, 119, 121–24, 142, 181, 210

imaginary, 9, 11–15, 18, 20, 22–24, 26, 31, 33–34, 37, 39–41, 55–57, 59–65, 80, 82–83, 87–90, 105, 107–11, 120–23, 126, 132–34, 147, 150, 163, 172, 179–80, 182–85, 187–88, 194, 196–97, 199, 204–05, 207, 209–12
intrusion complex, 9, 58–60, 182
IPA, 1, 7–9, 11, 28, 39, 70, 208, 212–213
Irigaray, Luce, 177–79, 203

Jakobson, Roman, 20, 27, 73, 76, 78
JanMohamed, Abdul, 5, 181, 185–88, 200, 215
Johnson, Barbara, 190–96, 200–01, 215
Johnston, Adrian, 42–43, 49
jouissance, phallic *jouissance*, feminine *jouissance,* 11–12, 20, 24–25, 27, 31, 33, 38–40, 55–56, 63, 65, 81–89, 94, 126–27, 133, 136, 140–41, 144, 162–63, 169, 172, 177–78, 180–81, 199, 208, 210–11
Joyce, James, 4, 40, 41, 95, 111–17, 128, 130–36, 138–40
(works of)
A Portrait of the Artist as a Young Man, 113–14, 130
Dubliners, 130
Exiles, 115
Finnegans Wake, 40–41, 111–13, 116–17, 128, 138–39
Stephen Hero, 114
Ulysses, 113–14, 116, 130

Kant, Immanuel, 16, 24, 27–28
Kirillova Olga, 142, 152–53, 163–64
Klein bottle, 29
Kurosawa, Akira, 145, 170

Lacan, Jacques
(works of)
Autres écrits, 48, 132, 206–07
Écrits, 1–2, 8, 15, 44–49, 52, 57–58, 64–81, 92, 95, 103–05, 126, 130, 132, 143, 145, 164, 182, 190–91, 195, 201, 206–07, 215
'Family Complexes in the Formation of the Individual', 58, 60
'Guiding Remarks on a Convention of Feminine Sexuality', 46
'Impromptu at Vincennes', 32
'Kant with Sade', 46, 95, 136
'*Le séminaire livre* XXVI: *La topologie et le temps*, 1978–1979', 42, 49
L'étourdit, 46
'Lituraterre', 46, 111, 132, 134, 137–40, 146, 168
'Logical Time and the Assertion of Anticipated Certainty: A New Sophism', 43
'Mirror Stage as Formative of the *I* Function as Revealed in Psychoanalytic Experience', 45, 57–58

My Teaching, 1, 5, 47
'On a Question Prior to Any Possible Treatment of Psychosis', 46, 64, 95
Radiophonie, 46
'Science and Truth', 46
'Seminar on "The Purloined Letter"', 45, 191
Television: A Challenge to the Psychoanalytic Establishment, 32, 46, 49, 202–03, 215
'The Case of Aimée, or Self-Punitive Paranoia', 96–99, 100–01, 130
'The Freudian Thing, or the Meaning of Return to Freud in Psychoanalysis', 46
'The Function and Field of Speech and Language in Psychoanalysis', 9, 46, 66, 69, 131, 182
'The Instance of the Letter in the Unconscious, or Reason since Freud', 21, 46, 66, 72
The Seminar of Jacques Lacan Book I: Freud's Papers on Technique, 1953–54, 11, 15, 95
The Seminar of Jacques Lacan Book II: The Ego in Freud's Theory and the Technique of Psychoanalysis, 1954–55, 15–18, 50, 131–32, 164, 193, 215
The Seminar of Jacques Lacan Book III: The Psychoses, 1955–56, 18–19, 50, 93, 95, 105–11, 117–23, 130, 216
'The Seminar of Jacques Lacan Book IV: The Object Relation, 1956–57', 19–20, 50, 95, 124, 126,
'The Seminar of Jacques Lacan Book V: The Formations of the Unconscious, 1957–58', 19, 21, 50, 60–63, 92, 211, 216
'The Seminar of Jacques Lacan Book VI: Desire and Its Interpretation, 1958–59', 21–22, 50, 132, 135, 149, 164, 216
The Seminar of Jacques Lacan Book VII: Ethics of Psychoanalysis, 1959–60, 24–25, 50, 132, 147, 165, 216
'The Seminar of Jacques Lacan Book VIII: Transference, 1960–61', 25–26, 50, 95, 124
'The Seminar of Jacques Lacan Book IX: Identification, 1961–62', 26–27, 50
'The Seminar of Jacques Lacan Book X: Anxiety, 1962–63', 11, 14, 27–28, 50, 95, 204, 216
The Seminar of Jacques Lacan Book XI: The Four Fundamental Concepts of Psychoanalysis, 1964, 10–11, 28, 43, 51, 66, 72, 92, 127, 182, 216
'The Seminar of Jacques Lacan Book XII: Crucial Problems for Psychoanalysis, 1964–65', 28–30, 51
'The Seminar of Jacques Lacan Book XIII: The Object of Psychoanalysis, 1965–66', 30–31, 51
'The Seminar of Jacques Lacan Book XIV: The Logic of Phantasy, 1966–67', 14, 31, 51
'The Seminar of Jacques Lacan Book XV: The Psychoanalytic Act, 1967–68', 31–32, 51
'The Seminar of Jacques Lacan Book XVI: From an other to the Other, 1968–69', 10, 33, 51
The Seminar of Jacques Lacan Book XVII: The Other Side of Psychoanalysis, 1969–70, 10, 33–35, 216
'The Seminar of Jacques Lacan Book XVIII: On a Discourse that might not be a Semblance, 1970–71', 35, 49, 132, 137, 163
'The Seminar of Jacques Lacan XIX: . . . Or Worse 1971–72', 11, 35–36
The Seminar of Jacques Lacan Book XX (Encore): On Feminine Sexuality, Limits of Love and Knowledge, 1972–73, 11, 13, 24, 36–39, 51, 53, 55, 66, 83–85, 92, 141, 143, 165, 177, 216
'The Seminar of Jacques Lacan Book XXI: *Les Non Dupes Errent*, 1973–74', 13, 39
'The Seminar of Jacques Lacan Book XXII: RSI, 1974–75', 13, 39–40, 89
'The Seminar of Jacques Lacan Book XXIII: *Le Sinthome*, 1975–76', 13, 40–41, 51, 95, 102, 111–17, 128, 130
'The Seminar of Jacques Lacan Book XXIV: *L'insu que sait de l'une-bévue s'aile à mourre*, 1976–77', 41–42, 52

'The Seminar of Jacques Lacan Book XXV: The Moment to Conclude, 1977–78', 42, 52
'The Signification of the Phallus', 46
'The Subversion of the Subject and the Dialectic of Desire in the Freudian Unconscious', 46, 73
lack, 19–20, 27, 31, 61–63, 79–80, 88, 115, 126, 147, 149, 162, 194–95, 200, 204–05, 209
lalangue, 36, 56, 81–88, 208
language, 9, 12, 18, 20–22, 24, 29–31, 34, 36, 38, 40–41, 44, 56, 63–71, 73, 76, 78, 80, 82–85, 87–88, 93, 107, 109–13, 120, 123, 128, 131, 145–49, 160–62, 168, 178–84, 192, 198, 204, 207–11,
law, 12, 18, 20, 23,31, 38, 56, 61–63, 82, 85, 94, 109–10, 114, 127–28, 147, 151, 179, 183, 198, 204, 207, 210–11
Leonard, Garry, 148, 150, 165, 216
letter, 17, 21, 35, 43, 45–46, 72, 74, 111, 132, 136–41, 144, 188–200
Lévi-Strauss, Claude, 28, 34, 203, 209
litter, 111, 137–40, 188
Little Hans, 4, 15, 20, 40, 124, 126
lituraterre, 4–5, 132, 134, 136–41, 188, 208–09
Loewenstein, Rudolph, 7, 95

Manicheanism, 182, 185, 187–88
masculinity, 38, 55, 83, 86–86, 134, 136, 147–48, 150, 155, 159–63, 180, 212
masochism, 93, 125, 127–28, 142, 211
matheme, 13, 34, 36, 85, 209
méconnaissance, 15, 57–59, 65, 197, 209
metaphor, 21, 27, 64–65, 67–68, 73, 76–79, 110, 146, 179, 209–10
metonymy, 21–22, 27, 67, 73, 75–79, 209
Miller, Jacques-Alain, 2, 5, 13, 28, 41, 44–45, 47–48, 52, 72, 166–67, 201–03, 216
mirror stage, 8–9, 11, 23, 31, 44–45, 57–60, 122, 133, 179–80, 182–83, 209
Moebius strip, 29–30, 35, 42
Molière, 131
Montrelay, Michèle, 177
mother, 12, 19–20, 22–23, 31, 59–65, 79, 89, 94, 100, 104, 122, 124, 126–27, 133, 142, 149, 172–74, 176, 178–80, 183–84, 197, 204–05, 210–11
Muller, John P., 2, 4, 52, 216

Name-of-the-Father, 10, 12, 18, 27, 35, 39–40, 64–65, 79, 89–90, 94, 104, 108, 110, 112–15, 117–18, 174, 178, 180, 183, 207, 210–11
negation (*verneinung*), 63, 103–04, 117–20, 188
neurosis, 18, 65, 68, 71, 90, 93–95, 103, 117–124, 126, 132, 135–36, 210–11, 213–14
Nietzsche, Friedrich, 16
Nobus, Dany, 52, 216

object, 11–12, 19–20, 23, 26–28, 30–31, 33–34, 41, 50–51, 60–64, 78–79, 86, 88, 100–01, 118–19, 122, 124–28, 133, 149–50, 152, 162–63, 169–74, 176, 183, 186, 199, 204–07, 210
Oedipus complex, 9, 18, 21, 58, 60–64, 89, 94, 104, 110, 126, 134, 142, 147, 173–74, 178, 204–05, 210–11
Other/other, 5, 16–18, 22–24, 27–30, 33–34, 46, 59–61, 65, 68, 70, 76, 80, 83–88, 107–111, 120, 126–27, 133, 148–51, 156, 160, 162, 169, 174–99, 206–08, 210

paranoia, 8–9, 93, 95–102, 105–07, 123, 211
Pascal, Blaise, 31, 33
passage to the act, 27–28, 31–32, 204
paternal function, 35, 89–90, 94, 107, 110, 124, 127, 210–11
paternal metaphor, 64–65, 78, 110, 178, 183, 210
perversion, 18, 68, 93–95, 124–29, 132, 136, 210–11, 213
phallic myth, 5, 39, 83, 87, 141, 143, 147–48, 150–51, 154–56, 158–59
phallus, 19–20, 22–24, 35, 38, 40, 60–65, 81, 84, 87–88, 126, 141, 147–48, 150–51, 177–80, 194–95, 204–05, 211
phobia, 20, 40, 93, 95, 124, 127, 210
Plato, 26, 28, 167, 175
pleasure principle, 82, 94, 208
Poe, Edgar Allan, 4–5, 17, 35, 131–32, 137–38, 188–201, 215
postcolonial, postcolonialism, 169, 181–88
postmodern, postmodernism, 132, 142, 144–45, 154, 169–72, 174
poststructuralism, 143–45, 170, 181
psychosis, 4, 8, 18–19, 35, 40, 46, 64–65, 89–90, 92–96, 99–102, 105–07, 110–13, 115, 117, 119–21, 123, 126, 132, 136, 138, 166, 201–03, 210–14

queer, 128, 181

Rabaté, Jean-Michel, 52, 130, 132, 137, 165, 168, 201, 217
Ragland-Sullivan, Ellie, 179–80 201, 217
Rat Man, 10, 15
Ray, Satyajit, 170, 201
real, 6, 8, 11–14, 16, 18, 20, 22–28, 30, 36–40, 55–56, 60, 62–63, 81–90, 100, 103–05, 111, 116–19, 122, 124, 127, 132–37, 140, 142, 145–48, 150, 154, 156, 158, 160, 162–63, 168, 171–72, 174, 176–77, 180, 188, 197–99, 204, 207–12
rebus, 44–45, 74
repression (*verdrängung*), 18, 20, 60, 68, 77, 88, 94, 104, 117–20, 174, 180, 183, 210
return to Freud, 1, 3, 46
Rose, Gilbert, 142, 152–53, 163, 165
Roudinesco, Elisabeth, 9, 44, 47, 52, 217

Sade, Marquis de, 24, 28, 131
sadism, 93, 125, 127, 211
Said, Edward, 181, 185
Sartre, Jean-Paul, 131, 203
Saussure, Ferdinand de, 27, 34, 68, 73, 75–78, 84, 87, 92, 150, 165, 209, 217
Schema L, 17, 194
Schreber, Daniel Paul, 4, 15, 19, 95, 106–111, 113, 123,
semblance, 35, 59, 137, 139–40, 147, 171
sexual relationship, sexual difference, sexual non-rapport, 5, 11, 31, 35–36, 42, 55, 60, 83, 86–87, 108, 112, 115, 134, 141, 143–44, 150–51, 171, 180–81
sexuation, 35–36, 55–56, 81–88, 115, 134, 212–13
SFP, 7, 9–10, 13, 207, 212
Sheridan, Alan, 45, 51, 92, 182, 206, 216
sign, signifier, signified, signification , 18–23, 27–29, 31, 33–34, 38, 53–55, 64–65, 68–69, 72–89, 96, 108, 111–12, 117–21, 124, 138–39, 141, 146, 150, 153, 158, 171–73, 179, 183, 192–96
sinthome, 11–12, 37, 40, 88–91, 95, 111–17, 138–39, 169, 194, 207, 212
Socrates, 16
Soler, Colette, 87, 92
Sophocles, 25, 131–32, 134, 198–99
specular image, 18, 56–60, 64, 179, 182–83, 209
Spooner, W. A., 136–37
SPP, 7, 9–10, 19, 212–13
subject, subjectivity, 1, 3–4, 12–42, 45–46, 53–91, 94–95, 100, 103–10, 116–20, 124–26, 133, 139–51, 156–63, 169, 172–88, 191–94, 198, 200
symbolic, 11–15, 18, 20, 22–28, 31–40, 55–56, 60–68, 80–90, 94, 103–11, 117, 120–21, 126, 132–34, 137, 145–47, 150, 155–57, 161–63, 171–72, 176–80, 182–88, 192, 194, 196–99, 204, 207–08, 210–13
symptom, 12, 18, 21, 40, 66, 68–71, 79, 88–91, 93, 97, 100, 103, 105, 112–26, 134–35, 148–50, 155, 158–60, 162, 168, 170, 173, 212

Thurston, Luke, 39–40, 51, 89, 92, 130
topology, 13, 29, 40–43
torus, 41–42
transference, 15, 25–26, 28, 32, 90, 153

unconscious, 2–4, 9, 16–17, 21, 24–25, 28–32, 39, 41–46, 53–57, 60, 65–84, 87–91, 102, 105, 107, 116–20, 127, 134–35, 139, 141–42, 145, 155, 168, 180, 183, 198, 205–08, 213

variable-length sessions, 1, 7, 9, 70, 212–13
Voruz, Véronique, 11, 37, 52, 217

Warburton, Eileen, 141, 153–54, 165
Wolf Man, 4, 10, 15, 95, 103–06
Woodcock, Bruce, 152–53, 163, 165
Woolf, Bogdan, 11, 37, 52, 217

Žižek, Slavoj, 5, 12, 53, 92, 144, 165–76, 196–201, 217
(works of)
Enjoy Your Symptom: Jacques Lacan in Hollywood and Out, 12, 196–201
Everything You Always Wanted to Know About Lacan (But Were Afraid to Ask Hitchcock), 165, 167, 169–176, 201, 217
How to Read Lacan, 166–67, 201
The Pervert's Guide to Cinema, 217
The Pervert's Guide to Ideology, 217